Marcus Ferrar is a former Reuters correspondent who covered Eastern Europe during the Cold War, living in East Berlin and Prague. He is the author of several books about Germany, Eastern Europe, Communism and World War Two: 'A Foot in Both Camps: A German Past for Better and for Worse', 'Slovenia 1945: Memories of Death and Survival after World War II' and 'The Budapest House'.

THE FIGHT FOR
FREEDOM

MARCUS FERRAR

CRUX
PUBLISHING

First published in the United Kingdom in 2016

by Crux Publishing Ltd.
This revised edition published in July 2018

ISBN: 978-1-909979-74-1

Copyright © Marcus Ferrar, 2018

Also available as an ebook:

eISBN: 978-1-909979-23-9

Requests for permission to reproduce material from this work
should be sent to

hello@cruxpublishing.co.uk

CONTENTS

INTRODUCTION

In the time it took to write this book, millions of people have won freedom and many others were exposed to new oppression. People have been fighting for freedom for thousands of years, and there is no sign of a let-up – on the contrary. This book tells the story of those who fought, and those who sought to put them down.

It recounts struggles that liberated whole peoples, not just by violence but also peacefully – by challenging customs, speaking out bravely, opening up government and breaking artistic conventions. It examines what drove human beings to push for more freedom, and the reasons for resisting it. It features heroes, villains, revolutionaries, scholars, clergymen, feminists, soldiers, demonstrators and a multitude of others who dared to think and act in defiance of the rules.

At a time when freedom both triumphs and is defeated, changing people's lives radically, this book addresses a number of pertinent questions. Is liberty advancing? Or is it a lost cause – as today's upsurge of illiberal populism may suggest? Can freedom justify beheading a king or sabotaging power stations? Is nonviolence the only ethical way to fight for freedom? That was the view of Mahatma Gandhi and Martin Luther King, but was it therefore wrong for Allied armies to liberate Europe from the Nazis by force of arms?

If we accept that human beings can be irrational or – as Christians may claim – that they are intrinsically sinful, then fighting for freedom may not necessarily lead to a better world. Liberty can certainly be put to evil use, but this book presents plenty of contrary evidence that mankind benefits enormously from the freedom that people have fought for.

My own times have born this out. My grandfather and father had to defend freedom in two World Wars, while I have been able to live my life as I wanted and never had to do military service. My German mother stood up against tyranny by refusing to attend Nazi rallies and, although she was expelled from her school, she won in the end because the Nazis were defeated. In East Berlin and Prague as a foreign correspondent, I experienced the bitterness of a people living under a foreign yoke, but later watched them take to the streets and wrest their liberty back. In Lisbon in 1974, I joined exhilarated crowds celebrating the overthrow of a dictatorship in a revolution which brought Portugal eventually into a European community based on liberal values. Experience has taught me to hold freedom fighters in respect.

This book does not purport to be a comprehensive history of the fight for freedom, which would stretch to several volumes. It gives an overview of the struggle in a few hundred pages, and focuses on a few individuals who have distinguished themselves in the modern times. The story starts off the coast of Greece, proceeds from Europe into America, Africa and Asia, and ends in the depths of Ukraine – and on into the future. Doubtless there is more to come.

MF
Oxford, June 2018

THE POLICE HAVE GONE

Don't go to school today. Come down to the square. You will never forget this all your life. Today is revolution.
– Budapest mother, 1956

The people are grumbling. But that's not unusual. It's been like that for as long as anybody can remember. They're getting angry. It's a bit much. Things can't go on like this. A spot of trouble, but nobody up there in the palace feels too concerned. The people have never understood. They can't be trusted to grasp the whole picture.

Crowds are out on the streets. They don't want to stay at home or at work. A newspaper, which for years has toed the official line, reports that the government has blundered – only on a trivial matter – but how does it get away with it? Something is changing.

The people congregate in the city centre. Some stay overnight. They light fires and put up barricades. Heavily armed riot police tramp up and try to move them away. They swing their truncheons and shove, but mostly it's a tense stand-off. Days go by, then weeks. By now it's not just the downtrodden, but also the thinking middle-classes who gather. People start talking about issues which matter to them, awakening from a long sleep during which nothing was discussed, because nothing could be changed. People are there who never before or afterwards would join a revolution. Young and old talk endlessly, and freely.

The despot holds fast, or so it seems. In fact his failure to put an end to the protests gradually undermines a power which is credible only if it is total. Numbers swell, orators whom nobody knows make speeches which are drowned in the hubbub. Rumours of provocateurs spread, passions rise, the police wade into the crowd and shots ring out. News spreads that people have been killed. Crowds chant: "We are the people." A bloodbath seems imminent.

Then suddenly the police have gone. Armed guards at the palace, the parliament, the military headquarters, the prison and the checkpoints turn mild and impotent. They hesitate, obstruct half-heartedly, and then the people push past and swarm through. By that time, the tyrant has fled – in a fluttering helicopter, an armoured car or a carriage with curtained windows – heading for oblivion. It's all over in a matter of minutes.

With a few variations, the fight for freedom has come to climaxes like these in Kiev in 2014, Tunis and Cairo in 2011, eastern Europe in 1989, Lisbon in 1974, Budapest in 1956, St Petersburg in 1917 and Paris in 1789.

At such moments, the fight for freedom is exhilarating and devastatingly effective. Tyranny collapses in an instant. All constraints fall by the wayside. No more repression, spying, threats or discrimination. The people take their destinies into their own hands and do what they want. They embrace each other, offer bouquets of flowers to strangers, and thrust carnations into soldiers' rifles. They marvel at marbled buildings through which they can roam at will. Events move at a breathtaking speed in directions no one can predict. Those who take part never forget the experience for the rest of their lives. It is as if they are responding to an age-old human instinct.

The fight for freedom not only overthrows political regimes, but brings change in all walks of life. It liberates people from enslavement, and lets them talk and write freely. They can worship as they wish, explore new paths in art, escape discrimination on the basis of race, gender or social class, and have a say in determining their lives by casting a vote. Sometimes whole nations or groups have won freedom, but at the heart of the concept is freedom of the individual, since communities too can oppress.

The struggle has defeated tyrants who subjugated peoples out of lust for power, greed or a desire to shape the world according to their wishes; it has ended misery and persecution for countless millions, but it has also enabled peoples who have suffered no particular cruelty to break free from well-wishing tutelage.[1]

Despite these undoubted benefits, people are wary of freedom's scope for abuse, even by leaders of liberation movements. Hardly anybody insists that liberty should be total. We should not be free to kill innocents or slander, and we therefore see a need for laws that curb our freedom of action. If we fear a dangerous and unpredictable world, we may even prefer to forego freedom and place ourselves under the protection of a strong power.

Yet placing faith in security is open to abuse too. Tyrants exploit those who dread the intentions of their fellow men and women, or who doubt their own capacity to effect change for the better. If human beings really did prefer to live in a secure and controlled world, then we would, and our society would be static. But we choose not to do that.

The urge for freedom bubbles away just below the surface, erupting from time to time like molten lava, often quite unexpectedly.

Freedom is subversive in that it undermines accepted "truths" and upsets our accustomed ways. It arouses passions for and against, and leads to constant argument. For example, who should decide laws, and how far should they go in constraining liberty? Over hundreds of years, politicians and philosophers have chewed ceaselessly at this bone. Today voters in a number of countries question whether the so-called "liberal international order" of recent years really serves their needs. The disputes are unsettling, but they too are manifestations of freedom, since they take place only when people can openly express themselves.

For better and for worse, freedom is intensely stimulating. It is empowering, since it gives us choice. It enlivens the spirit and helps foster progress. The fight for freedom engages the bold and the ambitious – people who want to change the world. Many humans consider it intrinsic to their very being.

Some struggles for freedom change the world forever in ways which are quite unforeseen at the time. Others build on achievements of the past, while yet others leave glorious memories, but change little.

Over the ages, one liberty after another has been fought for and gained. The world today is freer than it ever was and, despite all the drawbacks, this has benefited hundreds of millions of people. It has been a long and bumpy road, and the ways humans have chosen to make their way along it has never failed to surprise.

It all started with a sea battle some 2,500 years ago.

CHAPTER 1

THE BEGINNINGS

We are free to do as we wish.
– Pericles of Athens

Ancient Greece

In mankind's earliest history, we find little trace of people fighting for freedom. From what we know of the first men and women, their lives were governed by nature, customs and their unfaltering beliefs in the mystical. That left little scope for the exercise of free will. Most would have belonged to a group in which the stronger members were expected to protect the less able: the main concern being survival. And so, even when the first great civilisations emerged, some 5,000 years ago, the need to hold together in the face of immutable forces and constant danger took precedence over any concept of individual freedom.

In Ancient Egypt, governed by Pharaohs and priests, the cardinal virtues of society were obedience, resignation and patience. In the Far East, the prevailing religions of Hinduism and Buddhism similarly promoted ideals of subservience to deities and docility, while in China, Confucius (551-479 BC) held that human harmony is based on order and stability.

The Ancient Greeks of Athens, however, did feel that freedom was important, both for the individual and the community, and they were prepared to fight for it. In the year 480 BC, they won a battle for freedom that arguably changed the world. Confronted by the Persian Emperor Xerxes and a vast army, they were in grave danger. Xerxes was set on conquest and subjugation, and one Greek city after another gave way as he advanced from the north. Even the sturdy fighters of Sparta prepared to withdraw to their lands in the far south.

In the face of what seemed like certain defeat, the Athenians decided to defend their liberty come what may. Organised as a fledgling democracy for the past quarter of a century, they took key decisions in assemblies of 6,000 citizens. So when one of these assemblies resolved to evacuate the city and its surroundings, some 150,000 people, including the old, the sick, and women and children, moved en masse to the off-lying island of Salamis. When Xerxes rode into Athens, he found it practically deserted; they had fled their homeland, not out of fear, but as a strategic manoeuvre freely decided upon.[2]

The Athenian commander, Themistocles, decided that, rather than try to hold out against an invading army of some 200,000 soldiers, he would defeat the Persians in a decisive sea battle and thus break their resolve. His aim was not merely to resist, but to drive the enemy out for good. The Persians were confident because they outnumbered the Greek fleet, but they underestimated their opponent. Themistocles tricked Xerxes by sending a message suggesting the Greek navy was about to flee from its position in the Straits of Salamis, and that he himself was ready to change sides. Xerxes took the bait but, far from a foe on the verge of flight, the Persians found a Greek navy eager for battle. After feigning retreat, the Greeks turned their triremes to attack. As they advanced, the crews sang a battle hymn:

> *Forward, sons of the Greeks,*
> *Liberate the fatherland,*
> *Liberate your children, your women,*
> *The altars of the gods of your fathers,*
> *And the graves of your ancestors:*
> *Now is the fight for everything.*[3]

The Persian ships fell into disarray in the confined waters, and were either disabled or fled. It was a humiliating defeat for the invaders and thereafter Xerxes withdrew his troops from Greece, leaving the victors free from foreign occupation. Themistocles' daring ploy had worked.

The lasting significance of this victory at Salamis is that it opened the way for an astonishing flowering of liberty in Athens. After returning in triumph to their city, the Athenians made the most of the freedom they had defended by pioneering a society based on the rule of law by public consent – a novel idea then, but now the foundation of every democracy. Anyone with Athenian citizenship, even the lowly born crews of the warships at Salamis, could vote and be eligible for public office. The result of this bold new venture was a vigorous democracy which, although imperfect, inspired political leaders around the globe for centuries. If they had lost, they would have come under the heel of an oriental despot. Their liberal regime would never have developed, and civilisation today would have turned out very differently.

The Athenians consciously lived their freedom in many walks of life. In 431 BC, their political ruler Pericles boasted that his citizens had laws of their own, providing equal justice for all. "We are free to do as we wish," he proudly proclaimed. On the stage, the playwright Aeschylus celebrated Prometheus for defying the gods to bring fire to mankind, enabling humans to develop independently of divine intervention. Philosophers could discuss the nature of the world, morality and political systems, almost uninhibitedly.

It was the philosopher Socrates (470-399 BC) who particularly championed freedom of debate. He would walk the streets of Athens, engaging all and sundry in philosophical discussion, using these dialogues to compel people to think issues through to their logical conclusions. He exercised the right to think independently, speak freely and disagree ad nauseam, eventually provoking some powerful enemies. For all its ground-breaking liberalism, Athens was not immune to political conflicts, and Socrates' endless contestation finally landed him in court.

Accused of corrupting the youth and heresy – charges which have been levelled against freethinkers ever since – the philosopher argued that individual conscience took precedence over human laws, and insisted on the public value of free discussion. Famously declaring that "an unexamined life is not worth living", he insisted that he should be rewarded rather than punished for speaking freely. His opponents retorted that encouraging people to rebel against orthodox thinking would subvert Athens' democracy.

As was the custom in democratic Athens, a jury of fellow-citizens judged his case. They found him guilty by 280 votes to 220 and sentenced him to death. Socrates refused efforts by friends to arrange his escape. On principle he chose to calmly drink the hemlock that would kill him. Thus, one of the earliest struggles for freedom of speech came to a head: Socrates had to die, but his defence of freedom of debate has inspired people ever since.

The Athenian experience of freedom was neither complete nor long lasting. It was a right to be enjoyed only by male citizens of their own city, not by foreigners or women, and they saw no contradiction in owning slaves. Within two generations of defending their own freedom against the Persians, Athenians were punishing rebellious subjects with executions and enslavement.[4]

Athenian democracy lasted nearly 200 years before yielding to the military supremacy of Macedonia, under a leader, Philip II (359-336 BC), who skilfully exploited divisions among the Greek city-states. The great Athenian orator Demosthenes (384-322 BC) tried to rally his compatriots to resist conquest by "the pestilent knave from Macedonia."[5] But the Greek city states could not decide whether Macedonia or Persia was the greater threat, and they were not ready to sacrifice their autonomy to form a united front.

However, the seed of liberty had been sown and the Athenian ideal survived. Scholars in isolated centres of learning preserved its memory, handing it down to future generations. Awareness of the desire for freedom penetrated European culture and, although sublimated for centuries, it never faded away entirely. In the 18th century, Athenian principles of freethinking underlay the Age of Enlightenment; when the Founding Fathers of the United States of America drew up a new constitution, they too looked to Athenian democracy and adapted it for a larger community. Through into the 20th and 21st centuries, statesmen in western democracies were expected to be familiar with the great Athenian past, and its influence has meanwhile spread far beyond Europe.

Quite why the Golden Age of Athenian democracy flourished at a time when free forms of society were unknown elsewhere is not entirely clear. In this case, it was enabled by a bold and imaginative general (Themistocles); a politician who took freedom in government to new heights (Pericles); and a host of talented philosophers who gave free rein to their powers of reason. Above all, the Athenians derived a will to resist through the democratic decision-making they initiated in the crucial years before Salamis. Having tasted freedom, they fought bravely to keep it.

Freedom under Rome

This was not the approach taken subsequently by the Romans, who were, at best, ambivalent about freedom. Shortly before Athens fought at Salamis, Romans freed themselves from their autocratic king and set up a republic governed by two annually elected magistrates called consuls. The Roman concept of *res publica* – government for the people – was supposed to reconcile freedom within the constraints of law. As the statesman Marcus Tullius Cicero (106-43 BC) put it, "we are servants of the law in order that we may be free", while Emperor Marcus Aurelius claimed to "respect most of all the freedom of the governed".[6]

Yet, these protestations of freedom proved disingenuous. As power concentrated into the hands of military leaders such as Julius Caesar (100-44 BC), and later of emperors, Rome focused on expanding and consolidating its territory, and on exercising authority. The basis of its rule was power, used ruthlessly when its leaders saw fit.

The wars the Romans waged for these purposes caused fearful casualties. Julius Caesar boasted that one tribe that resisted him, the Helvetii, lost more than two-thirds of its people in battle. In another battle in 58 BC, the Romans killed almost the entire army of the German Suebi tribe as it tried to retreat across a river.[7] In his campaign to control Gaul (modern France and Belgium), Caesar captured some 50,000 locals and sold them on as slaves, reserving prominent captives to be paraded in chains through the streets of Rome. The Romans spoke of this as "pacification", but as they were forcibly depriving people of their liberty, the result was often far from peaceful.

Repression bred a desire to fight and to regain lost freedom, not least in newly conquered Gaul, where Celts had lived for centuries in well-established societies. As soon as Caesar returned to Rome, the local chieftain, Vercingetorix, led an uprising against the remaining Roman garrisons. He gathered tribes in a formidable army of 80,000 and waged guerrilla warfare, burning crops and farms so that the Roman occupiers ran short of food. Caesar hurried back and battle ensued with siege machines, boiling pitch, fire, hidden stakes and desperate hand-to-hand combat. The Gauls put up a fierce resistance, but were eventually cornered in a stronghold. Vercingetorix led a counter-attack, which almost broke through the Roman besiegers, but Caesar led his last reserves of cavalry to attack the enemy's rear. The Gauls fell back, the tide of battle turned and the Gallic chieftain surrendered. Dignified in defeat, Vercingetorix put his best armour on, adorned his horse, rode out of the gates and made a turn around the seated Caesar. He dismounted, threw off his armour and sat quietly at Caesar's feet, until he was led away.[8]

The name Vercingetorix meant "king of warriors", but Caesar humiliated his enemy by having him dragged through the streets of Rome in chains, paying the price for opposing the might of Rome. Five years later, Vercingetorix was beheaded, in celebration of yet another of Caesar's triumphs.

In Britain, it was a tall, red-haired warrior-queen, Boadicea (Boudicca) who led the fight for freedom. Having colonised Britain in AD 43, the Romans raised hackles by treating the British arrogantly, disarming several tribes and trying to suppress Celtic culture. After making grants to tribes to pacify them, the occupiers caused resentment by turning the grants into loans and exacting repayment.

Boadicea's husband was one of the tribal leaders burdened with such a debt, and he sought to settle it by leaving half his kingdom to the Romans in his will. When he died in AD 61, the Romans promptly annexed the whole kingdom, flogged Boadicea, raped her daughters, seized Iceni treasure and sold much of the royal family into slavery.

Thereupon, Boadicea rose up in rebellion, amassed an army of 100,000, and ransacked Colchester, London and St. Alban's. Her followers put tens of thousands of people to the sword – many of them Roman settlers. The effects of the devastation can still be seen today in half a metre of red and black debris, which lies beneath the cities of Colchester and London.

As in Gaul, the uprising caught the Romans by surprise, causing Governor Gaius Suetonius Paulinus to pull back his legions and leave the inhabitants of the Roman settlements to their plight. In Rome, a shocked Emperor Nero considered withdrawing from Britain altogether. But ultimately, this ad hoc tribal resistance stood no chance against the well-organised military power of the Romans. That same year, Paulinus marshalled his legions to defeat Boadicea as she advanced into the West Midlands from her tribal lands. He exacted terrible revenge: according to the Roman historian Tacitus, the Romans killed some 80,000 Iceni men, women and children.

As a warrior for freedom, Boadicea neither gave nor sought quarter; after defeat, it is said she took poison rather than surrender. She is still celebrated by Britons today for fighting to regain liberty and for leading as a woman commander in the Celtic tradition. Before the final battle, Tacitus relates that she urged her warriors to match her fighting spirit: "Win the battle or perish: that is what I, a woman, will do; you men can live on in slavery if that's what you want."[9]

Revolt of Spartacus the Slave

It was not just the "pacified" foreign populations who were deprived of liberty. Romans used tens of thousands of slaves as labour in their own homeland, and they too were often tempted to rise up in rebellion. Twice the Romans had to put down slave revolts on the island of Sicily, but the insurrection led by Spartacus in 73 BC was on a much larger scale, and took place in the Roman heartlands.

Spartacus was a slave who had been trained to fight as a gladiator for the entertainment of Roman citizens. As such, he and the 70 other slaves who broke out with him were desperate men – as gladiators, they were destined to die a violent death, sooner or later. They seized weapons and armour from their gladiator school in Capua, central Italy, and made off into the countryside, taking up positions on the slopes of Mount Vesuvius. Soon the slaves were besieged by Roman militia, who thought they had them cornered, but misjudged the enterprise and agility of men trained in gladiatorial combat. The rebels descended cliffs on ropes and ladders fashioned from vines, circled behind the besiegers and put them to the sword.

As a result of this victory, thousands of other slaves, discontented farmers and herdsmen joined the revolt, eventually swelling the rebels to an army of over 90,000. They ravaged large swathes of Roman territory, plundered food, valuables and stocks of arms, and made a mockery of the laws of the land. The support they attracted demonstrated widespread dissatisfaction with Roman rule, and their success in battle humiliated the Roman military leadership. Over the course of two and a half years, Spartacus distinguished himself as a brilliant general and defeated nine Roman armies. At one point, it seemed as if the slaves would try to capture Rome itself, and panic spread through the city.

Finally Rome appointed one of its toughest military commanders, Marcus Licinius Crassus, to mobilise the state's legendary fighting capacity. First he struck fear among his own 40,000 legionaries, making an example of one legion that had fled during battle by carrying out decimation – the execution of every tenth man.[10]

Crassus eventually cornered Spartacus and his army in Calabria, the toe of Italy. In the final battle, Spartacus fought his way up close to Crassus, but he was surrounded and died fighting, his body disappearing into an anonymous mass of corpses. To deter others from defying Roman leadership, Crassus had 6,000 captured slaves crucified along the Appian Way, leading from Capua northwards to Rome. They died slow, agonising deaths and their bodies were left to rot as a warning.

These uprisings in Gaul, Britain and Italy showed that the rule of the Romans was often cruel and oppressive, despite the perceived benefits derived from Roman law and order. As a result, the Romans were continually obliged to suppress uprisings all over their Empire; in the Jewish lands alone, they had to call in legions three times during the first few years of the first century AD.

These freedom fighters have inspired and motivated future generations. Vercingetorix is remembered as a hero in today's France, where liberty has become a cornerstone of the constitution. In Britain, Boadicea symbolises the sturdy independence of an island race determined to defend its freedom from foreign threats. As for Spartacus, his example as a freedom fighter and his resilience as a warrior continue to move people more than 2,000 years later. His revolutionary army was volatile and beset by divisions, but for two and a half years he inspired his followers to fight for noble goals – freedom, equality and prowess.[11] It was one of the greatest wars of resistance in the history of slavery.

However, for all the glorious defiance, it seemed that Roman law and order was destined to prevail. After the death of Vercingetorix, Gaul was tamed and adopted Roman ways of life. With the defeat of Boadicea, the once proud and prosperous Celts were pushed to the far west of Britain. As for Spartacus's uprising, it resulted in Roman slaves being treated somewhat less harshly, but another 1,850 years would pass before a slave revolt triumphed over a European power (see Chapter 5).

However, one man living under Roman rule started a movement that made an astonishing impact on the world. He offered liberation, not from slavery or foreign occupation, but from the oppressive nature of Roman societies.

Christianity – Freedom and Oppression

It was Jesus who offered people this freedom and salvation; he told them that all people were equal before God, promising the Kingdom of God to the poor rather than the rich. "Blessed are you who are poor, for yours is the kingdom of God... but woe until you who are rich," he preached, adding on a later occasion "it is easier for a camel to go through the eye of a needle than for a rich person to enter the kingdom of God."[12]

This directly challenged the wealthy minorities who exercised authority. His targets included Jewish kings ruling under Roman supervision, Roman governors intent on stamping out subversive religious movements, and the officials and associates who supported their authority.

Jesus also defied the Jewish priestly caste which enforced religious observance: he went into their Temple and overturned the tables of money-dealers authorised by the priests. While the clerics forbade people to touch lepers, Jesus laid hands on them and cured, if not the disease, then at least their ostracism. In a society that subjected women to permanent male control, he treated women followers honourably. In the face of Roman authority, he urged people to "render unto Caesar the things that are Caesar's, and unto God the things that are God's", which could be interpreted as asserting freedom to practise one's chosen religion.

The vision which Jesus offered to the poor, the destitute and the outcasts was of an egalitarian existence free from the repression under which they lived. Jesus was a revolutionary, and for this he suffered the habitual Roman punishment for such leaders – crucifixion.[13]

Jesus intended his liberating Kingdom of God to be for all people, not just his fellow-Jews, and after his death the Apostle Paul spread the faith among Gentiles as far as Rome. This led to an explosive growth in followers, laying the foundations for Christianity to become a world religion. Today, about a third of the world's population is at least nominally Christian, a greater number than the adherents of any other faith. Christians can be found in all social classes, but it is in the impoverished parts of the world that their numbers have grown the fastest.

As the Roman Empire declined, eventually offering neither freedom nor security, early Christianity filled the void as a self-contained dynamic force. As they grew in confidence, Christian preachers taught followers to assert their faith and think for themselves, rather than mindlessly repeat rituals. In a letter to a Christian community in the eastern Mediterranean, Paul urged followers to understand the meaning of what they prayed for.[14]

The Roman Empire generally tolerated multiple religions, but in later years Christians came under pressure because they refused to pay homage to Roman gods and challenged the divinity of the emperor. In the second century AD, Emperor Marcus Aurelius – who claimed to respect the freedom of the governed – put thousands of Christians to death in an attempt to break their defiance.

In the middle of the next century, Emperor Decius (249-251) tried to enforce conformity by ordering all citizens to perform a sacrifice to Roman gods and the emperor. When thousands of Christian bishops, priests, followers and even the Pope in Rome refused to do so, Decius had them all killed. Emperor Diocletian (284-305) followed on by destroying homes of Christians and sending them to be torn apart by wild beasts in arenas. These persecutions, however, did not work: the victims were admired as martyrs by fellow Christians, and as champions of freedom of belief by the wider population.

The new religion continued to expand, eventually penetrating the highest echelons of the Empire in the reign of Emperor Constantine (306-337). Believing that Christianity could hold the Empire together as a unifying force against barbarian invasions, Constantine ended the persecution in the Edict of Milan of 313 and decreed freedom of religion.

Constantine then sought to maximise the influence of Christianity by consolidating its beliefs. Hitherto, Christian leaders had heatedly disputed theological debates among themselves, but in 325 Constantine summoned them to the Council of Nicaea to agree on a single doctrine. It formulated a Nicene Creed (statement of beliefs), which, in an expanded version, is recited in Christian churches today. While Constantine tolerated other religions too, Christianity gradually acquired status as the state religion and Constantine himself was baptised in 337, just before his death.

As a result of Constantine's intervention, Christians no longer needed to fight for freedom to practise their religion, but they soon demanded that theirs should be the only authorised faith. They lobbied for the decree of religious tolerance to be cancelled, and eventually non-observance of Christianity in the Roman Empire became subject to the death penalty. Christian freedom fighters had turned into Christian enforcers, supported by the power of the secular state. For the next 16 centuries, Christianity would both advance and hold back freedom, though it would never entirely lose touch with the essentially liberating message of Jesus.

Christianity did not just promise the Kingdom of God to the poor, it also offered relief from the burden of guilt to all those who confessed their wrongdoings and sought redemption in heaven. This, however, required unquestioning faith, which was liable to exploitation by men who mistrusted freedom.

One of those was the Church leader Augustine (354-430). Setting out a new doctrine of obedience and exclusivity, he affirmed that all humans were born sinful, since Adam committed the Original Sin of disobeying God in the Garden of Eden. They could find salvation only by submitting to God's grace and being baptised into the Christian Church. Many people found comfort in this, but it demanded submission and left no scope for freedom of religious choice. Augustine's was the doctrine of a militant religion grasping for dominion over men's souls. Rather than freedom on earth, it conditionally offered life after death.[15]

As it reached the height of its powers in the Middle Ages, the Catholic Church in Europe exercised enormous influence. It presented its doctrine as a universal truth binding society together, and asserted that dissent exposed the community to God's retribution. This meant that freedom of religious belief was outlawed, and any conviction that departed from official doctrine was treated as heresy. However, heresies continued to proliferate, indicating a subversive readiness to defy authority and think freely.

In order to suppress the dissenters, Popes combined with kings and lords to establish Church courts known as the Inquisition. The first were set up in France at the end of the 12th century, spreading later through the rest of the Catholic Christendom. The Inquisitors could use torture to extract confessions and assumed guilt unless the defendant could prove innocence. The Inquisition decided whether the defendant was guilty, while the secular authorities set the sentence and carried it out.

In Spain and Portugal, the Inquisition came to a terrifying climax in the 15th century, when Christian monarchs sought to establish the predominance of their religion after driving Muslim rulers out of the Iberian Peninsula. The Inquisitors in particular targeted Jews and Muslims who had converted to Christianity under duress and were suspected of returning to their old faiths. The most flagrant heretics were condemned to burn at the stake – modern calculations of their numbers range from a few thousand to several tens of thousands[16] – but more common were a prison sentence, whipping, a penance, a fine and even occasionally acquittal. At the end of the Inquisition proceedings, the condemned were paraded and sentences proclaimed, often in front of hostile mobs. All in all, the Inquisition was a uniquely powerful instrument for suppressing freedom of religious opinion.

In the early 13th century, heresy threatened to get out of hand in southern France. The Catholic Church faced dissent there, not just by individuals, but by a widely followed religious sect – the Cathars. They were Christian, but engaged in banned practices such as contraception, and believed in a personal relationship with God without the intermediation of priests. To suppress these nonconformist practices, Popes and French kings waged a 50-year crusade in southern France, slaughtering some half a million people, dissenters and loyal Catholics alike. One of the crusaders, Abbot Arnaud Amaury, ordered: "Kill them all. God will know his own."

The Cathars were wiped out as a people and today it is almost impossible to find vestiges of their existence. But their spirit has lived on; the idea of a personal relationship with God was a central feature of Protestant doctrine 300 years later.

Humanity's underlying drive for liberty had surfaced and made itself felt in government, social order, speech and religion, but the movement encountered constant resistance. Whether by fear, scepticism or greed, plenty of people rejected freedom viscerally, grasping instead for security, order and discipline. They were to be disappointed, however. Instead of stability came more change and with change, more turbulence.

CHAPTER 2

FROM MAGNA CARTA
TO GUTENBERG

I am ready to defend my convictions even unto death.
– John Wycliffe

The Feudal System Opens Up

I n 13th century England, liberty was under threat, not only from a dogmatic Church, but from royal abuse of power. Under the feudal system, barons owed allegiance and military support to the king, and in return were consulted about important decisions. England's King John (1199-1216) ignored this arrangement when he unilaterally decided to wage war in France, lost many of the lands English kings owned there, and financed the expedition by raising taxation six-fold. As far as the barons were concerned, it was bad enough that he had led the country into a series of blunders, but that he exacted taxes without their consent violated the feudal pact.

Thus, in 1215, the barons rebelled against their king, leading to a showdown on the banks of the Thames at Runnymede, 20 miles upstream from London. The outcome of the tense meeting was Magna Carta, one of the world's first and most influential charters asserting fundamental liberties.

Three thousand five hundred words in length, written in Latin on a single sheet of sheepskin parchment, Magna Carta established the principles that a monarch was subject to the rule of law, and that the rights of individuals should be upheld against authority. Its most famous clause, 39, proposed that: "No free man shall be seized or imprisoned, or stripped of his rights or possessions, or outlawed or exiled, or deprived of his standing in any way, nor will we proceed with force against him, or send others to do so, except by the lawful judgment of his equals or by the law of the land."

For the first time, this established a right to trial by jury, and another clause safeguarded against justice being unfairly withheld, or administered by venal and ignorant officials. These important new liberties were not confined to the barons – the term "free man" included other classes (though not peasants). The document also forbade taxation "except by the common counsel of the realm", and, in an early affirmation of free trade, it decreed that merchants could come to England and trade without being subject to "illegal exactions".

King John set his seal to the document presented at Runnymede, but ignored it in practice and, in response to his appeal, Pope Innocent III annulled it and excommunicated the rebels. The barons responded by besieging the king's castles and occupying London, while King John laid waste to the northern lands of his opponents. At that point, Magna Carta seemed a dead letter, but within a year John had died, and the regent of his nine-year-old successor thought it wise to give the charter a new lease of life.

Over the eight centuries since its formulation, Magna Carta has often been disregarded, and most of its clauses are no longer relevant in today's society. However, as recently as

2008, members of the British Parliament cited Clause 39 to oppose a government plan to detain suspected terrorists for up to 42 days without charge. They also invoked it in the 17th century, in order to counter other monarchs who tried to exercise absolute power.

The principles of freedom, democracy and rule of law established in Magna Carta eventually spread far beyond England. Across the Atlantic, its language is to be found in the Bill of Rights drawn up by Thomas Jefferson in 1776 after Americans declared independence, and its principle of free trade now applies to commercial relations across much of the world.

Towards the end of the Middle Ages – in England and in the rest of Europe – social and economic changes also helped advance the cause of liberty. They undermined the feudal system, thus weakening the strength of the Church and the lords. So much so that when a plague reduced the supply of farm labour in the 14th century, surviving peasants were able to charge more for their work and acquire land. Also, when spices, silks and precious metals arrived in growing quantities from the eastern Mediterranean, towns in Italy, Germany and Flanders grew rich from the trade. For both peasants and townspeople, the ability to earn money meant greater power and greater freedom.

It was not long before towns turned into "city-states", in which adventurous minds freely explored new frontiers. In Germany, a number of them won recognition as Free Cities, no longer owing allegiance to local lords. Increasingly, individual citizens had their say.

The merchants on Europe's western seaboard turned their creative thinking to their exclusion from trading with Asia. Valuable goods coming in from China, India and the

Middle East passed through the Mediterranean to Italy and central Europe, leaving those in the west with meagre pickings. So traders in Portugal, Spain, England and Holland looked for ways to gain an advantage. In the new spirit of bold thinking and free enquiry, they came upon the counter-intuitive idea of reaching the east by sailing westwards out into the Atlantic.

Henry the Navigator, a Portuguese prince, gathered his best mathematicians, astronomers and navigators to develop a plan. Armed with complex calculations of winds and currents, his sea captains set off westwards over the horizon, doing their best to dispel their sailors' superstitious fears that they would fall off the edge of the earth.

The voyages of discovery made by Portugal, Spain, England, France and the Netherlands, from the 15th century onwards, brought new riches, and also victories for freedom of thought. Nobody before then knew there were ways around Africa and South America to the Far East, and very few people knew that the American continents existed at all. This led people to question conventional assumptions in all walks of life, stimulating their desire to make discoveries for themselves. What other truths had the guardians of knowledge missed, or concealed?

Protestants – Freedom from Rome

Those guardians were the Catholic clergy, whose authority was now weakened by changes in society and discoveries in which they had no hand. One of the first to challenge the Church's control of knowledge was John Wycliffe, a 14th century theologian at Oxford University. He declared that Holy Scriptures rather than priests should guide Christians, so he organised translation of the Bible into contemporary English to allow people to read it for themselves. In defiance of the Church hierarchy, Wycliffe declared that the Pope's authority was subsidiary to that of the Holy Scriptures. He preached that man could find salvation through a direct relationship with God, rather than through the Church.

This was revolutionary and challenged the Church head-on. Wycliffe attracted a large number of followers who relished the freedom to read, know and believe what they wanted. For the Church, however, he was a dangerous subversive.

A Church court charged him with heresy and placed him under house arrest, while Pope Gregory XI issued five Bulls (edicts) against him. The Church complained that making the Bible available in English to ordinary men and women would mean that "the pearl of the gospel is scattered and trodden underfoot by swine". To which Wycliffe replied: "Englishmen learn Christ's law best in English. Moses heard God's law in his own tongue; so did Christ's apostles."

He defended his convictions until he died a natural death at liberty in 1384, but was posthumously convicted on the heresy charge by the Church's Council of Constance, 31 years later. In 1428, Pope Urban VI had his remains disinterred, burned to ashes and thrown into a river.

Around the same time, the Czech priest Jan Hus was preaching the same liberating message in Prague. He too refused to accept papal authority and denounced the local Catholic clergy for immorality and corruption, writing: "The church shines in its walls, but starves in its poor saints; it clothes its stones with gold, but leaves its children naked." As a teacher at Prague's Charles University, he imported Wycliffe's texts and translated them into Czech.

Much of the population of Bohemia (today's Czech Republic) supported Hus, and civil war broke out in 1419 as Catholic kings and Popes sought to regain control. By that time, Hus himself was dead. He appeared at the Council of Constance but, despite guarantees of safe conduct, he was imprisoned and condemned in 1415 for heresy. Given a last chance to recant and be set free, he bravely refused and declared: "I shall die with joy today in the faith of the gospel which I have preached." He was singing and praying as flames fuelled by Wycliffe's books consumed him at the stake.

After the final defeat of the Hussites in 1434, the Catholic Church's crackdown on freethinking seemed complete; but Wycliffe and Hus were precursors of a much larger upheaval to come.

This was triggered by the invention of the Gutenberg printing press in 1439. Although printing was first developed in China, Johannes Gutenberg, a German living in Strasbourg, created a press with movable metal type which could print multiple copies faster and more cheaply. This transformed access to knowledge as drastically as the World Wide Web did at the end of the 20th century. Hitherto, almost the only people who could read and write were Churchmen, who laboriously recorded knowledge by hand in monasteries. They wrote in Latin, which no ordinary people could understand, enabling the clergy to filter what knowledge reached the wider community.

Gutenberg's printing press thus destroyed the Church's monopoly over knowledge. The number of books in circulation exploded and spurred a huge growth in literacy. Publishers began producing books not just in Latin, but in the languages spoken by the lay people, and it was they who became the main consumers of knowledge, not the clergy.

One man in particular used Gutenberg's invention to advance the cause of freedom and change the religious world forever. This man was Martin Luther, the son of a German copper miner. Ordained as a Catholic priest in 1507, he began teaching at the University of Wittenberg in central Germany and, like Wycliffe and Hus, rebelled against the fundamental practices and doctrines of his Church. He too insisted that people could attain salvation by personal faith in God, with no need for the Church's rituals and ceremonies.

Luther was particularly annoyed that a Church agent in Wittenberg was selling pardons known as "indulgences" to absolve people of their sins. The agent would even sell an indulgence for a sin that the payer intended to commit in the future. Half the proceeds went to Rome and the other half to a banker to whom the local archbishop owed a debt. Luther was furious at the corruption. Even more frustrating was that his congregation ignored his own orders to do penance for their sins, on the grounds that they had already paid for indulgences.

In 1517 Luther came out in rebellion by nailing a document of *95 Theses* to the door of the Wittenberg castle church. In it, he attacked the indulgences and a wide range of other Church practices which he found corrupt. There was no stopping the wave of religious liberty he released. The *95 Theses* were reprinted in huge numbers on Gutenberg presses; within two weeks they were all over Germany, and in two months all over Europe. Luther made fiery speeches, debated with Church scholars and preached provocative sermons in his Wittenberg church. When the Pope in 1520 issued a Bull rebutting the *95 Theses,* Luther burned it in public, together with books on Church law. The Pope thereupon excommunicated him and he was ordered to appear before a secular assembly, the Diet of Worms. When Luther refused to recant, he was declared an outlaw and a heretic.

At this point, he was saved by the ruler of Saxony, Frederick the Wise, who offered him a remote castle to cool down and avoid arrest. In his castle refuge, Luther wrote a German translation of the Bible, which was published in 1534. Thanks to the Gutenberg printing press, and his readily-accessible style of writing, it was an instant success. As with Wycliffe's Bible in England, Germans could read the word of God without the intermediation of the clergy, free to interpret it as they wished. Since then, the Bible has been translated into more than 500 languages.

Luther went on to publish an array of pamphlets, letters and sermons which spread rapidly around Germany thanks to the presses. The Catholic Church, operating slowly with Latin manuscripts copied by hand, could not compete. Then, in another bold act of defiance, he broke free from the constraints of clerical celibacy and married an ex-nun, with whom he had six children.

His attacks on authority prompted a revolt by German peasants against their lords. They protested that Jesus protected the poor, and that the Bible contradicted none of the reforms they demanded. Luther, however, was only interested in spiritual freedom, not political, so he urged the lords to suppress the uprising, which they did, at the cost of some 100,000 lives.

Nevertheless, the Protestant Reformation was now unstoppable, representing a huge advance in freedom of religious expression for millions of people. Northern and central Germany embraced the new Lutheran faith, and the decision to do so often involved a democratic process. The citizens of Ulm in Bavaria, for example, held a referendum to determine whether or not to follow Luther. In a free vote, citizens decided that their mighty Minster, the tallest church in the world, should abandon Catholicism for the new faith. The more conservative countryside of Bavaria meanwhile stayed Catholic.

In 1536, another Protestant leader, Jean Calvin, led the citizens of Geneva in a further break with Rome. Like Luther, he believed that salvation came through personal faith rather than Catholic sacraments. But Calvin was intent on enforcing a truly moral society rather than introducing religious liberty. He demanded absolute trust in God's providence, meaning no freedom to question the Church and no straying into new doctrines. He even claimed that God determined before birth who would be saved and who would be damned in the afterlife. Some people, according to Calvin, were predestined to go to heaven as the "elect".

This was a recipe for tyranny. Calvin legislated vigorously to compel a godly life and subordinated the state to his new Reformed Church. The word of the Bible became as absolute as the authority of the Popes had been, while adultery, blasphemy, witchcraft and heresy were deemed crimes punishable by death. In just four years, 58 of Geneva's population of 16,000 were executed for religious offences and a further 76 exiled. Drinking wine, swearing and merry-making were banned, as was all art and instrument-playing.

As an immigrant from France, Calvin had to fight to assert his authority in Geneva, which may partly explain why his rule was so autocratic. Despite the grim years of his rule, Calvin's break with Rome did offer some freedom in that it gave people an alternative to the Catholic Church. They were free from foreign interference and free from the Inquisition.

After his death in 1564, life in Geneva became less oppressive – but still stoutly independent. In 1602, troops of the Catholic Duke of Savoy tried to capture the city in a surprise attack at night, but citizens swarmed to the ramparts and repulsed them. Never again would Catholics threaten Geneva. Each year, its citizens commemorate the defence of their liberty by parading through the old town on horseback, bearing swords, lances and fiery torches.

Calvin inspired Protestant Churches in France, Scotland and the Netherlands, as well as the Puritans in England and settlers in America, while Lutheranism took root in the heart of Europe. Luther and Calvin both changed the world by creating forms of Christianity that were fundamentally independent in spirit. The focus on the Bible meant different interpretations of its texts could flourish – and that meant greater freedom of thought.

So despite their authoritarian tendencies, both Luther and Calvin are key figures in the fight for freedom, and their impact has been long lasting.

Renaissance – Freedom to Create

A new breath of freedom was also sweeping the world of the arts, where the medieval Church had stifled innovation. In the cities, affluent citizens were becoming more interested in their worldly lives, and this led artists to focus on the human being.

In the flowering of the Renaissance, between the 14th and 16th centuries, painters, sculptors and poets celebrated the nobility of the unconstrained human spirit. Men and women were worth representing for their own sake, rather than as iconic representations of a religious idea. Even if a subject was Biblical, the human qualities of the person depicted outshone the evangelical message.

Raphael's *Sistine Madonna,* painted in the 16th century, shows Mary as a beautiful young woman looking straight at the viewer, calmly and serenely. At a time when the Church frowned upon liberated women, the artist dares us to behold a self-assured young female, gracefully assuming her place in the world.

Another Madonna, painted by Fra Filippo Lippi in 1465, turned out to be a nun who absconded to co-habit with him and have two children. During the medieval time, a scandalised Church would have made sure the picture was never seen. But in this more liberal environment, Lippi's Madonna was acclaimed as a masterpiece because she radiated an uplifting human spirit.[17]

Neither of these paintings conveys submission to God. They portray women in elevated roles, rather than subordinate to men, and celebrate human beauty, intelligence and refinement. Renaissance artists depicted mortals who are free to aspire to greatness in the here and now.

Scholars began studying ancient Greek and Roman texts in ways the Church had hitherto discouraged. Instead of trying to deduce new truths about Christianity, as the monks did, the scholars found proof of the unbridled human spirit. They called themselves "humanists" and rediscovered free debate, the power of reason, respect for the individual and a confidence in human capabilities.

In the 15th century, the Popes joined in celebrating the human spirit by commissioning frescoes from Raphael and Michelangelo. Painters even felt free to create pictures that had no religious theme at all, portraying reclining beauties, merchants, artisans, servants, peasants, and even criminals. Across all of Europe, the human spirit flourished in newfound unrestraint.

The fight for freedom had thus made major advances by the end of the 16th century. The ancient Athenians created a free political democracy, Jesus launched a religion which gave hope to millions of the oppressed, Magna Carta introduced safeguards against rulers, Protestants defeated the absolute authority of the Catholic Church, and Renaissance artists freed themselves from the inhibitions of religious piety to celebrate humanity. Although Vercingetorix, Boadicea, Spartacus, the Cathars and the Inquisition's heretics were ultimately crushed, their courageous bids for freedom left a lasting impression on people's minds.

Despite these hard-fought successes, the benefits had not spread beyond Europe and they had been enjoyed by relatively few. Society was for many still hard, brutal and restrictive. Many more fights for freedom lay ahead.

CHAPTER 3

FROM PARLIAMENT TO ENLIGHTENMENT

Man is born free and everywhere he is in chains.
– Jean-Jacques Rousseau

Parliament versus the Monarch

O ne of the major challenges in the fight for freedom was holding on to any advances made. Victories were followed by defeats, and even the great achievements which would eventually change the world were susceptible to reversal.

Magna Carta, for example, was for hundreds of years only intermittently observed in England. Just a few dozen years after King John put his seal to the charter, his son Henry III flouted it by raising taxes for new foreign adventures without consulting his lords. In 1258, the lords responded with a coup d'état, forcing him to agree that Parliament should meet three times a year to discuss all matters of government. This body had grown out of earlier councils of lords, which had advised feudal kings for several centuries. First called Parliament in 1236, it would struggle with monarchs for supremacy for more than 400 years. The outcome would be a victory for

Parliament which liberated people more than anyone had originally imagined.

At first made up of lords and senior clergy, membership of Parliament was broadened in 1264 to include lower-ranked knights and "burgesses" – free men from the towns. Thus began what later became Britain's House of Commons, a freely elected representative body which today has greater powers than kings, lords and churchmen.

By the 15th century, legislation was no longer enacted in the name of the monarch, but by "authority of Parliament". Kings fought back, not just against the growing powers of Parliament, but also against the individual rights protected in Magna Carta. James I (1603-1625) asserted that he had a divine right to rule, declaring that kings were superior to other men. He felt he should heed tradition and God, but not Parliament, thus claiming the right to impose laws by royal prerogative. Parliament counter-attacked with a Petition of Right, which invoked Magna Carta to set out liberties that the king was forbidden to infringe. This Petition of Right was ratified by James's son, King Charles I (1625-1649), and is still in force today in Britain and parts of the Commonwealth.

The two sides, however, remained set on a collision course, since Charles too insisted that he ruled by divine right. Infuriated by the challenge to his authority, Charles dissolved Parliament, but was forced to summon it again when he ran short of money in a war against the Scots in 1639-40. He was told that Parliament would not vote in favour of taxes unless royal abuses were curbed. As a result, the king dissolved it again, but within a few months it was back, and this time it passed an act decreeing that it could be dissolved only if its members decided to do so themselves.

Charles marched into Parliament with armed guards in 1642 and attempted to arrest five leading members, but they had been tipped off and had disappeared. In a brave act of defiance, the Speaker of the House refused to say where they were.

Unable to enforce his will, Charles left London and declared that Parliament was in rebellion, after which both sides began raising armies. Thus began the English Civil War (1642-51), pitting Parliament against the monarchy. There were only a few large battles, but the bitter animosities aroused by constant warfare deeply wounded the nation.

After two inconclusive engagements, Parliament created a so-called New Model Army, which determined the future course of the war and set standards still observed by the British Army today. It was more professional, more democratic and more motivated than other armies of the time, which consisted largely of mercenaries. Officer ranks were no longer reserved for the higher echelons of society, but were appointed instead on the basis of ability – one commander had originally been a butcher.

Following defeat by the New Model Army in 1645, Charles surrendered to the Scots, who handed him over to Parliament in exchange for £400,000. Some Parliamentarians wanted to let the king continue to reign, on the condition he would give up abuses of power, but the New Model Army's commanders did not trust him. They marched on Parliament, arrested those members trying to negotiate and ordered Charles to be put on trial for treason.

Parliament appointed 135 men to a special High Court of Justice to conduct the trial, but only 65 turned up. Regardless of the meagre turnout, the prosecutors proceeded to make their case, arguing that Charles was entrusted to govern "by and according to the laws of the land and not otherwise". Charles refused to accept the court's jurisdiction, but was sentenced to death after being found guilty as "a tyrant, traitor, murderer, and public enemy to the good people of this kingdom".

As he stood on the scaffold, Charles continued to assert his absolute right to rule, declaring that if people wanted liberty they would have to be governed, but with no right to participate in that government. A hooded executioner then severed his head with a single blow.

An uneasy sigh arose from the watching crowd as the axe fell. Never before had an English king been put on trial and executed. The deed raised grave questions: for example, was it morally justified to behead a king if he stood in the way of liberty? Did the bloodletting not dishonour the concept of freedom itself? Such reservations must be seen in the context of the devastating Civil War England was undergoing. In those harsh times, killing had become commonplace and mercy was at a premium. If freedom was to be fought for, then at some time or another, blood would surely be spilled. By beheading their king, Englishmen showed they were deadly serious in asserting their will for liberty.

Unquestionably, it was a decisive moment in the history of England and in the fight for freedom. Government had replaced the absolute authority of a king and Parliament had established the primacy of rule by an elected assembly, a form of government that has become a cornerstone of liberty. This sent shock waves around Europe, particularly in France, where Louis XIV (1638-1715) ruled by divine right and dominated the rest of Europe. France and England were now on divergent paths, one resolutely committed to autocracy and the other moving towards greater freedom.

The liberties the English Parliament won during the Civil War came at the cost of 200,000 lives and the next 11 years brought little respite. The victorious Civil War commander, Oliver Cromwell, was appointed Lord Protector in 1649, and ushered in rigorous reforms to be imposed by Puritans. Theatres and inns were closed, sports were banned and fines were imposed for swearing. Women were persecuted for wearing make-up or colourful dresses and put into the stocks if found not attending church on Sundays, while Protestant zealots resumed the destruction of religious statuary and paintings that had begun a century earlier.

Cromwell arbitrarily arrested opponents and ruled as a dictator for the last five years of his life, having dismissed Parliament as "a pack of mercenary wretches". The English won freedom from the absolute rule of kings, and in exchange had to endure the tyranny of Cromwell and the Puritans. It was an unfortunate start to a new era. Sceptics about freedom have argued that it was ever thus, and that man has always been destined to subjugation, perhaps for his own good. However, this reflects an unduly pessimistic view of the capacity of human beings to decide their own fate. Admittedly, Cromwell's dictatorship demonstrated that a collapse of authority can be followed by a nasty period of transition, but it was no proof that tyranny was bound to prevail.

Soon after Cromwell died in 1658, the late king's son returned from exile to take over the throne as Charles II. A populace tired of austerity welcomed him jubilantly, but he too came into conflict with Parliament when it became known that he had made a secret treaty with the French king. Charles II suspended Parliament in 1681 and ruled on his own until his death in 1685. The crisis came to a head again in 1688, when the next king, his brother James II, adopted

Catholicism, dissolved the re-established Parliament yet again, and appointed Catholics to key positions in society.

Having been pushed to their limit, the Parliamentarians invited in a Dutch army, headed by William of Orange, to help rid them of the king. James raised an opposing army, but after many leading nobles deserted him, he fled to exile in France. Shortly afterwards, Parliament declared that James had abdicated and arranged for William and his wife Mary to take over the throne jointly. The choice was judicious: Mary was James's eldest daughter and William was a Protestant (as were most Parliamentarians).

Looking to avoid a repeat of their unstable history, Parliament voted a new Bill of Rights preventing monarchs from interfering with the law or raising taxes unilaterally. It also guaranteed free elections and freedom of speech in their chamber. This so-called "Glorious Revolution" permanently tilted power towards Parliament.

Parliament was thenceforth free to rule without significant hindrance by a monarch, whose position at the head of the state eventually became largely symbolic. With time, the House of Commons, which had led the rebellion against the crown, came to predominate over the House of Lords, which included many royalists. Power thus gravitated towards a wider spectrum of people, giving them greater freedom to govern their lives. With these new liberties established, albeit still imperfectly, England was energised to expand trade, industry and its overseas domains.

The Enlightenment Liberates Thought

Although England had become more liberal in the way it ran its government, the continent of Europe persisted in upholding the feudal pact between monarchs and lords. This led the once thriving Free Cities, such as those in Germany, to stagnate. The liberal spirit of the Renaissance subsided and authorities began imposing censorship to curb the free expression stimulated by the Gutenberg printing press.

The rise of Protestantism had enabled millions to free themselves from the authority of Rome. But despite this, both Catholics and Protestants still held that the Bible was an unquestionable font of knowledge about man and the universe. So, while the Bible became more open to interpretation, its overall authority could not be challenged. Moreover, rivalry between Catholics and Protestants plunged Europe in the first half of the 17th century into a devastating Thirty Years' War which trampled over individual liberties.

In keeping with its dogmatic approach, the Catholic Church continued to resist knowledge that did not conform to its doctrines, reinforcing its influence through the Counter-Reformation revival movement. According to the Church, the Earth was at the centre of the universe and the sun moved around the Earth. So in 1632, when an elderly Italian astronomer published a book asserting that, instead, the Earth revolved around the sun, he was dragged before the Inquisition and convicted of heresy. Despite being a devout Catholic, Galileo Galilei was sentenced to life imprisonment.

He had already been in trouble for making the same assertion 18 years earlier, having studied calculations made in the previous century by the Polish astronomer Nicolas Copernicus. Galileo had meanwhile made observations with a telescope he had built himself, and established for certain that Copernicus was right. For the Church this was decidedly awkward. The notion that the Earth turned around the sun undermined one of its basic tenets: that man was made in the image of God. If the Earth was no longer the centre of things, but just one planet among others in a solar system, man may be just one part of a much larger universe, and not necessarily of divine importance.

Despite the Church's efforts to silence him, new scientific discoveries merely confirmed that Galileo was right. Even so, the account of his experiments remained on the Catholic Church's Index of Forbidden Books until 1835.[18] Galileo did not contest the Church as such, but he was distressed that he was forced to repudiate an indisputable fact. He was denied the right to demonstrate the truth freely.

Across Europe, however, intellectuals began to fight for that right. In the 18th century, they spread freethinking, tolerance and the notion of equality, and brought about a more accurate understanding of man and the universe. In this century, the fight for freedom took the form of a fight for knowledge – based not on tradition and faith, but on reason; if something could not be logically demonstrated, the intellectuals dismissed it. Instead of blind faith, they propagated Enlightenment.

This flourishing of intense inquiry changed how people thought about science, religion and politics, and in particular weakened the Church's authority on the way the world was created. From the first chapter of the Old Testament, Genesis, it could be calculated that the world was created in one instance at around 4,000 BC. This did not tally, however, with new geological discoveries showing that the Earth experienced several natural catastrophes before its atmosphere could sustain life. It became apparent that life had existed far longer than could be reconciled with the Holy Scripture.

If the Biblical account of creation was fallible, would the Church's other teachings still hold true? If they too could be questioned, why submit to the authority of the Church at all, whether Catholic or Protestant? Enlightenment thinkers no longer felt helpless before a punishing God, but rather at liberty to inquire further.

This had revolutionary implications: if the Church's static view of the world was invalid, how credible was the divine right by which monarchs such as Louis XIV reigned? The Enlightenment's freethinkers questioned the relationship between the people and the government, and asked how much liberty should be allowed and how much authority was necessary.

Britain was already ahead in tackling such issues. Living during the English Civil War in the 1650s, Thomas Hobbes (1588-1679) assumed gloomily that men, like animals, tend naturally to fight with each other and cause anarchy, thus depriving individuals of freedom. He believed humans should therefore accept firm government by a sovereign, but on the basis of a "social contract" freely struck on the basis of equality. John Locke (1632-1704) asserted that a natural God-given moral law entitled men to be free and equal, and if governments violated individual rights, people may legitimately rebel. He favoured institutional checks and balances to limit government power.

In France, Voltaire (1694-1778) went even further. Declaring that "reasonable liberty permits the mind to soar", he championed complete freedom of conscience and expression, and demanded that church and state should be separated. His main weapon was biting satire, as a result of which he was imprisoned, his books were burnt and he was several times exiled. One million people attended his re-burial in Paris in 1791, and his influence far outlasted his epoch. In the weeks after Islamic fundamentalists launched a lethal attack on the French satirical newspaper *Charlie Hebdo* in 2015, Voltaire's *Treatise on Tolerance,* first published in 1763, returned to France's bestseller lists.

Jean-Jacques Rousseau, another 18th century French philosopher, similarly fostered individual liberty. He declared: "Man is born free and everywhere he is in chains," and to break those shackles he proposed a social contract between rulers and the governed. Rousseau considered that an individual's conscience was an infallible guide to moral action. He looked back to "noble savages" of primitive times and saw freedom as the natural state of being.

In Germany, ruled by autocratic princes, the poets Johann Wolfgang Goethe and Friedrich Schiller celebrated free-spirited individuals fighting against tyrants. The philosopher Immanuel Kant (1724–1804) told people to look inside themselves to decide their moral duty, rather than rely on God or any other authority. He saw the flourishing of rational thought in the Enlightenment as man's coming of age – his emancipation from parental guidance.[19]

This was a fight for freedom waged by intellectuals and was as effective as any uprising in undermining autocratic rule. Growing literacy aided the cause, as noted by a German visitor to Paris in the 1780s, who saw women, children, workmen, apprentices, coachmen and soldiers all reading books.[20] Even the nobility and clergy became avid consumers of literature; Marie-Antoinette, wife of Louis XVI, had books in her library that were banned by the censor.

It looked as if France might go through a liberalising, peaceful transformation, which would be widely accepted as in England in 1688-89. But alas, France did not take England's path and instead of gradual change came violent revolution, not only in France, but also in the New World.

CHAPTER 4

AN AGE OF REVOLUTIONS

Life, liberty and the pursuit of happiness.

Liberty, Equality, Fraternity.

*Workers of the world, you have nothing
to lose but your chains.*

America

———————

Having set the pace in opening up government to the people, it is ironic that Britain's Parliamentary democracy had to submit to the western world's first great revolution. The rebels were the families of English settlers who had crossed the Atlantic to settle on the east coast of America. Britain intended the colonies to be extensions of the mother country, helping to increase the home nation's wealth. In America, however, a number of the leading settlers were nonconformists who had fled England to escape religious persecution, and so felt little loyalty to their mother country.

As often before, the trouble started over taxation, in this case a move by Britain in the 1760s to tax the colonies directly. American colonists questioned its right to do so, since they had no representation in the British Parliament.

By 1773, the Americans mostly had things their way, but the British still tried to levy a minimum of taxation in order to assert their sovereignty. The dispute came to a head in Boston late that year, when protestors tried to prevent taxable tea from being unloaded from three ships. The British Royal Governor refused to allow the tea to be sent back to Britain, so the protestors boarded the ships and tipped all 342 chests of tea into the harbour.

News of this "Boston Tea Party" caused a huge stir. The British Prime Minister, Lord North, declared: "Whatever may be the consequence, we must risk something; if we do not, all is over," and ordered the port of Boston to be closed. Despite conciliatory gestures on both sides, the American War of Independence broke out in 1775, leading to the rebels' declaration of the independence in the following year. The British had to concede the loss of sovereignty after their final defeat in 1783.

How was it that the colonists succeeded against an established military power such as Britain? England's Magna Carta worked in their favour, since it safeguarded people's freedom against abuse of power, and specifically from being taxed without consultation. They were reinforced by a Royal Charter of 1606 which promised that "the persons which shall dwell within the colonies shall have all the liberties as if they had been abiding and born within this our realm of England."[21]

By the time the confrontation arose in the 18th century, the American settlers had Magna Carta hard-wired into their legal systems, and the knowledge that they were fighting for its principles was a strong motivator. The British, on the other hand, could not convincingly argue against a charter they had written themselves, meaning that even before the revolt started, the rebels held the moral high ground.

On their own territory and fighting for their freedom, the Americans were superior to the British in communicating and making use of intelligence. One of their leaders, Paul Revere, one evening overheard a stable boy say the British military would move on Lexington the next day to arrest colonial leaders and seize munitions in nearby Concord. He jumped on his horse and galloped 13 miles through the night to Lexington, knocking on doors at every settlement and rousing local militia – the minutemen. The news spread like wildfire as church bells rang out, drums beat and those alerted made off to wake up others. When the British troops set out to march to Lexington and Concord the next morning, they were astonished to encounter fierce resistance all along the way. They were soundly beaten and had to retreat. The great power was humbled by a band of locals, and the effect on the morale of both sides was immense.

Another advantage the Americans enjoyed was that the British counter-insurgency campaign lacked public support at home. King George III wanted the rebels put in their place, but he was subordinate to his ministers and Parliament, where opinion was divided. Some leading figures believed the colonists were justified in demanding "no taxation without representation", since this contravened a clause of Magna Carta. When Americans themselves would much later fight a war in Vietnam, they too would learn the same hard lesson about divided public opinion at home.

Also crucial to the rebels' success was the support they received from the French, who hoped to regain American territories they had been forced to cede to the British after defeat in Europe a few years earlier. With the help of French soldiers and a French blockading fleet, an American army forced the British to surrender at Yorktown in 1783. That too was a lesson that freedom fighters in the next two centuries took to heart: foreign support could effectively tip the balance of power. In this case, France gained the satisfaction of spiting an old foe, but exhausted itself financially.

Having defeated the British in the first encounters, the 13 colonies involved in the war set about forming a new state. The way this was done showed just how far humanity had progressed along the path of freedom. Instead of following military successes with orgies of torture, mutilations and displays of severed heads on pikes – as so often in the past – the Founding Fathers of the United States of America focused on the obligations of a state towards its citizens, considering how to balance authority with freedom. In doing so, they looked to the freethinkers of the Enlightenment for inspiration.

The man who probably influenced them most was the English philosopher John Locke, who held that every man had a natural right to defend his life, health, liberty and possessions – against an unjust government if necessary. When Thomas Jefferson came to draft the Declaration of Independence in 1776, he wrote in the Preamble:

> *"We hold these truths to be self-evident, that all men are created equal, that they are endowed by their Creator with certain inalienable rights, that among these are life, liberty and the pursuit of happiness."*

Thirteen years later, the Founding Fathers defined those rights more specifically in a Bill of Rights of 1789, which guaranteed freedom of religion, freedom of speech, freedom of the press and freedom of assembly. It also limited the government's powers in judicial and other proceedings. Absent was Locke's stipulation of the right to property, since not everybody believed it was a right, or that it was a freedom to be fought for. Interestingly, this was the view taken also by Rousseau, who argued that when man first enclosed ground and declared ownership, he opened the way to much suffering and misfortune. Rousseau asserted that "the fruits of the earth belong to us all, and the earth itself to nobody".[22]

The American Revolution, the Declaration of Independence and the Bill of Rights stand out as major steps forward in the fight for freedom. Rational and focused on the public good, they enabled a free and prosperous society to develop in America – disproving the cynical theory that overthrowing one tyranny must be followed by the sprouting of another. So successful were these new constitutional arrangements that they set standards other nations sought to emulate.

They were deficient in two respects, however; although it was self-evident that all men were created equal and had the right to liberty, this did not apply to slaves. Among the Founding Fathers, George Washington, Thomas Jefferson and Patrick Henry all owned slaves themselves. Secondly, American women were restrained from exercising the freedoms granted to men, since women did not have the vote. Only after World War I did full female suffrage come into force in the United States (see Chapter 12).

France

Even before the American Revolution, clouds began gathering over the archaic, authoritarian regime of France, the most powerful nation on the continent of Europe. Louis XV (1715-1774), like his predecessor Louis XIV, claimed the divine right to rule. But he committed one blunder after another, compounded, as far as the population was concerned, by bad harvests and two wars (1740-48 and 1756-63), both culminating in defeats for France.

Louis XV's reign was a catastrophe, and by the time he died in 1774 to be succeeded by his son, Louis XVI, France's finances were in dire straits and the absolutist monarchy was extremely unpopular. The nation's system of government no longer corresponded to the needs of the times. Merchants, manufacturers and professionals were generating prosperity through trade and business, but were excluded as commoners from the political process. Peasants were stuck in a feudal system which kept them in hopeless poverty, while the king and the nobility remained cut off from reality in antiquated rituals at the Royal Palace of Versailles.

Desperate to find a body that would sanction new taxes, the king summoned the Estates General, which had not met for 175 years and was comprised of clergy, nobility and commoners. That was more representative of France as a whole, but was still weighted against the social class to which most of the population belonged – the commoners. In June 1789, the king issued a charter promising freedom of the press, reform of the law and internal free trade, but he held out against social equality, insisting on the old prerogatives for nobility and clergy.

It was too little, too late; the commoners responded by splitting off to form their own National Assembly, declaring that they represented the French people, and they swore not to disperse until they had formed a new constitution. With this, the king began gathering troops to regain control, and on 14th July 1789, as panic and rumours swept the populace, a mob stormed the Bastille prison where political prisoners were detained. The crowd found only seven prisoners inside, but the assault captured the imagination of the public as a momentous act of liberation. The French Revolution had erupted, and there was no holding it back.

A month later, inspired by the American Declaration of Independence,[23] the French National Assembly voted a "Declaration of the Rights of Man and the Citizen" proclaiming liberty, equality, fraternity, and the right to resist oppression. It effectively did away with France's old system of government and by enshrining basic liberties and human rights, it reinforced the concept of individual freedom.

The king refused to sanction the decrees and remained aloof in his Palace of Versailles, on the outskirts of the capital. After a large crowd of Parisians gathered menacingly outside the palace, Louis gave in and returned to Paris, where the Assembly continued its work dismembering his regime and destroying the powers of the Catholic Church.

The National Assembly reorganised the administration of France along rational grounds, declared farmers and peasants to be free of feudal obligations, and abolished a tax known as the tithe, which required people to give one-tenth of their income to the Church. Church lands were nationalised and sold off to the benefit of the national exchequer, and the Church was legally separated from the State.

In 1792, power began passing from the National Assembly to more radical groups of insurgents, who plundered the king's palace in Paris and detained him and his family. They then replaced the Assembly with a Convention elected by free male suffrage, and this new body abolished the monarchy and declared a republic.

As the Revolution began to turn violent, thousands of aristocrats and clergy fled abroad, where they rallied alarmed foreign powers to wage war against France to restore the old regime. French revolutionary leaders responded with a call to arms, urging citizens to fight for their newly won liberty, their way of life, and their fatherland. The duty to fight was the corollary of their rights – two parts of the same democratic equation.

Foreign forces penetrated France's frontiers, but French soldiers eventually triumphed, due to levels of motivation which the opposing armies could not match. Revolutionary France thus pioneered a tradition of patriotic military service by every able-bodied male – a practice that eventually spread to the rest of Europe and America.

However, the foreign threat had another impact – it radicalised the French Revolution even further. Fanatics set on defending the Revolution at any cost replaced earlier leaders inspired by the Enlightenment, and the country descended into a Reign of Terror. Carts rumbled through the streets taking aristocrats, clergy and other "public enemies" to be guillotined before crowds roused by blood lust. Many were executed after show trials or no trial at all, and when infighting broke out among the revolutionary leaders, some of them met the same grisly fate.

Although the new constitution safeguarded freedom of worship, mobs plundered Church buildings, venting their hatred for an institution that had become repressive and corrupt. In the cathedral of St. Denis, burial place of French kings, the tombs are now nearly all empty, their contents desecrated and destroyed. At Cluny in Burgundy, once one of Europe's most magnificent monasteries, only the transept of the church remains, the rest having been pulled down and carried off as building materials.

In January 1793, after an abortive escape in a curtained carriage, Louis XVI was tried for "conspiracy against the public liberty and the general safety". In the Convention that found him guilty, 321 voted for imprisonment, but 361 for execution. The larger vote carried the day and the king was beheaded in the centre of Paris to cries of "*Vive la République! –* Long Live the Republic!" It took the revolutionaries some time to take this fatal step, but like the English Parliamentarians 150 years earlier, they were finally prepared to sacrifice their king for a new order that better represented the people.

The rest of Europe looked on in horror and the Reign of Terror was seen as a catastrophic setback for the freethinkers who had tried to set up a fair and logical system of government. Instead of being able to take their lives freely into their own hands, people were subjected to fear, violence and death. The thrill of breaking out into *liberté, égalité* and *fraternité* gave way to an awful fascination with the welter of killing and destruction leading the country into anarchy. By the end of the century, unemployment, taxation and inflation were soaring, and the revolutionary regime had lost control over much of the population.

Waiting to seize his opportunity was Napoleon Bonaparte, who had made a reputation as a defender of the new republic at the head of its victorious armies. Sensing a desire for a return to order, he seized power in 1799 in a coup d'état against the civilian government, and proclaimed himself First Consul and then Emperor in 1804. Napoleon thereafter ruled as a dictator, invaded much of Europe and won one battle after another against rival powers.

Some of the defeated peoples at first welcomed the French incursion, firstly as a means of emancipation from their own oppressive rulers, and also because Napoleon introduced honest, efficient administrations, a fairer legal code and improved education. Napoleon professed to be spreading the French Revolution's noble principles of liberty, equality and fraternity; but the French occupation soon became associated with conscription, discrimination, censorship and police repression. Millions of Europeans lived in terror until he was overthrown in 1815 by an alliance of the peoples he sought to dominate. The anarchy of the Revolution had opened the way for him to impose his tyranny, but his defeat gave force to the maxim that the oppressed will not be downtrodden forever.

The French Revolution also lent weight to the opposing sceptical view that a fight for freedom would inevitably lead to disaster, with extremists exploiting the collapse of a previous order. However, it is hard to see how the much-needed change could have been brought about without any force at all. The monarchy and the nobles aimed to preserve their privileged positions by whatever means they could, so without the violence of the unruly masses, France may have remained in a decaying, oppressive regime, unable to release the potential of its people.

Along with the baying mobs and public executions also came freethinking, hopes and new ideas. The principles of liberty, equality and fraternity that the revolutionaries formulated have stood the test of time. They are among the key values of the European Union's 28 member nations, and are espoused by millions of other people around the globe.

So, at the cost of a king's head and a few years of anarchy, the French revolutionaries made good use of their liberty in laying one of the great milestones in mankind's long fight for freedom. By the 1870s, France settled into a form of democratic republican government, which, despite further shocks, has survived until today. French statesmen still wear the revolutionary tricolour, sing the *Marseillaise* revolutionary anthem and celebrate the anniversary of the storming of the Bastille as their National Day. They are proud that their compatriots of two centuries ago changed the world.

Reaction and New Uprisings

The reaction of Europe's rulers to the French Revolution and Napoleon's adventures was to strengthen their powers over their own populations and clamp down on liberties. Even the government of England, much admired by the French reformers, introduced laws prohibiting Treasonable Practices and Seditious Meetings. It suspended habeas corpus (legal protection against detention without charges) and legislated against trade unions and other reform groups.

After Napoleon was defeated in 1815, Europe's conservative rulers came together at the Congress of Vienna, at which they agreed to cooperate in keeping the peace and stifling liberal reform movements – there should no more Napoleons and no more revolutions. France restored the monarchy and came under the rule of the reactionary Charles X; Austria suppressed movements for autonomy by Slavs within its empire; and in Russia, after a brief experiment in liberal reforms, Tsar Alexander I returned to traditional autocratic ways.

The new conservatism, however, proved incapable of fulfilling the changing expectations of society, and the pendulum swung back towards liberal reform. In England, public opinion was outraged when soldiers at Peterloo, in Manchester, killed 18 industrial workers demonstrating against lack of representation in Parliament. Despite its claims to represent the people, the English Parliament in 1832 was still elected by only two per cent of the population, largely landowners.

In reaction to this Peterloo Massacre, Parliament passed a series of Reform Acts, giving more men the right to vote and thus influence the way they were governed. Between that year and the eve of World War I, successive Reform Acts extended suffrage to the middle and working classes, so that, by 1914, two men in three could vote (but still no women – see Chapter 12).

On the continent, the battle between freedom and repression swung to and fro. A series of uprisings by liberals and revolutionaries in 1830 brought in a new, reform-minded monarchy in France, while Belgium could free itself from the Netherlands, and Greece from the Ottoman Empire. In Germany, Italy and Poland, however, the movements were forcefully suppressed.

In 1848 another round of agitation for liberty turned into full-scale insurrections in Paris, Berlin, Vienna and Budapest. The French overturned the monarchy again and made suffrage universal for men. Central parts of Italy became free from Austrian rule and declared an Italian republic, but elsewhere unrest was again put down by force.

It was cut and thrust, but despite the setbacks, liberalisation was winning the battle. After defeating Austria in 1859, the Italians were able to unite their whole country as an independent kingdom. They called their struggle for national liberation the Risorgimento (Rising Again), later immortalised in the operas of Giuseppe Verdi.

The most charismatic Italian freedom fighter was Giuseppe Garibaldi, who led his guerrilla bands all over the country to fight foreign occupiers and reactionary local kingdoms. When they triumphed, he held plebiscites in Naples and Sicily, so that the populations could decide by whom they would be ruled. Meanwhile, across the Atlantic, Simón Bolivar and José San Martin led similar movements to free parts of South America from Spanish colonial rule. Brazil also wrested independence from Portugal in 1822.

In the midst of this ferment, John Stuart Mill (1806-73) published the book *On Liberty*, which remains one of the most influential works on the subject. Seeking to extend the field of freedom, he declared that individual liberty could not be legitimately infringed – whether by government, society or individuals – unless the action in question would harm other people. Mill affirmed that liberty allowed personal growth and self-realisation, and was a necessary condition for civilisation, social progress, education and culture. There should be free debate of opposing views, even if one of them turns out to be false, and accepted views should be constantly challenged to test their validity. Government should not impose censorship, and individuals should not bow to the prevailing prejudices of society.

Such freedoms may seem unexceptional in our liberal, free-speaking societies of today, where opinions whizz unchecked around Twitter and Facebook, but he was writing in England in 1859, when society was still beset by all sorts of impediments to freedom. Liberty was seen as a luxury, but Mill insisted that it was a necessity, only to be hindered if there were clear reasons to do so.[24]

Economic Liberty and Revolution

As the century took its course, the focus moved from individual liberty to questions of economic freedom. For capitalists, this meant liberty to conduct business according to the principles of free enterprise; for workers, however, it meant liberty from exploitation.

The economist Adam Smith (1723-90) argued that economies that evolved freely created more prosperity than those subject to government controls. The downside of his concept was that those who invested capital in businesses could exploit the workers for as much as they could get out of them. In practice, the mass of workers flooding into the cities from the countryside had no bargaining power against their employers. The free-market economy did drive economic growth, but it concentrated wealth in the hands of the few – the capitalists – while many of the rest lived in penury.

People began to ask whether freedom should also mean freedom from economic exploitation. One English commentator of the time, William Cobbett, expressed doubts that the social pact between citizens and rulers would hold if men were driven to desperate violence by poverty.[25] Earning one's wherewithal may be seen as a personal responsibility, but some of the working classes appeared to have no opportunity to do so. They were, it seemed, imprisoned in deprivation, which diminished their freedom as human beings.

Karl Marx and Friedrich Engels reacted to these miseries in 1848 with the famous call of their Communist Manifesto: "Workers of the world unite! You have nothing to lose but your chains." Marx and Engels urged workers to liberate themselves from the capitalists by seizing ownership of the means of production. They asserted that economic change generated a class struggle that would inevitably end in victory for the new class of industrial workers. The two developed this into a theory of human history, which they insisted was based on science and therefore irrefutable and assured of success.

Two concepts of freedom thus came into conflict: on the one hand, Adam Smith argued for a free-market economy with little or no regulation, while on the other hand Marx and Engels pressed for workers to free themselves from the free-market capitalists. To this day this dichotomy has not been fully resolved, and in many countries it can still be seen in the conflict between parties of the left and the right.

At the time, the prospect of liberating a downtrodden proletariat proved a powerful enticement towards revolution, and an opportunity soon presented itself. In 1870, France was defeated in a war by Germany and its government subsequently collapsed. In the aftermath of a siege causing near-starvation, the working class people of Paris set up a Commune that was a prototype of an ideal "Communist" society. It refused the authority of any government and operated as freely elected local bodies in which each man had an equal say. Workplaces were turned into cooperatives and the Louvre museum became a munitions factory run by a workers' council.

Despite setting up barricades of furniture and carts in the narrow streets of Paris, the Commune lasted only two months before soldiers of the reconstituted government swept it away in a flurry of retribution. About 20,000 insurgents were killed, and tens of thousands more were imprisoned or deported. It was a cruel end to a utopian experiment that pushed liberty to the verge of anarchy, but inspired future generations. The sight of revolutionaries manning barricades against the forces of repression moved Victor Hugo to write *Les Misérables,* a novel that has since been turned into a popular stage musical and film.

It was in Russia that a party representing the industrial proletariat was first able to seize the means of production – that is, factories, land and natural resources. Marx expected revolution would come first to advanced economies such as Germany or Britain, not Russia, with its masses of peasants. But the old order in Russia could not withstand the defeats and terrible losses of World War I. Tsar Nicholas II abdicated in early 1917, and with him went the old Russia of Tolstoy, Dostoevsky and Pushkin, of Tchaikovsky and Stravinsky, of the magical Russian ballet of Nijinsky, and the aristocracy with its vast estates worked by millions of serfs.

Power passed into the hands of mutinous soldiers drawn from the humblest of classes, no longer willing to fight for the Tsar. Into the vacuum of power came revolutionary committees modelled on the Paris Commune of 1871, with no leaders, no rules and no structures; accepting no authority but their own and calling themselves Soviets. A provisional government, drawn from the left and right, tried to set up a parliamentary democracy, but it was half-hearted and its authority rapidly disintegrated. With disorder spreading throughout the country, Russia became engulfed by revolution.

However, any hopes that revolution would lead to new liberties came to nought. One evening in autumn 1917, an American journalist named John Reed went to the outskirts of St. Petersburg to join a group of radicals called the Bolsheviks, who were about to bring the revolution to its climax. He found himself following a crowd, flowing like a black river through the streets, and then swarming through open gates into the brightly lit Imperial Winter Palace.[26] Based on this, Reed wrote a celebrated book called *Ten Days That Changed the World* – and they certainly did that, but not in the direction of liberty.

With the Winter Palace in the hands of revolutionary groups, the Bolshevik leader Vladimir Lenin coined the slogan "All power to the Soviets!" That meant sweeping away the provisional government and Parliament, but he had no intention of repeating the impotent anarchy of the Paris Commune. He wanted sole power for the Bolshevik Party, which was to rule by dictatorship. The Party duly seized the means of production, as Marx had directed, but the workers could not throw off their chains. As in the French Revolution, extremists seized power, but this time the new tyranny would last much longer.

The eruption of World War I brought to an end the freedom fighting of 19th century Europe. New liberties had been won, but in the face of constant opposition by conservatives defending privileges or concerned about anarchy and a collapse of moral values. Outside Europe and America, much of the rest of the world had been colonised by European powers, and these subject peoples could not be counted as free. Ironically, many were kept down precisely by those European civilisations that were finding ways to freedom for themselves.

The one great nation that did fully embrace the idea of freedom was the United States of America. In this vast New World, opportunity was boundless, one could become rich irrespective of class, and for those who wanted unbounded adventure, the Far West beckoned. Typically the first explorers staked out land, cleared it, sold it and then moved on westwards to virgin territories. Nobody put any restraints on this freest of enterprises, except occasionally the native Indians, who were ruthlessly brushed aside.

America drew in millions of Europeans, who suffered from economic deprivation and saw little opportunity to better themselves in their homelands. They abandoned homes and villages, pulled together a few meagre belongings and made their way across the Atlantic in primitive vessels. The shining beacon of the Statue of Liberty greeted them on arrival, symbolizing what they could expect as new Americans: a land of freedom.

Yet America was not completely free – not for all. It relied heavily on slavery, a dark part of its history that scars its society even to the present day. America would go through much agony and travail in dealing with this fundamental denial of liberty. Slavery would raise awkward questions about the very nature of American society and, before the issue was resolved, it would tear the nation apart.

CHAPTER 5

FREEING THE SLAVES

I was born a slave, but nature gave me the soul of a free man.
— Toussaint-Louverture (liberator of Haiti)

Early Slavery

S ince the dawn of humanity, tribes that went to war put their captives to work as slaves. There was no question as to whether this was right or wrong; it was a natural phenomenon, much the same as keeping domesticated animals. Slaves were first recorded in Sudan in 2,500 BC, in the Hebrew Bible and Babylon some 700 years later, and in present-day Spain from 850 BC.[27]

Slaves were generally the property of the owner, and could be bought and sold at will. Some, however, were serfs, who could be sold only in conjunction with the land. This status gave them greater permanence, since they could stay in their homes. The Greek state of Sparta functioned with serfs from the 9th to the 2nd century BC. Known as "helots", they were owned by the state, bound to a patch of land and assigned to work for individual Spartans; their masters could neither free them nor sell them.

Most slaves, however, were chattels belonging to their owners rather than tied to the land. In these early times, they were primarily put to work in the fields, since land was abundant and labour was in short supply. Others worked in irrigation, mining, tending furnaces and as household servants or entertainers.

The Athenians of the 4th century BC introduced remarkable liberties for their citizens, but had a blind spot as far as their slaves were concerned. The Athenian philosopher Aristotle preached the value of community and fellowship, but held slavery to be "natural". Athenians had 30,000 slaves working in their silver mines alone, and the city police force consisted of 300 enslaved Scythian archers. In 166 BC, the Greek island of Delos was said to be trading 10,000 slaves per day.[28]

Slavery also flourished in ancient Egypt, the Roman Empire and among the peoples of China and Central Asia – indeed in almost all the known world. The Arabs, who conquered large swathes of the Middle East and North Africa, became probably the greatest slave traders of all. Between the 8th and 19th centuries AD, some 10 to 20 million people from Europe, Asia and Africa are estimated to have been enslaved by Arab traders; taken across the Red Sea, Indian Ocean and Sahara desert to be sold. Women were put to work as domestic servants, wet nurses or sex slaves. Men could become sailors in Persia, pearl divers in the Gulf, workers on the saltpans of Mesopotamia (modern Iraq) or end up as eunuchs in courts. Some, such as the Ottoman Empire's Janissaries (captured Balkan boys) and Egypt's Mamluks (slave warriors), became powerful military castes, and if settled in Muslim lands, Islamic law granted slaves a certain legal status. This did not, however, ease the mortality rate, which for those brought from Africa was extremely high.

In Christian lands, slavery was for many centuries just as endemic. Despite the preaching of Jesus on behalf of the downtrodden, early Christianity did nothing to end the practice. The Christian theologian Augustine saw slavery as part of a divine plan, teaching that it resulted from the Fall of Man following Adam's disobedience of God. His only recommendation was that masters should treat their slaves decently.

By the Middle Ages, however, Church leaders began to preach that slavery was contrary to the Christian sense of charity and justice. As a consequence, after his invasion of England in 1066, William the Conqueror outlawed enslavement of Christians, and the use of slaves to till the fields was replaced by serfdom. Serfs were obliged to cultivate the land on which they lived on behalf of their masters, but they had a right to protection in return.

Despite this first step taken in England, slavery continued to proliferate elsewhere: pirates based on the Barbary Coast of North Africa are estimated to have taken over one million Europeans captive between the 16th and 19th centuries.[29] They were ransomed, sold or set to row until they died on galleys. The United States regularly paid phenomenal ransom sums demanded by the pirates; in 1795 alone, it handed over nearly a million dollars, naval stores and a frigate to ransom 115 sailors from the pirate ruler of Algiers.[30] Within a seven-year period, Britain lost 466 merchant ships to the Barbary pirates, who also raided coastal settlements in Ireland and south-west England.

In 1444, Portugal became the first European country to import slaves from Africa, after which the practice remained unchallenged in Europe for another 300 years. In the 18th century, however, public opinion began to consider slave owning as an archaic denial of liberty, deserving to fall out of use. Even in autocratic Russia, the institution was abolished in favour of serfdom in the 17th and 18th centuries. In China, the practice also declined, even if decrees outlawing it were often flouted.

Slavery in America

In the Americas, however, slavery flourished as never before. The New World, full of rich land ready to be cultivated, developed a voracious appetite for slaves. The new plantations of sugar, cocoa, coffee, tobacco and cotton fed growing consumer demand in Europe – indeed they stimulated it. Use of slaves was a particularly cost-efficient means of exploiting these commodities for profit; they were considered as a business resource, not as members of society with rights.

Europeans may have no longer owned slaves themselves, but their seafarers were happy to enrich themselves by trading slaves. The Europeans established trading posts down the west coast of Africa, where frequent wars between indigenous empires yielded a plentiful supply of captives. Britain, France, Portugal and the Netherlands together developed a massive Atlantic slave trade, which came to be dominated by the British as the leading sea power.

The English maritime heroes Sir Francis Drake and Sir John Hawkins were early pioneers in the business, and by the 18th century slave trafficking had taken pride of place in all British trade. Transporting slaves was part of a triangular trade: ships left Europe with exports for sale at the African trading posts, and the boats were then re-stocked with slaves to be transported across the Atlantic and sold to the colonists

– in Brazil and the Caribbean, and later in the United States. On their return to Europe, the ships carried the sugar, cocoa, coffee, tobacco and cotton which had been produced on the plantations by the slave labour.

The slave trade was enormously lucrative, with a profit turned at each stage of the trip. London, Bristol, Nantes, Bordeaux, Le Havre, Amsterdam, Cadiz and Lisbon owed much of their growth and prosperity to this cruel commerce. The unrivalled European capital of the slave trade, however, was Liverpool. It organised 5,000 slave voyages, twice as many as London and Bristol combined. In this highly competitive business, Liverpool merchants undercut rivals on costs, excelled in fast turnarounds of ships and cultivated close relationships with African traders, who were eager participants in the business. If captives from African wars were lacking, the local traders sent raiding parties inland to kidnap new prisoners and drive them to be detained in coastal forts. Some of those strongholds were surrounded by impaled skeletons to deter escape attempts.[31]

Some 12 million slaves were shipped from Africa across the Atlantic between the 15th and 19th centuries. At least 10 per cent are estimated to have died on the six-week voyage, for which they were packed like sardines, forced to lie in their own excrement and provided with minimal food and drink. The survivors staggered ashore disorientated, anguished and fearful, their spirits broken and in no fit state to resist. As such, in the eyes of the buyers, they were well suited for the forced labour that was to be their fate.

The large majority of slaves were sent to the Portuguese colony of Brazil and to the British West Indies. In Brazil, African slaves had an average life expectancy of only eight years, since they lacked resistance to local tropical diseases and often suffered from malnutrition. Most were male, and the lack of females prevented reproduction. As a result, slaves in Brazil had to be constantly replaced, and their overall population did not grow significantly. In these two top destinations, the slave population far outnumbered the rest of the inhabitants – the colonists and the natives. In the Caribbean islands, there were 10 times as many black slaves as white people.

In America, fewer slaves were brought into the country – between 600,000 and 650,000 – but the inclusion of women meant the slaves reproduced. Although it seemed evident to Jean-Jacques Rousseau that all men are born free, the offspring of these American slaves were born into bondage. By 1860, there were four million slaves in America, 99 per cent of whom were born into enslavement in the "land of the free."[32]

On arrival, slaves were paraded for inspection, usually naked as if they were animals. There were terrible scenes of grief as husbands and wives were split, or mothers and fathers saw their children sold off to other owners, never to be seen again. Slaves could form new couples on the property of their owners, but their relationship had no legal standing, and owners were liable to split them again by selling one member of the couple elsewhere. One slave marriage in three in the United States was afflicted by forced separation.[33] In the southern United States, the internal slave trade was the second most important business after the plantations themselves.

Owners ruled over the slaves absolutely, regulating their rising, eating, working, resting and sleeping. Newly imported slaves were subjected to cruel induction regimes, and thereafter violence and terror kept teams of men and women working in the fields from dawn to dusk. Punishments included whippings, brandings and amputations of fingers and ears, while women were frequently raped by their proprietors.

Slavery was a heinous offence against human liberty and it is ironic that its perpetrators included some of America's Founding Fathers, who had fought for freedom themselves, proclaiming liberty to be among the principles on which their state was founded. In 1774, Thomas Jefferson owned 187 slaves; George Washington, the first president, was recorded as owning 416, among them carpenters, spinners, drivers, stable boys, smiths, seamstresses, a wagoner, a carter, a gardener and domestic servants. Six out of the first 12 American presidents were slave owners.[34]

The spirit of free enterprise weighed against the idea of giving up this lucrative practice. Those running slave businesses saw the doctrine of unregulated economy and free trade as a carte blanche to make money, untrammelled by other concerns. For owners of slaves, their victims were property and a means to make profit. For the shippers, they were a commodity to be traded like tea, spices or cotton.

In Britain, the moneyed classes cared little that the slaves they traded were abused, since they treated their own lower classes little better. Moreover, there were good opportunities to re-invest profits, as the capital accrued from the slave trade helped to finance the Industrial Revolution, which in turn made Britain the greatest world power.[35]

Abolishing the Slave Trade

Yet consciences began to stir, as the Enlightenment spread new ideas of liberty and the rights of man. This inevitably led to a questioning, not only of slave ownership, but also of the slave trade itself. In 1792, 300,000 Britons boycotted British West Indian sugar, while religious movements preached the inherent unity of all mankind, seeking to bring slaves within the Christian embrace. An increasingly liberal and expanding middle-class began to question all established institutions: from the monarchy, hereditary privilege and large landed estates, to slavery.

Britons wanted to show other nations that they were civilised and progressive – in contrast to their great rivals, the French. Having dominated the Atlantic slave trade for more than 100 years, the British also no longer found it edifying to collaborate with American rebels. Britain had profited handsomely from the slaves in the West Indies, who at one time helped to produce 55 per cent of the world's sugar, but the cheap commodities available from the American slave plantations risked undermining Britain's trade.

The chances of passing a law ending the slave trade seemed slight, however, since the British Parliament consisted of landowners and conservatives with vested interests. But it was precisely in one of those conservative politicians that the fight for abolition found an unlikely champion. As the son of a rich merchant, William Wilberforce (1759-1833) led a life of luxury as a young man, gambling, clubbing, theatre-going and horseracing. As a Cambridge undergraduate, he made friends with William Pitt, a future Prime Minister, and joined Parliament at the age of 21, establishing a reputation as an eloquent speaker. A few years later, he underwent an intense religious conversion to evangelical Christianity and decided to dedicate his work from then on to God's service.

He became convinced that his life's mission was to abolish the British slave trade – and this he did, with the help of some powerful supporters. Wilberforce set up the "Society for Effecting the Abolition of Slavery", which campaigned through pamphlets, public meetings, press lobbying and boycotts. As Prime Minister, William Pitt encouraged him, as did wealthy Quaker entrepreneurs, who held the slave trade to be unethical and inefficient. Josiah Wedgwood, the renowned potter, supported the movement by creating a logo of a kneeling slave with the inscription "Am I not a Man and a Brother?"

Wilberforce introduced his first motion to curb the slave trade in Parliament in 1789, but it failed, and when he proposed legislation to abolish it in 1791 and 1793, he was again defeated. Unluckily for him, British public opinion had become alarmed by the excesses of the French Revolution, and turned against liberal reforms of any kind.

The campaign for abolition thus remained dormant until a major slave revolt in the French West Indies colony of Saint-Domingue put the whole institution of slavery in jeopardy. Towards the end of the 18th century, Saint-Domingue accounted for a third of the entire Atlantic slave trade. Its slaves produced about 40 per cent of the sugar consumed in Europe and 60 per cent of the coffee. By the time they rose up in rebellion in 1791, some 790,000 slaves were working on the Saint-Domingue plantations.

Led by François-Dominique Toussaint-Louverture, a slave who had been granted freedom, the uprising led to the abolition of slavery on the island two years later. Although Saint-Domingue remained nominally a French colony, Toussaint-Louverture became its effective ruler for the next nine years. After Napoleon sent an army to re-assert authority on the island in 1802, the French arrested Toussaint-Louverture and deported him to a prison in

France, where he died the following year. But it was to no avail: the French had to abandon the fight after yellow fever devastated their forces in 1804, leaving Saint-Domingue free to gain independence and change its name to Haiti.

It was the first time a European nation had been forced to give way to a slave uprising, and the shock waves spread throughout the rest of the West Indies and the Americas. Toussaint-Louverture showed that, contrary to general assumptions, a black ex-slave could govern wisely and efficiently. In the years that he held sway over the island, he introduced paid labour to the plantations, kept a well-disciplined army and negotiated trade treaties with Britain and the United States.

Toussaint-Louverture was inspired by Spartacus, the leader of the slave revolt against ancient Rome, and also by the French Revolution and the Enlightenment. When rallying the islanders in 1793, he declared: "I want Liberty and Equality to reign in Saint-Domingue... Unite yourselves to us, brothers, and fight with us for the same cause." He correctly foresaw that the fight for freedom could not be kept at bay forever. When he was arrested, he told his captors: "In overthrowing me you have cut down in Saint-Domingue only the trunk of the tree of liberty; it will spring up again from the roots, for they are numerous and they are deep."[36]

The British, then locked in war with France, rejoiced that the slaves of Saint-Domingue had humbled their foe. Thereafter, ending slavery seemed the modern idea. Wilberforce introduced a new bill to abolish the British slave trade in 1807, telling the House of Commons: "You may choose to look the other way, but you can never again say that you did not know." The bill passed into law with large majorities in both the Houses; tears streamed down Wilberforce's face as he heard the voting numbers.

Even then, the slave trade did not end immediately, since ships from other nations were unaffected by British laws. As an imperial power, however, Britain was able to enforce its will on the high seas, and from 1807 the Royal Navy mounted a large-scale interdiction operation off the western coast of Africa. Over time, it yielded significant results: from 1867, no more slaves reached Cuba, which had been one of the most important destinations. Altogether, the British Navy freed 150,000 slaves from arrested ships, and its operation lasted into the 20th century, costing the lives of 5,000 British seamen. On the diplomatic front, Britain pressured the Netherlands and Portugal into banning the trade of slaves, in 1814 and 1815.

Ending Slavery

Ending the trade, however, did not mean slavery itself was stopped, and here too Britain played a leading role. In 1833, the British Parliament passed a law outlawing slavery within the British Empire, as a result of which 800,000 slaves were freed. The government paid tribute in Parliament to Wilberforce as the inspiration behind their bold move – but tragically he had died one month before the law was enacted.

The British government then proceeded to pay extraordinary sums to the large number of slave-owning Britons in compensation for liberating their slaves, altogether representing £16.5 billion in today's money. The father of a future Prime Minister, William Gladstone, received the modern equivalent of £83 million, while other unlikely beneficiaries included the Bishop of Exeter and the

Anglican Church's Society for the Propagation of the Gospel in Foreign Parts.[37]

When the Spanish colonies in Latin America freed themselves from Spanish rule over the next 10 years, the British government insisted it would recognise the new regimes only if they ended slavery. They did, and there too the British helped subsidise compensation for the owners. France outlawed slavery in its colonies in 1848, and gradually the other European colony-owning powers followed suit in order to convey the message that their imperial rule had a civilising influence.

The British paid a price for their support of freedom: production of sugar in the British West Indies fell by 25 per cent after the slaves were freed, while production soared on the slave plantations of competing territories. Banning slavery in its colonies is estimated to have cost Britain 1.8 per cent of Gross National Product annually over the following 60 years.[38]

In America, slavery was undermined when the British gave freedom to escaped slaves who joined them during the war of American Independence. George Washington then bequeathed freedom to his American slaves in his will (although it turned out some belonged to his wife, so they were excluded), while Thomas Jefferson signed a law banning the import of slaves in 1807. In the 30 years after Independence, most northern states outlawed the practice.

Significantly, however, the Constitution of the United States did not mention the word "slavery", and in southern states it grew by leaps and bounds, largely due to births inside the country. By 1810, the slave population of the United States was twice the size it had been in 1770, and in the south it accounted for one-third of all inhabitants.

New technology, such as steam power and the cotton gin,[39] made it faster and cheaper to produce textiles from cotton. As a result, demand for this raw material soared and, as plantations expanded, the demand for slaves grew too.

Churches in the south preached the Christian virtue of obedience rather than equality of all people before God, and on the plantations owners would read the Bible aloud, but not allow their slaves to read the book for themselves. The blacks meanwhile developed an "invisible church" of their own, focusing on Christianity as a religion for the oppressed, and incorporating their call-and-response singing, which harked back to their African roots.

Despite the gradual divergence in worship, churchgoing did, at times, provide a common experience for owners and slaves. They were segregated in church, but together they heard the same sermons and attended the same burials. Unlike the vast estates of Russia, where absentee owners had little or no contact with their serfs, most of the owners in the American south were residents, and formed a community with their slaves, albeit an unequal one. Black and white children played together until the age of eight, often unaware of the master-slave relationship.

Any idea of liberating the slaves, however, was viewed with horror by the southern whites, who claimed it would lead to poverty, rape and banditry. They believed the slaves were, in their very beings, unsuited to freedom. At best, they were to be treated like children.

The north and south became divided – the north urbanising and investing in factories, transport and modern mass media, while the south continued living off the plantations, basing its economy on slavery – helped by a sharp increase in the world price of cotton in the

1850s.

However, since the successful slave revolt in Saint-Domingue, the threat of insurrection loomed over the whole slave-plantation business. On Christmas Day 1831, some 60,000 of Jamaica's 300,000 slaves went on strike, burning and looting plantations. It was the largest slave uprising in the British West Indies, and the colonial army managed to suppress it only after 300 slaves and 14 colonialists were killed.

That same year, the American slave Nat Turner had a vision of gaining his freedom by force, and launched a bloody uprising in Southampton County, Virginia. After killing his master's family as they slept, he and other slaves moved from house to house, killing over 50 whites with clubs, knives and muskets. A militia force had to be raised to put down the rebellion, which ended with the execution of Turner and 55 others.

Then in 1841, African slaves aboard the Spanish ship *Amistad* off the coast of Cuba mutinied and killed most of the Spanish crew. They intended to sail back to Africa, but the ship was seized by the U.S. Navy and taken ashore in Connecticut. Spain demanded the return of the slaves, but a judge ruled that they had been kidnapped and had the right to free themselves by whatever means necessary. The prosecutor appealed, but the Supreme Court upheld the verdict and, with the help of donations from abolitionists, the Africans were able to return to modern-day Sierra Leone.

The scale of the uprising was small – there were 63 slaves on board – but what was significant was that the Supreme Court of the United States had vindicated them in their fight for freedom. It was a momentous ruling against the institution of slavery, showing that winds of change were blowing across the United States.

American Civil War

Such small-scale uprisings were mere skirmishes. The fight to free American slaves would be settled only in a Civil War that would cost the lives of some 620,000 American soldiers and change America forever.

In the middle of the 19th century, tensions between the north and south came to a head over the morality of slave owning. Increasingly, public opinion in the north favoured its abolition, while the south was determined to maintain a practice that had proved lucrative. When Abraham Lincoln (1809-1865) of the anti-slavery Republican Party was elected president in 1860, southern states feared he would outlaw slavery across the nation, so 11 of these states seceded from the United States of America to set up a separate Confederate state. After the rebels captured government forts and Lincoln sent troops to counter-attack, the ensuing Civil War pitted three million soldiers against each other, in 237 battles that extended over a vast front. The number of soldiers killed between 1861 and 1865 was nearly as many as those who died in all the other wars Americans have fought, before and since.

Lincoln's immediate goal was to force the rebel states back into the Union, but after a time it became a moral crusade to end slavery across the United States. Early in 1863, Lincoln issued an Emancipation Proclamation, which declared slaves in the rebel southern states to be free. It had no direct consequence, since the south was not then under Lincoln's control, but it encouraged slaves to run away and 180,000 joined the Unionist armies of the north.

After the Battle of Gettysburg in the summer of 1863, Lincoln made a speech to commemorate the 51,000 soldiers who died in the encounter, which proved the turning point of the war. He reminded his listeners that "four score and seven years ago our fathers brought forth on this continent a new nation, conceived in liberty, and dedicated to the proposition that all men are created equal." He resolved "that this nation, under God, shall have a new birth of freedom".

The Confederates finally lost the deadliest war in American history, and Lincoln's Gettysburg address set the direction for the future. The Unionists of the north freed all the slaves in the south and set up Republican Reconstruction Governments in every southern state. These were tasked with establishing civil and voting rights for the blacks, and restoring political and economic life. As a result of this emancipation, Freedmen's schools were established and former slaves could form legal families.

Much of the rest of the world was following suit. In 1861, Tsar Alexander II ended serfdom in Russia, freeing 50 million people. He believed the practice was holding back Russia's development and told his reluctant nobles: "It is better to begin to destroy serfdom from above than to wait until that time when it begins to destroy itself from below." In Brazil, the outlawing of slavery saw the release of 750,000 slaves in 1888. The trend also continued in the 20th century, with China abolishing the practice in 1906, followed by the U.N. Universal Declaration of Human Rights of 1948, prohibiting slavery and the slave trade in all their forms.

However, Lincoln's triumph in fighting for the slaves' freedom immediately triggered a counter-attack by conservatives defending their interests. The white southerners were outraged and humiliated at being forced to free human beings whom they considered to be their property. Five days after the American Civil War ended in 1865, a Confederate sympathiser assassinated Lincoln.

The Ku Klux Klan was formed to restore white supremacy and deter blacks from exercising their voting rights. The Reconstruction Governments were also gradually removed from power, as new white legislators brought in voting laws so complex that they effectively disenfranchised black people. They reduced spending on black education, curbed civil rights, and segregated races in schools, public transport, theatres, eating places, hotels, parks, hospitals, waiting rooms, drinking fountains and burial grounds. Racism became virulent.

The Reconstruction Governments had not redistributed any land, so the liberated blacks remained at a disadvantage compared with the whites. They were freed from masters and plantations, but many were left hungry, destitute and "slaves to the rains and frosts of winter".[40] Together with the rising discrimination and violence, this caused deep disappointment and despair among black people. The south slipped into lethargy, corruption and ignorance, with a long recession in the 1870s depressing spirits further. The fight to liberate the blacks seemed to have yielded very little. No longer were they formally slaves, but their right to equality and freedom remained severely curtailed.

Despite the lack of progress, abolition of slavery as an institution represented a breakthrough; the idea that enslaving our fellow-man was ethically justifiable had been broken forever. Although many obstacles remained, from now on it was clear that black people were entitled to be treated as free human beings. What they needed was a charismatic figure to open up freedom in its entirety, and that man would come (see Chapter 13).

CHAPTER 6

WORLD WARS – LIBERTY DIES AND IS REBORN

*Man can now go to the moon, but I
still can't go to West Berlin.*
– anonymous East Berliner, 1972

Darwin Distorted

Throughout the 19th century, the battle between reformists and conservatives went to and fro but, despite setbacks, the cause of freedom made great advances. In the first half of the 20th century, however, Europe was plunged into turmoil which caused tens of millions of deaths and nearly extinguished freedom altogether. At times, it seemed as if the progress achieved in the struggle for liberty over two millennia would come to nothing.

When the scientist Charles Darwin published *The Descent of Man* in 1871, he inadvertently sowed the seeds of two World Wars. Darwin argued that man was descended from apes, rather than created in the image of God. Predictably this upset the Church, since it challenged the Biblical account of creation. Bishop Samuel Wilberforce (son of William Wilberforce) declared Darwin's theories to be "incompatible with the word of God",[41] and the Vatican Council of 1870 re-affirmed that God created all life on earth.

More ominous were the interpretations made by Europe's nationalists for baleful purposes, focusing on Darwin's assertion that all species developed in competition with others. Although the scientist described only physical evolution, politicians abused his concept of "the survival of the fittest" to foment enmity between nations. Until then, scientific discovery tended to further mankind's fight for freedom, but now it was being perverted to incite hatred.

Thus, when Germany, Austria, Hungary, Russia, France, Britain, Italy, Serbia and Turkey engaged in World War I, nationalists depicted the conflict as an epic struggle for the survival of their respective peoples. Mass mobilisation forced millions of Europe's young men to abandon peaceable pursuits and submit to the iron discipline of military authority. Meanwhile, at home, governments curbed freedom of speech, news reporting and business enterprise.

WWI may have been a dark time for freedom, but the powers upholding liberty – France, Britain and the United States – eventually triumphed, and autocratic Germany was defeated. The break-up of the Austro-Hungarian Empire also freed Czechs, Slovaks, Romanians and Southern Slavs to form their own independent states (Czechoslovakia, Romania and Yugoslavia).

Totalitarian Russia

Russia, by contrast – now renamed the Soviet Union – was subjected to a totalitarian regime that suppressed liberties more than ever. Lenin decided that his Bolsheviks, or the

Communists as they re-designated themselves, should take the lead in the struggle against capitalists, which in practice meant crushing all opposition. Energetic and brutal by nature, Lenin ordered a "Red Terror" involving tens of thousands of executions, imprisonments and deportations during a three-year civil war that followed the Communists' takeover.

Things became worse after Lenin died in 1924, as he was succeeded by Josef Stalin, a sinister ex-seminary who became one of the cruellest tyrants in history. He caused the deaths of between 10 and 20 million Russian citizens in a reign of even greater terror, which required people to believe unquestioningly and submit completely.[42]

Stalin headed off potential challenges by having his leadership comrades murdered,[43] staging thousands of show trials and engendering a climate of chronic suspicion. In the Ukraine, he starved over three million peasants to death for being "disloyal", which is bitterly recalled by today's Ukrainians as Russia again jeopardises their autonomy.[44] Even those who had no real intention of exercising individual liberties were denounced, tortured, executed or sent to Gulag prison camps in Siberia, where the inmates were to all intents and purposes slaves. Some 18 million prisoners are estimated to have passed through the Gulag, and nearly three million died.[45]

Slavery thus returned to Russia with a vengeance, 90 years after serfdom had been abolished. Gulag convicts were typically dumped in the middle of uninhabited frozen tundra in Siberia, left to create rudimentary shelters and set to work logging. In the far east of Siberia, the Kolyma road built by Gulag prisoners became known as the Road of Bones, because the bodies of those who died were incorporated into its surface, rather than buried in the hard permafrost.

Between 1931 and 1933, 126,000 Gulag convicts were forced to dig a canal over 141 miles to the Baltic Sea. Over 10,000 of them died, but the passage served little purpose since it was too shallow for most seagoing vessels. For about 30 years, the slave labour provided by the sprawling network of Gulag camps formed an integral part of the Soviet economy. Camps were slowly wound up after the death of Stalin in 1953, but the last was only closed in 1987.

Despite the intimidation and punishments, a few brave souls did speak out, even against the dreadful Gulag. One was Alexander Solzhenitsyn (1918-2008), intellectual, deeply religious, the son of an officer of the Russian Imperial Army and a convict in the Gulag for eight years. He had been sentenced in absentia for writing critical comments about Stalin in a private letter in 1945.

After his release, Solzhenitsyn wrote a novel entitled *One Day in The Life of Ivan Denisovich,* which depicted the dismal life of a Gulag prisoner as it had never been told before. He offered it in 1961 to the editor of the *Novy Mir* literary review, Alexander Tvardovsky, who read it from cover to cover in one night, and realised he had a bombshell in his hands. If he could publish it, millions of Soviet citizens would know what a tyrant Stalin had been.

Thus far, nobody had dared to speak out, and Tvardovsky knew the book would be blocked if he passed it through normal publishing channels. Luckily he was on personal terms with Stalin's successor, Nikita Khrushchev, and took the book straight to the new leader. As it happened, Khrushchev wanted to open up society, and so he gave the go-ahead after reportedly telling his comrades in the ruling Presidium: "There's a Stalinist in each of you; there's even a Stalinist in me. We must root out this evil."[46] Holding the first proof copy in his hands, Tvardovsky exclaimed: "The bird is free! The bird is free!"[47]

One Day In The Life of Ivan Denisovich became a best-seller around the world, and Solzhenitsyn became an overnight hero in the fight for freedom; emotional letters from grateful former inmates of the prison camps flooded in. Until then, it was unheard of in the Soviet Union to discuss politics openly, let alone something as controversial as this. So although repression continued, he had won the freedom to tell the truth, even if just once, and nine years later this earned him the Nobel Prize for Literature.

Liberalisation was Khrushchev's own personal venture, so when he was toppled from power in 1964, the window of opportunity that Solzhenitsyn had prised open slammed shut: the new leaders had no interest in pursuing it. In the meantime, the writer completed his seven-volume *Gulag Archipelago,* and fought a gruelling battle with Soviet authorities to have it published. He was publicly supported by western authors such as Jean-Paul Sartre, Graham Greene, W.H. Auden, Truman Capote, Arthur Miller and John Updike. But in 1974, a year after the first editions appeared abroad in translation, he was arrested, charged with treason and deported to the west.

Solzhenitsyn was a curmudgeonly fighter, devoted to the ideals of old Russia, and if any freedom was to be gained in the face of a pitiless security regime, it had to be fought for with all the ferocious obstinacy that a man such as he could muster. In his unbending intransigence, Solzhenitsyn was the man of the moment. Although his fight for freedom was cut short, it was not before his searing indictment of one of the Soviet Union's core institutions provoked indignation around the world. Harassed and demeaned for much of his life, he emerged victorious in the end; he outlived the Soviet system by 17 years and was able to return to Russia in his old age.

Another prominent champion of civil rights and liberties was Andrei Sakharov (1921-1989), designer of the hydrogen bomb which enabled the Soviet Union to rival the United States. He argued against the arms race, and then against suppression of free speech, travel restrictions and censorship. At first he spoke out within the privileged circles to which he belonged, but his activities soon escalated to writing clandestine pamphlets and publishing articles in the west.

He was awarded the Nobel Peace Prize in 1973, but his wife Yelena Bonner had to receive it on his behalf, as furious Soviet authorities refused to let him travel to Oslo for the ceremony. Seven years later, after publicly criticising the Soviet Union's 1979 invasion of Afghanistan, he was sent into internal exile in the town of Gorky (now Nizhny Novgorod), 250 miles east of Moscow. There, Sakharov went on hunger strike in an attempt to force authorities to allow his wife to travel to the United States for heart treatment. Isolated from friends and subject to frequent house searches, he was under constant threat from the Soviet police. Only his renown as a nuclear physicist, and the admiration he aroused in the free world, protected him from worse.

Like Solzhenitsyn, he too had the last word. When the Soviet Union began to crumble in 1986, a new Soviet leader, Mikhail Gorbachev, personally telephoned him in Gorky to say he was free to return to Moscow. Gorbachev, whose own family had served time in the Gulag, then introduced many of the civil rights and liberties for which the scientist had fought. Sakharov had succeeded, and when he died three years later, the European Union created a *Sakharov Prize for Freedom of Thought* in his honour.

Nazis and Resistance Fighters

Prospects for freedom in Europe after World War I were scarcely any better outside Russia. Although the three great liberal democracies of the Allied forces (Britain, France and the United States) had triumphed over the Central Powers (Germany and Austria-Hungary), the tolerance and solidarity required for freedom to flourish failed to emerge, even after the guns fell silent. The victors imposed vindictive reparations on Germany, and movements such as *Freikorps* military veterans and Hitler's brown-shirts rampaged through German streets bent on revenge. Spurning democracy and liberty, they sought to impose unquestioning discipline and the authority of the storm-trooper. In parts of the dismantled Austro-Hungarian Empire, German speakers and Hungarians who previously held the upper hand became oppressed minorities. Unrest was widespread and liberty under constant threat.

When depression hit Germany at the beginning of the 1930s, Hitler took his chance. Although Germans had known for 10 years that he was a dangerous rabble-rouser, to their everlasting shame, in 1932-33 they voted him into power. Within just a few weeks, his Nazi regime then established a dictatorship that would give rise to a new world war and enslave most of Europe. Not only did the Germans allow their own liberties to be crushed, but they also inflicted the same fate on a multitude of other nations. Ironically, this hammer blow against freedom was struck by a nation which had played an honourable role in Europe's 18th century Enlightenment.

At the height of World War II, peoples from the Atlantic to the eastern reaches of Siberia had very little personal autonomy. The German army exacted deadly reprisals against occupied populations to crush resistance. In Yugoslavia alone, one in 10 of the population was killed. At home, the Nazis created concentration camps in which anyone deemed an opponent was imprisoned, starved and maltreated, often until death. Six million Jews from all over Europe were sent to be murdered in extermination camps.

It became extraordinarily dangerous to exercise free will or voice an opinion. A few German individuals with strong personal values nevertheless did dare to. Joachim Fest, an eminent post-war German historian, remembered how his father refused to recant his democratic ideals after the Nazis dismissed him from his post as a schoolmaster. His mother countered that "small people" coped with tyranny by pretending to conform. His father retorted: "In such matters, we are not small people," and quoted St. Peter as saying: "Even if all others do so, I do not."[48] The son later entitled his own autobiography *Ich Nicht* – 'Not I'.

Defiance was not common, as the majority of the German population accepted Nazi dictatorship quite willingly, and even helped enforce it. In fact, most of the people whom the Gestapo secret police arrested were denounced by acquaintances. Those who tried protest were quickly neutralised; a White Rose group, formed among Munich students, distributed anti-Nazi leaflets in 1942 and 1943, but the ringleaders were captured and beheaded. In July 1944, conspirators led by Claus von Stauffenberg exploded a bomb in a room where Hitler was meeting generals, but when it failed to kill him, they were quickly discovered and gruesomely tortured to death. Rather than weakening as a result of the plot, the Nazi dictatorship became even more ferocious.

Beyond the borders of Germany, the nations under the Nazi heel did not wholly resist the loss of liberty either. Many people were fearful of social change and disarray in their own societies, so uncomplainingly accepted the order imposed by the Nazis. In occupied France, for instance, there was widespread collaboration, and French authorities readily rounded up Jews for dispatch to Auschwitz.

Nevertheless, a resistance movement did build up in France, and it had its heroes. The most celebrated was Jean Moulin, whom the collaborationist Vichy government dismissed from his official post after he refused to purge left-wing subordinates. After a brief period under arrest, he joined the Resistance in 1941, and travelled covertly to London to meet General Charles de Gaulle, who had set up Free French forces in exile to fight for France's liberation. On de Gaulle's orders, Moulin parachuted back into occupied France in 1942 to unify the various Resistance groups, but he was betrayed, captured and horribly tortured by Klaus Barbie, the head of the Gestapo in Lyons. He held out without betraying his comrades or giving away information, but died of his injuries in July 1943.

As president of France, de Gaulle had Moulin's ashes moved in 1964 to the Pantheon, where the remains of other great French champions of freedom are interred. At the Pantheon ceremony, culture minister André Malraux spoke of the terrible traces of torture on the face of the hero who had died for his country's freedom, and said: "On that day, his was the face of France." Today French schools acclaim Jean Moulin as a model French citizen – a freedom fighter with a civic conscience.

The French Resistance had an uphill task organising any effective disruption, since the Germans cowed the population with spying, punishments and threats. Also, the enemy had tanks, aircraft, field guns and machine guns which far exceeded the few rifles and bombs at the disposal of the freedom fighters. To begin with they were few in numbers, but when German authorities began sending French men and women to Germany as forced labour, the Resistance gained thousands of new recruits. They became known as the *Maquis,* after the rough scrub where they hid.

In the winter of 1944, some 450 *Maquis* grouped on the Plateau of Glières, in the French Alps, to gather supplies and weapons parachuted in from Britain. After successfully repelling the militia attacks of French collaborators, the defenders became overconfident. Rather than slipping away into the wilds, as guerrillas were taught to do, they confronted German troops of 4,000 men, armed with field guns, armoured cars and heavy machine guns. The *Maquis* stood no chance and almost all were killed. Even at that late stage of the war, it was suicidal for insurgents to do battle with well-armed, well-trained troops.

Despite this disaster, the gallant fight by the doomed *Maquis* of Glières prompted the British and Americans to take the French Resistance seriously and develop coordinated strategies. When the Allies poured on to Normandy beaches in June that year, the Resistance provided valuable intelligence, sabotaged German supply depots and railways, and attacked German reinforcements. As a result, the Allies could advance more quickly than their military planners expected. Thus, the men and women of the French Resistance did indeed help liberate their country.

In occupied Yugoslavia, partisans under Communist Josip Broz Tito fought a guerrilla war against the German occupiers with the help of arms and military advisers parachuted in by the British. The guerrillas struggled to make headway against German troops, only winning control of the country once the enemies retreated to defend their homelands.

Even after hostilities ceased, the bloodbath continued. The indoctrinated partisans, who treated their wartime British liaison officers as class enemies, assassinated thousands of collaborators, local mayors and civil society leaders so that they could enforce Communist rule. As many people were killed in Yugoslavia *after* the war as Britain lost during the whole of its six-year duration.

Though this did not exactly represent liberation, Tito and the partisans were credited with ridding their country of Nazi occupation. Unlike other East European countries, Yugoslavs did not depend on the Soviet Red Army to chase the Germans out, and Tito's break with Stalin in 1948 confirmed that Yugoslavia was free of foreign influence. Tito also allowed his people to emigrate if they wanted to; that too Yugoslavs saw as a significant liberty.

Further east, in the occupied parts of the Soviet Union, some 180,000 Soviet partisans operated behind the German lines. With nearly all their forces gathered on the front lines, the Germans were hard put to cope with these "bandits", as they called them. But once the Germans retreated, the Soviet secret police re-established totalitarian control over the whole population – thus, the partisans won no freedom at all.

As the Soviet Red Army entered Poland in 1944, some 40,000 Polish Home Guard, who had been preparing to free their nation for years, rose up against the German occupiers in Warsaw. They hoped that the Soviet Red Army, which had stopped opposite Warsaw on the far side of the River Vistula, would come to their aid. But Stalin was not interested in helping to liberate Poles, particularly since the Home Guard was loyal to the Polish government-in-exile in Britain. Instead, he waited for the Germans to crush the resistance, and then moved in to impose Communist rule.

Like the French *Maquis*, the Polish freedom fighters had to learn the harsh lesson that irregulars stood no chance against a well-organised army. Over 200,000 Poles (many of them civilians) died as a result of the 63 days of desperate fighting. The Germans systematically destroyed Warsaw, before evacuating as the Red Army resumed its advance. Only 15 per cent of Warsaw's buildings were still standing by 1945, and Poland would not be free for another 45 years.

Prisoners-of-war made daring bids for personal freedom from the camps deep behind German enemy lines. Their chances of success were small, but as military personnel they were duty-bound to try to escape and re-join their units. In autumn of 1943, three British servicemen escaped from *Stalag Luft III* camp in south-eastern Germany after digging a tunnel from underneath a portable vaulting horse that they brought daily into the exercise yard. They crawled out and eventually reached England via neutral Sweden.

Six months later, Air Force prisoners of several nationalities in the same camp made a mass breakout, known later as The Great Escape. From one of the huts they dug a tunnel 336 feet long, using bed-boards as supports, old tin cans rigged together as ventilation systems, and purloined cable to provide electric lighting. To dispose of the shovelled sand, prisoners walked around the prison yard letting it trickle out of bags hidden in their trousers.

After a nerve-wracking battle of wits against German spies in the camp, 76 prisoners hauled themselves through the tunnel on the night of 24th March 1944 and made off through the surrounding forest. Three German-speakers equipped with civilian clothing and forged papers made it back to Britain, but the others were recaptured. Hitler was furious and had 50 of them executed.

As an escape to freedom, it was largely a failure, but as news trickled through to Britain, it had two important psychological effects. The daring of the escapees captured imaginations and bolstered morale, while the horror at Hitler's lethal retribution – which contravened the rules of war – steeled Britons in their determination to overthrow him. News of further escapes by French, Polish, Dutch and British prisoners-of-war from the forbidding castle of Colditz had the same effect.

In the dark days of Nazi-dominated Europe, there was little else to celebrate except agents parachuting into France to help the Resistance, partisans blowing up Balkan railway viaducts, Polish freedom-fighters stumbling through sewers to liberate their capital, and prisoners-of-war making valiant attempts to come back and fight on. At a time when there was frustratingly little the Allies could do to defeat the Nazis, such daring bids for freedom, however ill-fated, strengthened resolve and gave hope that the human yearning for liberty would triumph in the end.

Finally, it would be the massed armies of heavily armed regular soldiers that proved decisive in freeing Europe. Back in the summer of 1940, this was just a distant hope, as there was only one nation in Western Europe willing to continue waging war against Hitler – that was Britain, protected by

25 miles of sea separating it from the continent. When the British Army was forced to withdraw from France in June 1940, some members of the British government wanted to sign peace on Germany's terms. Winston Churchill, the newly appointed Prime Minister, would have none of it. Although no liberal by nature, he was the man of the moment when his people's freedom was in danger. As others wavered, he took to the radio to rally his compatriots:

> *"We shall go on to the end, we shall fight in France, we shall fight on the seas and oceans, we shall fight with growing confidence and growing strength in the air, we shall defend our island, whatever the cost may be, we shall fight on the beaches, we shall fight on the landing grounds, we shall fight in the fields and in the streets, we shall fight in the hills; we shall never surrender."[49]*

Marshal Pétain, the French collaborationist leader, sneered that Britain would soon "have its neck wrung like a chicken". Speaking to the Canadian Parliament shortly afterwards, the portly Churchill retorted: "Some chicken, some neck!" It earned him a standing ovation, and helped win support in America for Britain's battle to remain free.

Liberation and New Tyranny

In 1943 and 1944, huge Allied armies advanced on Germany from the east and west to liberate Europe from Nazi tyranny. In the east, liberation was a hollow boast, since one dictatorship was replaced immediately by another. But in the west, the battles waged by British and American armies did bring freedom, and they were fought on a colossal scale. Just for the crossing of the Rhine in March 1945, British and American armies threw more than a million men into the assault. The liberation was extraordinarily violent and brought fearful casualties, not only among the fighting soldiers, but also among civilians caught up in the hostilities. 500,000 Germans lost their lives in the bombing of German cities, as did 20,000 French when the Allies bombed Normandy during the D-Day landings of June 1944.

The liberation of Europe at the end of World War II refuted the idea that the only valid fight for freedom is a nonviolent one. It also once more belied the assumption that a fight for freedom must inevitably be followed by a new tyranny. After the war ended, the countries of western Europe, including the western half of Germany, benefited from free voting, free speech, free press, free opinions and free enterprise. Freedom was thrown to the winds during the two World Wars, but once the fighting had ceased, it returned to the west and endured.

"Liberation" by the Soviet Red Army, on the other hand, meant military sequestrations, pillage and rape. Some two million German women were violated in the months after the German defeat in 1945. Stalin declared that after all the sacrifices – the Soviets lost millions of men – "Ivan should have a little fun with a wench."[50] The Soviet soldiers, however, did not limit their brutality to Germany – they also raped systematically in Poland and Hungary; for them, this was part of the spoils of battle, but by no stretch of the imagination can rape be considered "liberation".[51]

The Soviet ideologues portrayed the Nazis as a movement of bourgeois industrialists. So in their eyes, "liberation" justified excluding the bourgeois classes from power in the countries they occupied. They used this self-serving distortion to legitimise the establishment of proletarian dictatorships in eastern Europe, and the imposition of an "Iron Curtain" insulating the inhabitants from the free ideas of the west.

In the immediate post-war years, Stalin went back on a promise to allow free elections in Poland, with the result that the Communists there gained sole control, as they did in Hungary. In Czechoslovakia, the Communists at first ruled with pro-western parties, but used their command of the police to undermine their partners and seize power on their own. By 1948, it was clear that the decisive political influence in each country was the intimidating presence of the Red Army.

The Communist regimes slavishly carried out Stalin's ideological directives to confiscate private property, requisition crops, repress religion and monopolise the media, using the secret police to enforce compliance. In East Germany, the Stasi (Ministry for State Security) spied on citizens by following them, listening through hidden microphones, tapping telephones and opening 90,000 letters a day. Those whom the Stasi classified as enemies it persecuted with torture and imprisonment. In Hungary, secret police jailed nearly one citizen in 10, executed thousands more and kept files on one million people.

Nowhere were the differences between the two systems more stark than in Berlin, half of which was controlled by the western Allies and half by the Soviets. In the western sector, people could vote freely, move around freely and express themselves freely. In the east, elections were rigged to give the Communist Party 99 per cent of the vote, the Party controlled what was published and secret police intimidated people into silence. On one side of Berlin were shops full of consumer goods, and on the other side shortages and queues.

Wherever Europeans could vote freely, they never

elected a Communist government, and in Berlin people could vote with their feet. Communist East Germany lost a steady stream of doctors, teachers and other qualified workers to the west, because it was possible to walk without hindrance from one sector to another.

In 1948, Stalin tried to eliminate the pocket of freedom represented by West Berlin by blocking its land routes through East Germany to the west. He hoped to starve the western part of the city into submission and force the western Allies to withdraw, but the U.S. military governor, General Lucius Clay, decided to defend West Berlin's liberty by organising an airlift. Planes flying in from the west landed every few minutes, in fair weather and foul, bringing essential supplies of food, medicines and coal. After a year, Stalin gave up.

The success of the Berlin airlift convinced Germans in the west that Americans were determined to defend their freedom. Their champion was Clay, a hard-bitten American general who only a few years earlier had been fighting against them in the world war. For the children of West Berlin, the greatest heroes were the American air crews who scattered sweets on their landing approaches. The British, for their part, helped the West Germans to set up free broadcasting and press.

West Berlin was safe, but the Communist regime in the east still could not stop the flow of refugees crossing over to the west in search of freedom. That loophole was not to last: one warm August night in 1961, paramilitary workers on the east side started putting up a barrier of breeze-blocks and barbed wire across the middle of the city. By the morning, the Communists had built the first structures of the Berlin Wall and West Berlin was sealed off. Berliners found themselves separated from friends and family on the other side of the city, and over time the Wall became a massive structure. Guards with dogs and machine-guns shot to kill when anyone tried to cross over, reinforced by mine-strips and scatter-guns that could bring down escapers in seconds. The Berlin Wall epitomised the imprisonment of citizens by cruel masters.

U.S. president John F. Kennedy later reassured West Berliners of their liberty, with a rousing speech near the Wall in which he declared: "All free men, wherever they may live, are citizens of Berlin, and, therefore, as a free man, I take pride in the words *Ich bin ein Berliner* – 'I am a Berliner'."

Kennedy's speech was received with tumultuous applause by the West Berliners, but for East Germans, stranded on the other side of the Wall, it brought little comfort. A few made daring escapes, including one young border guard with steel helmet, tommy-gun and jackboots, who leaped over the half-erected barrier while his comrades were still building it. A few individuals tentatively lowered themselves from windows facing on to the western side, and in 1978 two families floated over the border in a rudimentary hot-air balloon made with scraps of cloth and a foot-powered sewing machine. But the chances to escape were few, and most East Germans resigned themselves to their captive state. As one gloomy East Berliner on the street put it to a western reporter in 1972, "man can now go to the moon, but I still can't go to West Berlin."[52]

The despotic practices of Russia continued to hold sway in eastern Europe for 40 years after World War II. With a few notable exceptions, the concept of man as an individual with a free will remained a distant dream for people who could scarcely imagine better. That is until everything changed, unexpectedly, all in the space of one year (see Chapter 11).

CHAPTER 7

FREEDOM FROM EMPIRE

First they ignore you, then they laugh at you,
then they fight you, then you win.
– Mahatma Gandhi

India

———

The 20th century saw a struggle for freedom not only in Europe, but also in the colonies that the European powers had set up in Africa and Asia. In the 18th and 19th centuries, the Europeans had seized large parts of the rest of the world in order to exploit them commercially. As time wore on, this ever more blatantly contradicted the principles of liberty that they professed in their own countries. As a result, their empires were not sustainable in the long run, and even a leading democracy such as Britain was eventually contested by the peoples over which it ruled.

During the last quarter of the 19th century, the European powers competed with each other to colonise whichever of the globe's territories were still available. Britain, France, Belgium and Portugal finished with the largest shares, and in Africa they were joined by Italy and belatedly Germany, all seizing whatever domains they could, irrespective of traditional boundaries. In Asia, India was in the hands of the British, and various European powers colonised China's coastal trading points (which the British callously used to fuel Chinese drug addiction by smuggling in Indian opium). Russia, meanwhile, had been colonising its Siberian hinterlands since the 16th century.

Most colonies started as little more than coastal trading posts, and subsequently grew in size as the colonists made alliances with local chiefs to expand trade inland. Only later, as the map was divided up, did the European powers feel obliged to exercise authority over the territories that were recognised as theirs.

For the inhabitants, otherwise under the sway of local rulers with scant respect for liberty, colonial government by Europeans did not necessarily make their lot worse. In some cases, it even freed them from being enslaved or conquered by neighbouring peoples, but that was an incidental benefit, not resulting from any freedom of choice. Nobody asked the indigenous populations whether they wanted to be governed by foreigners, and as such, colonialism was de facto a negation of freedom.

Most of the benefits that foreign rule brought with it were reserved for the European powers, which sought to maximise gain by exploiting commodities such as cocoa, coffee, tea, sugar, cotton, rubber, copper, gold and diamonds. In fertile countries like Kenya, white settlers took over land to farm, while Belgium's King Leopold II exploited vast territories in the Congo, not on behalf of the Belgian state, but as his own private business.

As the number of its colonies grew, Britain considered more carefully how it ought to rule them. Until the middle of the century, India was run by the East India Company, a trading enterprise which left the local princes to continue administering, but under the shadow of British military power. The princes went along with this, since their privileges were protected and they too could enrich themselves from the developing trade. This loose relationship changed in the 19th century as the British became increasingly proud of their civilisation, and felt honour-bound to export their ethical and democratic principles to their colonies. They condescendingly assumed superiority, and in India their reforming zeal led them to interfere in traditional customs which they had hitherto tolerated.

British trading practices also began to anger the Indians, whose artisanal cotton industry produced colourful, high-quality textiles. In the 17th and 18th centuries, the East India Company made a fortune importing them into Britain, but the Industrial Revolution enabled British factories to manufacture textiles at a lower cost because production became more efficient. The trade reversed and cheap British garments flooded Indian markets, putting local producers out of business.

Matters came to a head in 1857, when the British Army introduced a new rifle requiring soldiers to bite off the ends of lubricated cartridges. Rumours spread that they were greased with pig or cow fat, which offended the religious sensibilities of Hindus and Muslims. Indian troopers mutinied, slaughtered their officers, took control of Delhi and massacred white women and children. It took the British more than a year to put the rebellion down, and they meted out ferocious punishment, bayoneting the mutineers en masse, even tying some to the muzzles of cannons.[53] Determined to impose its authority more rigorously, the British government wound up the East India Company and began ruling most of India directly.[54]

The British were shocked that the paternalistic influence they sought to impose met with opposition from the supposed beneficiaries. The Indians let it be known they did not want to be patronised, and they questioned the alliances that their undemocratic princes made with the British. A new generation of Indians began to think in more modern westernised terms, and these terms included the notions of freedom and independence.

Despite the tensions, the Indians and British continued to be attracted by each other. The Indians were drawn to British education, for example. Mahatma Gandhi, the independence leader, studied law in England, and Jawaharlal Nehru, the first Prime Minister of independent India, went to school and university there. The problem for the British was that education also bred freethinking, and this led to questioning of the established order.

The British, for their part, took to the lavish ruling habits of the Indian princes. Queen Victoria became Empress of India with great pomp, while her grandson King George V travelled to Delhi in 1911 for a magnificent ceremony called the Durbar, in which bejewelled elephants, dashing horsemen and soldiers in flamboyant uniforms paraded in obeisance. The extravagant effect was only slightly spoiled by the king trotting along on a small horse because he was nervous at mounting an elephant.

The days of imperial dominion were nevertheless numbered. An Indian National Congress party was set up in 1885 to campaign for independence, and Indians grew in confidence after one million of their citizens fought on the victorious side in World War I.[55] They were encouraged in their desire for freedom by American President Wilson's proclamation of the principle of self-determination for peoples.

Sensing a need to involve Indians in government, the British granted the vote to five million well-off Indians in 1919, but that represented only a small percentage of the nation's vast population. They handed certain responsibilities to Indians, but kept control of taxation, law and order, envisaging an India that would be largely autonomous but still an integral part of the empire. For the leaders of the Congress Party, this was not enough. They wanted to be entirely free from British rule, and they perceived these half-measures as a weakening of British resolve.

The British themselves faced mounting resistance from conservatives who were horrified at the prospect of losing "the jewel in the imperial crown"; they feared their whole empire would unravel if they lost India. In a rash act of repression in that same year, a hot-headed British brigadier ordered his troops to fire on unarmed Indian protesters in Amritsar, northern Punjab, killing 379 and injuring 1,200. The British quickly removed him from his command, but the damage to their relations with Indians was irreversible.

The British seemed to have reached an impasse; while on the one hand they wished to be appreciated for their civilising influence, on the other hand, they felt compelled to crack down on dissent. It was a quandary every colonial power faced; it was impractical and too costly to rule absolutely over vast territories and widely scattered populations, yet the more they sought amicable arrangements, the more the inhabitants were tempted to seek autonomy. Ruling over people who did not freely give their consent was in the long run destined to fail.

During World War I, Mahatma Gandhi (1869-1948) took leadership of the Indian National Congress, and roused Indians to fight for independence in a way that would inspire future liberation leaders around the world. His tactic was not to fight at all. Instead he chose nonviolence and showed it could achieve its goals as effectively as insurrection. Nonviolence did not imply passive endurance; as far as Gandhi was concerned, it meant taking on the British at every opportunity through a campaign of non-cooperation and civil disobedience. Violence, he believed, would just lead to repression, while nonviolence would provoke the British into making political blunders.

Millions of Indians – among them, the protesters present at Amritsar – took part in his first protest campaign, against a law authorising incarceration without trial for Indians suspected of sedition. Two years later, he started urging Indians to strike, to resign from government employment, and to boycott British goods, educational institutions and law courts.

Gandhi excelled in devising imaginative forms of protest. To defy the British monopoly on salt production, he led thousands of Indians in 1930 on a march over 250 miles to the sea, where they began to make their own salt out of seawater. Gandhi scooped up a handful of mud from the beach and declared that he was shaking the foundations of the British Empire. The British reacted by arresting tens of thousands of men and women, but the salt initiative caught the public eye, and showed that Indians could both disobey the British and poke fun at them. When protesters then began making bonfires of British cloth and withholding rents, the British realised they would have to negotiate with their tormentor.

After talks with the viceroy in Delhi, Gandhi was invited to London in 1931 for a Round Table conference, giving Londoners the chance to gape at this slight, bare-footed figure in his meagre cotton wrap. All the other delegates wore formal morning dress, and Winston Churchill scorned Gandhi as "a half-naked holy man". But there was no better way of conveying to the British that a new regime was in the offing.

The British were at a loss as to how to deal with this extraordinary character. They imprisoned him four times between 1922 and 1942, but he staged several hunger strikes which, as he well knew, alarmed his captors, since his death in prison would have caused pandemonium. The British detained thousands more Indians, but for the hundreds of millions whom they sought to deter, the prisons could never be large enough.

The Indians only had to wait: World War II finally opened up their road to independence. After the British surrendered Singapore and Burma to the Japanese in 1942, they had to call on large numbers of Indian soldiers to help them reverse the defeats. Britain's authority over its empire was dealt a heavy blow, and as Indians celebrated victory, they knew that their aspirations to live freely in their homeland could not be resisted much longer.

A month before the war finished, the old imperialist Winston Churchill was defeated in an election by the British Labour Party, which was ready to let India go. The prospect of freedom from colonial rule fulfilled a long-standing aspiration, but it also threw up an ominous question: could the free Indians live peacefully together? As the unifying effect of British rule faded away, communal hatred surfaced between the majority Hindus and the minority Muslims. As a result, the Muslim leaders insisted on a homeland of their own; so when India became independent on 15th August 1947, two new independent states were born – India and Pakistan.

On the eve of independence, India's new Prime Minister, Jawaharlal Nehru, spoke of India awakening to life and freedom, and the soul of the nation finding utterance. These were brave words, but tarnished by the killings that set in as 12 to 14 million Hindus, Muslims and Sikhs were displaced from one part of the partitioned territory to the other. Some of the trains that left India packed with migrants arrived in the new state of Pakistan with only dead bodies on board. Between about 500,000 and 1.5 million people died in this bloodbath, which was a grim precursor of post-independence horrors to follow elsewhere.

Gandhi's efforts to stop the partition of India, and indeed to stop the fighting, were to be the cause of his death. It was not in the struggle for independence that he perished, but because a fanatical Hindu decided he must die for trying to reconcile Hindus and Muslims. The assassin fired three shots point-blank into Gandhi's chest on 30th January 1948 as he walked to prayers. In the end, his people appreciated the liberty he brought them, but in the weeks following their independence, many turned away from the nonviolent methods through which he had achieved it.

Gandhi demonstrated that nonviolence could be an effective strategy in the fight for freedom, but in India he was up against opponents who had themselves fought on the side of liberty, and were losing the will to maintain an empire. Once the British realised independence was inevitable, they did not attempt to fight to the bitter end. If Gandhi had instead confronted a merciless tyrant such as Stalin or Hitler, his campaign of civil disobedience would have stood no chance.

Nevertheless, Gandhi succeeded in rallying a highly disparate people for their first time behind the cause of freedom. He channelled their growing urge to be free and brought it successfully to fruition. That was perhaps his greatest gift to his people.

Subsequently, India developed a democracy in which citizens could freely elect their governments. As the free play of elections testifies, today's Indians are not subservient, and they are ready to remove rulers who they consider serve the people poorly. With some significant exceptions, they embrace a concept of personal liberty in which everybody has a say.[56] In that respect, their fight for freedom under Gandhi's guidance achieved its goal.

Africa

With the "jewel in the imperial crown" gone, it was not long before the rest of the nations within the British Empire – most of which were located in Africa – achieved their independence. By 1951, an imprisoned independence leader exploited a legal loophole to stand in an election in the Gold Coast (now Ghana). To his own surprise, Kwame Nkrumah won a landslide victory, and the next day he was released, invited to the British Governor-General, and emerged a few hours later as Prime Minister. Nkrumah could hardly believe how fast things had changed, and as he descended the steps of the Governor's residence, he felt that: "I was stepping down from the clouds and that I would soon wake up and find myself squatting on the prison floor eating a bowl of maize porridge."[57]

On 6th March 1957, the Union flag of Britain was lowered and the new independent state of Ghana was born, with Nkrumah as its president: freely elected, charismatic and with six years' experience of running a government. Its cocoa-based economy was booming, its civil service was efficient and, with a well-to-do middle class, it seemed set fair for the future. Bathing in the glory, Nkrumah saw himself as the leader of an emancipation movement that would embrace the whole of Africa. The following year, he staged an All-African People's Conference, attracting liberation movement leaders from all over Africa. Now that one colony was free, they set on lighting fires of freedom across the continent.

As far as the British Crown was concerned, no one stood in the way of independence any longer. The British had originally intended to stay in control for 10 to 20 years, while they prepared locals to govern; but they jettisoned the timetable when it became clear that Africans would not wait. In 1960, British Prime Minister Harold Macmillan toured Africa, warning white settlers to prepare for a "wind of change".

Events gathered pace, and the British moved with almost undignified haste to rid themselves of an empire that had once been their great pride. By 1968, all their colonies had achieved independence and British officials were hard put to prepare so many new constitutions, elections and legislations in such a short space of time. In Zambia, for instance, negotiations over mineral rights were still going on behind a tea-tent just before a garden party celebrating the transfer of powers.[58]

So fast was the changeover that some of the new leaders initially hesitated to strike out on their own. Milton Margai of Sierra Leone burst into tears when asked by a British official which date he wanted for independence, declaring that he never expected to live to be asked that question. The incoming president of Kenya, Jomo Kenyatta, paid tribute to the British legacy: "We do not forget the assistance and guidance we have received through the years from people of British stock: administrators, businessmen, farmers, missionaries and many others. Our law, our system of government and many other aspects of our daily lives are founded on British principles and justice."[59]

In the French territory of Algeria, however, decolonisation took a very different path. By the mid-1950s, the French white settlers, popularly known as *pieds-noirs* (black-feet), had accumulated nearly all political and economic power. The Muslim Arabs and Berbers who had always lived there had a few seats in the French Parliament, but the whites controlled employment, commerce and agriculture, leaving the locals little or no capacity to determine their own affairs. Also, while the native inhabitants were reproducing much faster than the settlers, most lived in slums around the big cities, largely illiterate and jobless.

In 1954, the winds of change blowing through Africa reached the north African coast. Catching the French by surprise, an organisation calling itself *Front de Libération Nationale (FLN)* launched a series of attacks on police stations, barracks and telegraph lines in Algeria. The French Army cracked down and restored calm for a few months, but the FLN struck again, committing atrocities against Muslims who collaborated with the French. The French poured in troops, and violence escalated in an infernal spiral.

While Britain was ready to cede its empire, France had no intention of giving up Algeria. Since surrendering to the Germans in World War II, it was set on restoring its standing in the world. However, in that same year it suffered a blow to its shaky prestige when Communist guerrillas defeated French troops at the battle of Dien Bien Phu in Indochina (now Vietnam). This humiliation emboldened the Algerian rebels to begin targeting white settlers in

1955. They tossed grenades into cafés, dragged motorists from cars and killed them, and went from house to house slaughtering men, women and children. The French Army responded by shooting indigenous Algerians at will, and the colonists formed vigilante groups that went on killing sprees. The struggle for independence turned into a full-scale insurrection, with no quarter given on either side.

Young Frenchmen conscripted into the French Army tortured and murdered FLN suspects in interrogation centres, and were tormented for the rest of their lives by their guilty secrets. It became known as "the dirty war", and at home, government after government collapsed as the will of the people to keep fighting flagged. French generals finally took over in Algiers and demanded that General de Gaulle, hero of the French resistance in World War II, assume power at the head of the French government. He did so in 1958, and the generals thought he would stand fast on their side.

De Gaulle paid a visit to Algiers and told a cheering crowd of white settlers: *"Je vous ai compris!* – I have understood you!"* The settlers thought that these words clinched his support for *Algérie Française* – Algeria as an integral part of France – but in fact they committed him to nothing. In 1962, de Gaulle negotiated independence for Algeria, having decided that subjugating foreign people to an empire was an anachronism and a lost cause.

The General almost paid for this with his life at the hands of an *Organisation de l'Armée Secrète* – a terrorist movement of white settlers who were forced to abandon their livelihoods in Algeria. They seethed with resentment at what they saw as gross betrayal, and sought to track him down and assassinate him. De Gaulle narrowly escaped several attempts on his life, but continued liberating France's other colonies in west Africa, while still maintaining ties of cooperation with the mother country. The conservative old soldier turned out to be an unlikely champion of freedom, and he convinced his compatriots that they could still be proudly French, even if they cast off an empire.

The fires of freedom set alight at Nkrumah's 1958 All-African People's Conference next reached the Belgian Congo. The Belgians had efficiently exploited its vast underlying riches – in 1959 Congo produced 10 per cent of the world's copper, 50 per cent of its cobalt, and 70 per cent of its industrial diamonds. But they ruled with great brutality, causing hundreds of thousands of deaths, and they did little to educate the native inhabitants or give them a say in the country's affairs.[60]

That suppression did not survive Nkrumah's conference. A young Congolese liberation movement leader, Patrice Lumumba, proclaimed on his return from the gathering that he was seeking emancipation of the Congolese people from Belgian rule. "We wish to bid farewell to the old regime, this regime of subjugation... Africa is engaged in a merciless struggle for its liberation against the coloniser."[61]

Rioting broke out with a suddenness that caught the Belgians unprepared and, as in other revolutions, events moved unbelievably quickly. The Belgians belatedly offered political reforms, but these were rejected as inadequate. Fearing a full-scale colonial war, they hastily granted independence to the Congo in 1960, but the country soon fell into disorder. The remaining Belgian officers and mine-owners fell out with Prime Minister Lumumba, and conspired in the secession of the mineral-rich Katanga province.

This culminated in the murder of Lumumba by his Congolese enemies, aided by Belgian soldiers who dissolved his body in sulphuric acid. All over the rest of Africa, Lumumba became an instant martyr of the fight for freedom, but in the Congo his fight was in vain. After further chaos, a coup brought to power a military officer, Joseph Désiré Mobutu, who ruled as a rapacious dictator until his death in 1997.

The Congo's independence was a disaster, partly because Belgians dominated the population more ruthlessly than the British did in their colonies. Conditions ahead of independence offered little scope for the nonviolent path of civil disobedience taken by Mahatma Gandhi. In the face of an explosive desire for liberty, Belgian public opinion swung between panic and a vindictive desire to undermine the new independent state; and in a country as large and diverse as the Congo, this was a recipe for catastrophe.

Portugal

By the end of the 1960s, the only European power to retain colonies in Africa was Portugal, holding on to Angola, Mozambique and Portuguese Guinea. There too the winds of change were blowing. It soon found itself pitched against guerrilla movements armed with Soviet weapons, driving Volvo trucks funded by anti-imperialist Swedish foundations, and supported by a growing number of Cuban troops.

Like other colonial powers, the Portuguese were learning that an empire could be a poisoned chalice. Instead of yielding riches from trade and commodities, it drew them into an endless battle which sapped morale and national wealth. To escape lengthy military service fighting dangerous opponents in jungles, many young men emigrated, and with just nine million inhabitants and a backward economy,

Portugal could barely cope.

Yet the reactionary dictator who ruled Portugal for 36 years, Antonio Salazar, resisted the global trend towards decolonisation. He held his own people in check through secret police, censorship and suppression of political rivals. His successor, Marcelo Caetano, offered a few timid reforms, but this only encouraged the opposition building up against the regime.

With no possibility for the people to exercise their free will, revolution was the only means of effecting change. That duly broke out on the morning of 25th April 1974, when citizens of Lisbon woke up to find soldiers controlling the main points of the capital. Young captains of the colonial army had staged a coup d'état, not only against the dictatorship, but also in defiance of their own generals. Only a few hundred troops were involved initially, but other regiments rallied one by one and, within the space of a few hours, the dictatorship was finished.

In the early evening, Prime Minister Caetano handed over authority to a rebel officer, begging him "not to let power slip into the gutter". As the day wore on, people realised they were free from the oppression and autocracy of the old regime, and in their euphoria thrust carnations into the rifle barrels of the soldiers. The paramilitary police disappeared from the streets and the regime's numerous spies melted away into anonymity.

Unlike the officer-class in many other countries, the revolutionaries were no right-wing elite. Conscripted to fight in the colonies, they were poorly paid and just as disenchanted with the war as the soldiers they commanded. Youthful, clad in jungle fatigues and determined to take affairs into their own hands, they had much the same romantic appeal as the

African guerrillas against whom they had fought.

Over the next 18 months, these officers forced through revolutionary change amid great tumult; banks and industries were nationalised, farmlands were seized and redistributed to peasants and thousands of government officials were purged. Radical leftists took over the media and impromptu revolutionary committees requisitioned empty dwellings. Week after week, growing crowds demonstrated on the streets, while shootings and explosions disturbed the nights.

Some of the officers wanted to continue with perpetual revolution, and this brought them into conflict with the civilian political parties which had been allowed to operate as soon as the dictatorship was overthrown. But the radicals lost support among their military comrades and, as the country slid toward anarchy and economic disintegration, the revolution collapsed from one day to the next during the autumn of 1975. The civilian political parties could then move into the void and establish the same democratic institutions as elsewhere in western Europe. Portugal thereafter found its place in the modern world as a member of the European Union.

So the revolution brought freedom to the Portuguese at home, but just as importantly, it ended Portugal's colonial domination over the territories it ruled in Africa. Decolonisation was a top priority of the revolutionary young captains and, like the British, French and Belgians, they saw no other option but to hand over to the liberation movements that had resisted Portuguese rule. By the middle of the 1970s, it was becoming apparent that liberation movements did not necessarily bring freedom to the people, but for weakened Portugal there was no choice: no other indigenous organisations were capable of assuming power.

Portuguese Guinea on the west coast of Africa was the

first to win independence as Guinea-Bissau in 1974. After a desultory parade in a jungle clearing, the colonial army packed up and departed, leaving behind a swampy pocket of land, mired in destitution and tribal rivalries which have persisted until today. A few months later, the Portuguese handed over Mozambique to a Marxist-Leninist guerrilla movement, and finally in Angola, rich with oil and diamonds, they transferred sovereignty to a leftist independence movement, which had to fight for supremacy against rival groups backed by the U.S. and South Africa.

Angola was an ugly exercise in decolonisation. In the civil war which ensued, hundreds of thousands of white settlers had to abandon their livelihoods and evacuate with nothing but a suitcase. In the long run, however, shedding the empire released the Portuguese from an enormous burden, and enabled them to modernise their own society. Without first liberating themselves from dictatorship – achieved with little shedding of blood – that would not have been possible.

As for the people of their former colonies, although they were not yet fully free, they had at least shed foreign tutelage. That left South Africa, where the white apartheid regime now found itself exposed to the wind of change at its frontiers. There, an inspired freedom fighter awaited his moment of destiny (see Chapter 14).

CHAPTER 8

FREEDOM AND DICTATORSHIP IN THE EAST

Never take the lead – but aim to do something big.
– Deng Xiaoping

If a goat can get through, so can a man; if a man can get through, so can a battalion.
– General Vo Nguyen Giap

China

O ver the past hundred years, the Chinese people have been subjected to fearful oppression, causing tens of millions of deaths. Yet China too has had its freedom fighters.

At the beginning of the 20th century, the country was in a sorry state; its emperors were feeble, warlords held sway over whatever land they could seize, European powers ruled the trading ports, and peasants toiled in conditions of great poverty and exploitation. Worse was to come after the last emperor, aged only six, was deposed in 1911, and the people had to endure over 30 years of anarchy, civil war and an immensely cruel Japanese occupation.

When the Communists, led by Mao Zedong (1893-1976), finally defeated their foes and assumed power in 1949, the people might reasonably have expected that they could at last resume normal lives, free of the constant threats to their existence. Instead, they were subjected to the mercurial dictatorship of Mao, occasionally alleviated by the brave attempts of his Communist comrades to protect their people from the worst of his excesses.

Mao was no ordinary Communist ruler. According to his doctor, he did much of his business dressed casually, sitting in bed or by his pool in his Beijing compound. The unorthodoxy of his rule attracted romantic radicals in the west, enchanted by his daring, his unpredictability and his breaking of the mould. In comparison with grey functionaries of western governments, they found him liberating.

Mao himself insisted that the Communists aimed to bring freedom to society, but in reality his image as a champion of freedom was entirely fanciful.[62] His slogan "political power grows out the barrel of a gun" betrayed his belief that salvation must be forced upon the people, and he set out to do this as soon as he took power. As promised at its first Congress in 1921, the Communist Party imposed single-party rule, seized ownership of the means of production and set about destroying the bourgeoisie. To consolidate their authority, the Communists ordered the killing of several million landowners, officials, businessmen and intellectuals – in fact, anybody suspected of not favouring the Communist takeover. It was shockingly ruthless, but Mao argued that the end justified the means.

Then, surprisingly, Mao himself introduced a dose of freedom. Influenced by Khrushchev's liberalisation of the Soviet Union, in 1956 he launched the *Hundred Flowers* movement, inviting people to offer their opinions about the Party and, as he put it, "let a hundred flowers bloom" so that the nation could flourish. It unleashed a torrent of free debate and open criticism; wall posters denounced every aspect of the Communist government, while students and professors verbally attacked Party members. Advocates of autocratic government in Asia have often argued that Asians are readier to accept discipline than those in the west. The *Hundred Flowers* movement showed on the contrary that, given the chance, the Chinese would eagerly exercise their liberty to contest the wrongs of their government.

Mao had not anticipated the threat to Communist supremacy and brought the experiment in free speech abruptly to an end. He then saw to it that those who criticized him were forced out of their jobs, imprisoned or sent to do manual labour in the countryside.

To divert attention from his blunder, Mao forced his compatriots to embark on a revolutionary change to agricultural and industrial production. Launched in 1958, the so-called *Great Leap Forward* turned into a catastrophe, causing some 30 million Chinese to die of famine. New agricultural methods imported from the Soviet Union failed to produce adequate crops, but instead of taking relief action, Mao diverted millions of peasants from tilling the fields to smelting iron and steel in homemade furnaces. However, the low-quality metal was unusable, and political commissars compounded the peasants' suffering by requisitioning the reduced amounts of grain for the cities.

The programme was called off after three years, and the disaster opened the way for Mao's more liberal-minded comrades to push him aside from government. Deng Xiaoping (1904-1997) and Liu Shaoqi (1898-1969) halted the excesses of *The Great Leap Forward* and, in doing so, liberated the population from immense pressures on their everyday lives. Both remained loyal to the Communist Party, but for providing respite from Mao's revolutionary despotism they won widespread public recognition. In the Chinese tradition, they acted cautiously and avoided unnecessary confrontations, biding their time until the moment came to make their moves. But their cautious method led to significant changes, such as the more liberal economic policy that Deng introduced, providing material incentives and allowing managers to act independently of Communist ideology.

Mao made a comeback in 1966 by launching a *Cultural Revolution* – another alluring idea which caught his opponents on the back foot. The idea was to keep the country in a state of permanent revolution, in order to take power back into his hands. Red Guards, brandishing a *Little Red Book* of Mao's thoughts, dragged people in positions of responsibility before makeshift revolutionary tribunals and humiliated, beat or killed them. They forced millions from the cities into the countryside for "re-education", and wreaked immense damage to China's cultural heritage.

The comrades who had stood against Mao now felt the brunt of his revenge. Liu Shaoqi was denounced as a traitor, an enemy agent and "the biggest capitalist-roader in the Party". He was arrested, publicly beaten, denied medication for his diabetes, and died in 1969. Deng Xiaoping was removed from all his positions and sent to work in the countryside, while his eldest son was crippled for life by jumping out of a window to escape torture by Red Guards.

Another Chinese leader, Prime Minister Zhou Enlai, became widely respected for protecting victims from the excesses of the Red Guards. He was a veteran Communist who never openly challenged Mao, but in the eyes of the people he was a moderate and principled leader, shielding them from the hysterical violence of Mao's revolution. He created a little more space for freedom in their lives.

When Zhou died in early 1976, there was a great outpouring of public grief, which brought the battle between the fanatics and the liberalisers to a climax. Deng spoke an eloquent eulogy at Zhou's funeral, and riots broke out in Beijing after authorities hastily cleared away all the wreaths, posters and banners overnight. Tens of thousands of people poured on to the streets in protest, invaded government offices, overturned vehicles, lit fires and threatened police.

A so-called *Gang of Four,* including Mao's wife Jiang Qing, ordered a counter-attack by the police and workers' militia, which violently suppressed the protest and arrested several hundred participants. They blamed Deng and his liberalisations for the disorders, stripped him of his positions again, and denounced him as a "capitalist roader". The *Gang of Four* could act against Deng because Jiang Qing persuaded her husband that the revolution was in danger, but in August 1976 Mao died, and within a year the *Gang of Four* had been expelled from positions of power. It was the end of an era of revolutionary adventures forced upon a population in the name of inhuman ideology.

The death of Mao allowed Deng to make another comeback, and over the next four years he became the dominant figure in the Chinese leadership. For a time, China could breathe freely, as he allowed open criticism of the *Cultural Revolution.* Deng also abolished restrictions preventing children of former property-owning classes from holding responsible positions – primarily because he wanted to liberate those classes to create wealth. While Mao insisted that the Party control all economic development, Deng chose to give freedom to individual entrepreneurs, remarking: "It doesn't matter if a cat is black or white – so long as it catches mice."

Deng decided that the Chinese people should be free to make money, but not to have a voice in politics. He told visitors later that he believed the Soviet Union fell apart in 1990 because it could not satisfy the material needs of the population, not because it repressed liberty. However, Deng's theory that the Chinese would be satisfied only with material gains has not been tested, because the people have been given no other choice. When the peoples of eastern Europe were given the freedom to choose, they voted the Communists out of power, even though the transition caused them economic pain.

One of Deng's protégés, Hu Yaobang, became Party Chairman and went on to replace discredited Maoist ideology with a more flexible policy of "seeking truth from facts" – which meant free debate. Yet again, this stirred hardliners in the Party to fight back. In 1987, after several weeks of student demonstrations demanding more liberties, Hu was forced to resign for "mistakes on major issues of political policy". Once more, the Party clamped down on freedom of speech.

The Chinese people had sniffed the scent of liberty, however, and when Hu Yaobang died in April 1989, his funeral triggered even greater demonstrations for freedom in Beijing. Chinese journalists joined in, chanting "no more lies", and judges paraded with demands that they be free to administer the rule of law rather than Party edicts. Art students erected a makeshift effigy of New York's Statue of

Liberty in the central Tiananmen Square, and the numbers of protesters swelled to over a million.

For a few weeks, the principles of liberty pioneered in Europe and the United States flourished in China's capital. Suddenly, the whole of China's modern history was called into question. Why did Mao still lie embalmed in a mausoleum at the far end of Tiananmen Square? Why did the Party stifle the truth about the horrors of his *Great Leap Forward* and *Cultural Revolution*? What values did China represent as a state, now that Mao was dead?

Another reformist, Zhao Ziyang, who had been Communist Party General Secretary, went to talk with students in Tiananmen Square. At 5am on 19th May 1989, he appealed to them to disperse, with a vague assurance that their demands would eventually be met. But the students did not believe a Communist could really liberalise, and they refused to listen.

Although his speech was broadcast by state television, Zhao Ziyang knew that hardliners in the Party were planning a crackdown. He himself had been ousted from the leadership overnight and all he could do was save lives by urging the students to go home. The leadership had split between reformers and hardliners, and the tiny, wizened Deng had tilted the balance. He was a reformer at heart, but he could not countenance a movement threatening the very foundations of the Communist Party, which had never known democracy. Deng came down on the side of repression, the authorities decreed martial law, and on 4th June troops opened fire on the protesters in Tiananmen Square, killing hundreds of them.

The protest was crushed, but one lone resister was captured on film refusing to move. As a column of tanks crawled up to him, he stood there, shopping bags in hand, and refused to get out of the way. The leading tank halted – to shoot down a little man with shopping bags seemed ridiculous. The tank driver manoeuvred to left and right, but the protestor shuffled over with it. Then he climbed on top of the turret of the tank and began to berate the crew, until eventually he jumped off and was arrested.

Images of this man went around the world, and showed that a seemingly insignificant human being valued freedom enough to stand in the path of a tank. For a few minutes, he held up the might of China's modern army. To the discomfort of the government, the most memorable moment of this grim episode of Chinese history has been precisely this one. The Chinese authorities followed up with a wave of arrests and expulsions of foreign journalists, and Zhao Ziyang was put under house arrest until he died in 2005. So sensitive is Zhao's liberal reputation that, even posthumously, his name remains erased from most Chinese public records and textbooks, and his face airbrushed from photos.

To this day, Tiananmen Square in Beijing is dominated by Mao's mausoleum. The Party has stifled debate about the causes of the 1989 uprising by labelling it as a "counter-revolutionary episode". It refuses to re-open discussion of the disastrous *Great Leap Forward* or the *Cultural Revolution*, of which many living Chinese have memories. In fact, much of its recent history is a vacuum.

Freedom of enterprise has enabled the Chinese economy to roar ahead, mostly by providing cheap manufacturing to the developed world. This has enabled the 300 million Chinese who rank as middle class to earn their livelihoods more or less as they wished, but if growth peters out, they may lose their enthusiasm for economic liberty.

The Communist Party no longer positions itself as the vanguard of a social revolution; instead it poses as the guardian of order and the defender of China's sovereignty against foreigners, in the hope that feisty nationalism will win popular approval. Beyond the economic sphere, China still represses other liberties on a large scale. It is among the countries that execute the most people each year, it outlaws the Falun Gong spiritual movement as an "evil cult", and it stamps on dissent by Tibetans and ethnic minorities. The Communist Party of China has the final say on anything it considers important.

Hong Kong, which Britain handed back to China in 1997, has shown that absence of political liberty can still be a live issue. In the last four months of 2014, its citizens staged mass demonstrations and street sit-ins in protest at changes in the local electoral law empowering the central government in Beijing to vet candidates. Under the changeover agreement negotiated by Deng Xiaoping, Hong Kong citizens have been allowed to keep more civil liberties than people elsewhere in China, and as many as 100,000 turned out to resist the electoral change. After streets in the city centre had been blocked for 79 days, police moved the demonstrators out. The authorities refused to make concessions, but for nearly three months the people had openly defied a government which otherwise brooked no dissent.

Through all the repressions, certain Chinese leaders continued to push for freedom. Communist Party reformers such as Deng Xiaoping, Hu Yaobang, Zhou Enlai and Zhao Ziyang did so discreetly, waiting for the propitious moment. In this they followed an ancient Chinese tradition, favouring peaceful, low-key persuasion over direct confrontation. Deng Xiaoping told his followers: "Never take the lead – but aim to do something big." But it was a fight all the same, and did achieve more freedom for the people, even if limited to what Party discipline would allow.

Deng's own reputation is mixed. He was a champion of the opening up of the economy, which undid the revolutionary straitjacket imposed by Mao. On the other hand, when confronted by the crisis of Tiananmen Square, he chose the political repression which is typical of any Communist movement and continues to determine Chinese society today.

As for the Chinese people, for more than half a century they proved ready to fight vigorously for freedom if given a chance. Whenever cracks appeared in the absolute authority of the Communist Party, they descended on to the streets to demonstrate for more liberties. In doing so, they showed that the undercurrents of freedom run as strongly in the east as anywhere else.

Vietnam

In the early 1940s, a young Vietnamese exile in China was eagerly reading Mao's treatises about guerrilla warfare. When he returned to his home country in 1954, Vo Nguyen Giap (1911-2013) used what he had learned to liberate his people from their French colonial masters. During World War II, the Japanese had driven the French out of Vietnam – then known as Indochina – and after Japan's defeat, the French came back hoping to resume where they left off. However, the world had changed; the Soviet Union was a nuclear superpower and China was a Communist People's Republic. So when the local Communists decided to resist the return of the French, they could count on powerful foreign friends.

With their modern, professionally trained army, the French did not expect any great difficulty in dealing with Asian guerrillas. General Giap thought otherwise, and the death of his father and first wife under torture in French prisons gave him a strong personal motivation. He taught the soldiers he led that they were fighting to liberate their country, while the French troops consisted mainly of colonial recruits.

Giap trained his men to live off the land and travel on foot and by bicycle over forest paths; this enabled them to negotiate the steep jungle-clad mountains around the fortified French strongpoint at Dien Bien Phu. Moving in single file, 55,000 of his troops took up positions around the camp in 1954, aided by 200,000 porters and 12,000 bamboo rafts. They took artillery guns to pieces to pull into position, and dug trenches and tunnels up close to the French lines. Battle ensued and, despite inflicting huge losses on the attackers and being supplied with food and ammunition by air, the exhausted French capitulated after most of their soldiers were killed or wounded.

Giap's insurgent victory had its greatest impact psychologically, since it destroyed the French resolve to continue the war. Over its seven-year duration, the war cost the French dearly; 90,000 members of the French armed forces were killed, and the expense severely strained the post-war French budget. A few weeks after the surrender at Dien Bien Phu, France announced it would withdraw from Indochina, and a 1954 international conference divided the country into North and South Vietnam. The Vietnamese were thus free from French colonial rule, but in the north the outcome was a Communist dictatorship influenced by China and the Soviet Union, and in the south a corrupt government which refused to hold elections and existed on support from the United States.

General Giap took his orders from North Vietnam's political leader, Ho Chi Minh (1890-1969), who had immersed himself in Communist doctrine as a young man in France, the Soviet Union and China. In organising resistance, first to the Japanese and then to the French, Ho Chi Minh saw himself as waging a class war against capitalism. Taking the battle to the American-sponsored regime in South Vietnam was thus his next logical step. He ordered General Giap and his guerrillas to infiltrate along jungle trails to support the local Viet Cong Communist movement in subverting the southern government. As in the struggle against the French, the invaders lived off the land and hardened themselves to primitive conditions. Giap quoted the words of Napoleon that "if a goat can get through, so can a man; if a man can get through, so can a battalion". They harried the enemy into frustrated helplessness, terrorised the local population into allegiance and learned to be patient.[63]

The Americans responded by pouring in regular troops to bolster the South Vietnamese regime. When the professionals were not enough, they drafted young men into compulsory military service "to defend freedom". However, the conflict had now turned into struggle between the two superpowers. The Soviet Union gave significant aid to North Vietnam, and the Americans feared that if the south fell to the Communists, there would be a "domino effect" toppling other regimes in south-east Asia. The Vietnamese people themselves had no scope to determine the course of events. They had become pawns in a superpower conflict.

As the war ground on, with mounting losses and no prospect of victory, the U.S. government and military lost public support at home. Freedom of the press meant American journalists could roam where they wanted, witnessing the atrocities, disillusionment and setbacks for themselves. Their coverage contradicted the positive reports of victories and clearances coming from the American military command – not to mention the inflated body counts. Rioting by students broke out at American universities, and the portrait of Ho Chi Minh appeared in student dormitories across the country. Ho, whose name meant "Bringer of Light", was a hard-as-nails Communist, caring nothing for individual liberties. But for the rebellious students threatened with the draft, he was a gutsy underdog taking on a modern superpower.

A major offensive in 1968, during which the Communist fighters penetrated the U.S. embassy in Saigon, broke the will of President Lyndon B. Johnson to continue the war. He did not stand for re-election and, after a settlement negotiated in 1973 collapsed, the Communists took control of all of Vietnam. The last helicopter took off from the roof of the U.S. Saigon embassy in 1975 with desperate Vietnamese trying to escape by clinging to its skids. The image vividly demonstrated America's failure in a war it proclaimed as a fight for freedom.

Why did the Americans not succeed in Vietnam? Counter-insurgency wars had been won before. For example, the British defeated Communist guerrillas in Malaya in the 1950s by isolating them and nurturing local villagers. However, the Americans could not prevent the Soviet Union giving outside help to the Vietnamese Communists. With that aid flowing freely, the Americans would have had to risk a nuclear conflict to head it off. Moreover, the Americans were not focused single-mindedly on the cause of liberty, however much their own state promoted it as a justification for war. Their underlying motivation was to counter the challenge of the Soviet Union, and that overrode scruples about propping up an undemocratic government in South Vietnam. Global realpolitik was more important than protecting individual liberties.

For the rest of the 20th century, the United States largely refrained from exporting its libertarian principles by force of arms. Only after the 9/11 attacks of 2001 did President George W. Bush abandon this reticence and launch invasions of Afghanistan and Iraq. He too declared he was bringing freedom and democracy, and he too failed to do so.

The ideals of freedom, however, did not die. After the war, Vietnam lapsed into the rigid mismanagement and repression typical of a Marxist-Leninist state. The Communist Party assumed dictatorial powers, and soon tens of thousands of its citizens were trying to escape on rickety boats. The "boat people" arriving on coasts and islands of nearby countries demonstrated the bankruptcy of the Communist cause. They had left to find freedom elsewhere.

The "dominos" in the end did not all fall. Laos and Cambodia went the same way as Vietnam, but other south-east Asian states steered clear of Communism and kept on friendly terms with the United States. For them, the principles of political liberty, free markets and free international trade – even if not always faithfully observed – proved more attractive than inefficient and overbearing Communist regimentation.

Although Vietnam is still ruled by the Communist Party of Vietnam, in Ho Chi Minh City (former Saigon) young people openly flaunt the American way of life. The Party at first privileged workers and peasants, but has now opened up the economy to entrepreneurs operating as free capitalists.

Despite losing the Vietnam War, the United States still exercises a powerful influence in south-east Asia, and for all its setbacks and cold geopolitical calculations, remains a force for liberty and human rights in the region. Ho Chi Minh and General Giap, though they freed Vietnam from colonial rule, have by contrast left a legacy of oppression, which today's leaders are still seeking to moderate.

CHAPTER 9

REVOLUTIONARIES ON THE DOORSTEP

I have just done one of the hardest tasks I have ever had to do. I have had to condemn to death one of the finest characters I have ever come across.
– British officer Charles Blackader, sentencing Irish rebel leader Patrick Pearse

We cannot liberate by ourselves a country that does not want to fight.
– Che Guevara

Ireland

As war clouds gathered over continental Europe in 1914, the British government was even more concerned by a crisis right in its backyard. After centuries of suppression by the English, the Irish people were threatening to rise up and claim their freedom.

From the end of the 12th century, English kings had counted Ireland among their territorial possessions, and from the 16th century onwards England sent in Protestant settlers to take over lands belonging to the Catholic Irish. Soon they dominated the local parliament, and in 1649-52 Oliver

Cromwell occupied Ireland by military force, subduing it with great cruelty and loss of life.

The Irish seethed with discontent as Protestants overrode their liberties, but it took 150 years for the British government to realise that its oppressive regime could not go on indefinitely. In 1801, the government formally incorporated Ireland into the United Kingdom so that the Irish could elect members to Parliament in London and thus have more say over their own affairs. This merely fed a desire for greater autonomy, and the British felt compelled to make more concessions. In 1829, a ban on observance of the Catholic religion was lifted and, later in the century, "Home Rule" Bills were twice introduced into Parliament – but failed both times.

English landowners in Ireland and Protestant Irish living in the north-eastern corner constantly blocked change, and although Parliament finally did pass Irish Home Rule legislation in 1914, it was suspended when World War I broke out. At the last moment, the exasperated Irish were thus, once again, denied their freedom.

With no resolution in sight, a rebel Irish Republic Brotherhood decided to take advantage of Britain's pre-occupation with World War I to seize power and declare a free and independent Ireland. In response to a plea for help, Germany sent a ship laden with arms to Ireland, together with Irish ex-diplomat Roger Casement, who had raised an "Irish Brigade" among prisoners-of-war in Germany to fight against Britain. However, the British Navy intercepted the arms ship and Casement was arrested as he landed in Ireland from a German submarine.

After this setback, the Irish cause was unexpectedly helped by the introduction of military conscription in

Britain in 1916. Many Irishmen had volunteered to join the British Army at the outset of war, but they objected that the British were now forcing them to fight. Feeling that they had the benefit of public support, the Irish independence fighters sensed that their moment had come, and staged an uprising on Easter Monday 1916 in Dublin to establish a free Irish state. They caught the British by surprise, but the revolt quickly turned to fiasco. The rebels seized the General Post Office but failed to take railway stations, the port, the armoury or Dublin Castle (the seat of British rule). After five days of street fighting, the Irish surrendered, leaving 318 Irish and 116 British dead.

It happened so quickly and unexpectedly that Dubliners were taken aback and initially blamed the freedom fighters for the death and destruction. In that moment, the British could perhaps have swung opinion to their side by granting a few more liberties. But despite the British Prime Minister, H.H. Asquith, advocating leniency, the local British general exacted harsh reprisals, turning the population against him. A British firing squad executed 18 ringleaders, one of whom had to be lashed to a chair because he was injured and could not stand. Casement was hanged for treason in London, and over 3,500 Irish men and women were arrested.

The repression was a fateful mistake, since it brought Irish public opinion firmly back to the side of the freedom fighters. In the British elections of 1918, Sinn Féin, the Irish independence party, won a landslide victory in Ireland, but refused to take up seats in the Parliament in London, and instead declared Ireland's independence. The president of the new revolutionary Irish Republic was one of the leaders of the 1916 Easter Rising, American-born Éamon de Valera, who escaped from a British jail to take up his post.

Once again the bid was thwarted; the British refused to accept the Irish declaration and the Irish War of Independence broke out. The British recruited thugs in England and Scotland nicknamed the "Black and Tans", who roamed the countryside, killing and torturing whoever might conceivably oppose British rule. A British Labour Party commission expressed shame at witnessing the "insolent swagger" of the Tans, whom they described as "rough, brutal, abusive and distinctly the worse for liquor".[64]

With the population now behind them, the Irish independence fighters were mostly one step ahead of the British, and succeeded in infiltrating Dublin Castle with spies. The guerrillas drove police out of most of the countryside within a year, and crowds stoned British troops, who shot back at random. Prisoners went on hunger strikes, the independence fighters mounted ambushes and the authorities responded with curfews.

As the fight dragged on into 1922, public opinion, both in Britain and America (home of many Irish immigrants), put pressure on the British government to end the war. The outcome of negotiations was a divided Ireland. The independence fighters won the right to form an "Irish Free State", which would, however, still be a "dominion" within the British Empire.

That was not to be the end of it. Almost immediately the Irish independence movement split, between those accepting dominion status and those who wanted to cut all ties with Britain. Civil war broke out, with the British supporting the "Free Staters", and the other side claiming betrayal of the Republic. It was another ugly war, resulting in even more casualties than the War of Independence. The Free Staters eventually won, but in 1937, a Republic was declared after all, completely independent of Britain, and this time the British did not resist. Protestants in the north-east corner (Northern Ireland) refused to submit to the Catholic government in Dublin, so their region remained an integral part of the United Kingdom.

The question was still not settled, with Irish Republicans objecting to the rule of Protestant Northern Ireland directly by Britain. For them that meant full independence was still denied. So in the 1960s, an Irish Republican Army began another guerrilla campaign in Northern Ireland, fiercely opposed by Protestant Unionist militias. The British sent in troops, and the ghastly cycle of assassinations, maiming and lawless violence began again. This time, however, the British mounted a better intelligence operation among the insurgents and, after a time, they achieved an uneasy calm.

It took several decades before all parties in 1998 reached a "Good Friday Agreement", which provided for power sharing in Northern Ireland and the de-commissioning of paramilitaries and their arsenals. The Republic of Ireland, by far the largest part of the country, continued to rule itself independently of Britain, while in the Protestant-dominated north, the feuding parties agreed to share power and give up violence. Peace then gave people in Northern Ireland the chance to live according to their individual wishes, rather than as hostages to tribal loyalties. The outcome showed that even when a fight for freedom degenerates into bloodshed and hatred, it is possible to emerge both free and at peace. As such, the Irish struggle for independence testifies to the capability of the human spirit to deal with freedom wisely – if only after a very long time.

In 2011, Britain's Queen Elizabeth II, at the age of 85, paid the first state visit to independent Ireland by a British monarch. From the moment she stepped off her plane wearing an outfit in emerald green, the national colour of Ireland, her visit was a triumph. As someone endowed with no direct political power, but considerable moral stature, she was able to inspire true reconciliation. Paying tribute at a memorial to slain resistance fighters in Dublin, she declared: "I extend my sincere thoughts and deepest sympathy. With the benefit of historical hindsight, we can all see things which we would have done differently, or not at all." It was all but an apology for past wrongs.

Three years later, she invited Martin McGuiness, a former IRA guerrilla leader and member of the power-sharing government in Northern Ireland, to a banquet in honour of the visiting Irish head of state. She shook McGuiness's hand in welcome as he arrived at Windsor Castle. It seemed the natural thing to do.

Cuba – Liberation, Dictatorship and a New Opening

For many a long year, the United States exercised hegemony over Latin America, influencing governments to keep in line with its interests, and they scarcely expected that they too would find hostile freedom fighters on their doorstep. That assurance was rudely shaken in 1959, when a band of revolutionaries struggled ashore from a leaking boat to overthrow the dictatorship of General Fulgencio Batista in Cuba.

Batista, a former sergeant, was a corrupt tyrant who favoured rich landowners at the expense of poor peasants. But he was America's man, and now a group of leftist desperadoes had forced him to flee an island that lay scarcely 100 miles offshore from Florida. At the head of the rebels was Fidel

Castro, illegitimate son of a wealthy sugar-plantation owner, one-time Havana lawyer, and a guerrilla fighter schooled in the tactics of Mao Zedong.

Castro had been a candidate for an election his party was expected to win in 1952, but Batista staged a coup before it could take place. With the democratic path blocked, the next year Castro led a group of sympathisers in an attack on the Moncada barracks in the east of the country. He hoped to spark an uprising amongst the sugar-cane harvesters, but it was a debacle, and Castro was lucky to escape with his life. He was sentenced to 15 years in prison, but released under an amnesty in 1955 and exiled with fellow-dissidents to Mexico.

The following year they returned, making their way slowly over the Gulf of Mexico aboard the elderly yacht *Granma,* made for 20, but overloaded with 82 rebels, as well as food, arms and ammunition. When they came ashore in eastern Cuba, they found Batista's air force looking for them and an army patrol attacked two days later as they headed for the Sierra Maestra mountains. Only 20 survived and made it to safety in the forested heights.

Thus began a revolution that was to capture imaginations around the world. The survivors built up their numbers with a "hearts and minds" campaign among the peasants, helping out on farms, setting up schools and clinics, and re-distributing any land they could seize. It was a recipe tried and tested by Mao, whom they also emulated by capturing and executing anybody suspected as a government supporter. Castro's motivated guerrillas proved superior to the troops Batista sent into the mountains to destroy them, so government soldiers started deserting to the rebels.

Once they realised Batista was a lost cause, the Americans abandoned him and he fled to the Dominican Republic. From then on Castro was unstoppable, even though he still had only 800 guerrilla fighters. He marched on Havana, rallying crowds by invoking Cuba's war of independence from Spanish colonial rule (1895-98). In the capital, cheering crowds welcomed him as the nation's liberator.

However, the regime that Castro, his brother Raúl and Che Guevara set up was Marxist-Leninist, following the Communist doctrine that revolutionaries must enforce their authority absolutely. Castro and his comrades duly rounded up Batista officials, police and officers to put them before firing squads. Over the next half-century, they imposed their authority by imprisoning political opponents, suppressing dissent and monitoring subversive talk through neighbourhood vigilante groups.

Americans were not pleased at finding radicals inspired by their Cold War enemy on their doorstep. In retaliation, they stopped buying Cuba's sugar and providing experts to keep the economy going, subsequently breaking diplomatic relations and applying embargoes on trade and travel. As a result, Castro turned to the Soviet Union, which was happy to build a position of influence so close to the United States. In exchange for Cuban sugar, fruit, fibres and hides, Castro received Soviet oil, fertilisers, industrial goods and a $100 million loan. American-owned refineries on the island refused to process the Soviet oil, so Castro nationalised them, along with most other American assets on the island. The break was complete. Cuba was free of American hegemony – at a price.

Castro did not totally abuse the freedom the revolutionaries had won. He brought literacy and learning up to standards of the developed world, and introduced free, modern healthcare, which dramatically reduced infant mortality. His new regime gave 200,000 peasants deeds to confiscated property and banned foreign ownership of land. Much of this was conducive to liberty, and visitors could observe that the creation of a socialist society was generally well accepted. When U.S. President John F. Kennedy authorised an invasion of Cuba by a force of 1,400 combatants in 1961, it prompted no popular uprising against Castro and they were easily defeated.

Fidel Castro and his close comrade, Che Guevara (born in Argentina), were not just chasing Communist illusions; for them, what they had seen of Latin America in their youth gave them powerful motives to revolt. Landowners enriched themselves from vast tracts of land, while peasants owned little or nothing and were worked to exhaustion. The governments which had grown out of the liberation from the Spanish colonialists had become corrupt. Wealth was concentrated in the hands of a very few, and American businesses squeezed the countries for profits with little concern for the repercussions. The large mass of the population led lives that, in the eyes of Castro and Guevara, made them economic slaves. They passionately believed it was their vocation to end this exploitation.

Castro and Guevara cultivated a quixotic charisma as fighters for bold ideals, appealing to young people frustrated by the constraints of conventional society. Their Cuba seemed unique, a totally different presence on the world stage. The newly independent leaders of African states flocked to Castro's company, his *guerrillero* swagger reminding them of the times when they themselves had been struggling for national liberation. The dark, good-looking Guevara projected a paradoxical image as a revolutionary with an iron fist and a warm heart. After the fall of Batista, he would go to a prison in the morning to shoot members of the old regime, and on his way back home would spend an hour arranging food and shelter for a beggar he came across on the street.[65]

The two could hardly have been more different from the other Latin American leaders of the 1960s and 1970s. While Castro and Guevara posed for photos in jungle fatigues, the military rulers of Argentina, Chile and Brazil stood to attention in uniforms bedecked with medals, staring grimly through dark glasses. While Cuba was inciting revolution, Chile's General Augusto Pinochet overthrew the democratically elected government of Salvador Allende; Argentina's General Jorge Videla killed thousands of political opponents, notably by ejecting them alive from aircraft over the sea; and Brazil's military dictatorship committed systematic murder and torture.

Castro and Guevara were convinced that their Cuban style of revolution could also free oppressed peoples elsewhere. In 1965, Guevara went to the Congo to train leftist guerrilla fighters in one of the internal wars that followed the end of Belgian rule. He and Castro had succeeded in Cuba after starting from nothing, but his African venture came to nought after less than a year. With only six of his original companions still alive, he crossed back over Lake Tanganyika to safety in Tanzania. He wrote of the exploit: "There is no will to fight. The leaders are corrupt… we cannot liberate by ourselves a country that does not want to fight."

The next year he went to Bolivia to mount an insurgency against the pro-American government, but there too he failed completely. Hounded by government troops assisted by American commandos, he and his band of fighters stumbled through the jungle, ill, poorly fed and unable to win over the local population. Guevara was captured and shot in 1967, and his bedraggled body was photographed to be promulgated around the world. He was then buried at a secret location. As was always the risk for a *guerrillero*, his end was obscure and wretched.

Like those before them and others who would follow, the Cuban leaders learned that liberating one's own people from oppression was one thing, but attempting the same for people in foreign lands was likely to be less welcome. Meanwhile, back in Cuba, freedom from American-style capitalism brought greater equality, but also hardship. The Cuban peasants were forced into agricultural cooperatives, which meant arduous work for little recompense, and for everybody the rupture with the United States led to shortages and restrictions. Large numbers of doctors, lawyers and other professionals resented the regime imposed by the revolutionaries, and chose freedom by emigrating to the United States.

The Soviet Union collapsed in 1990, leaving Cuba's Marxist-Leninist regime as an isolated anachronism. The rest of Latin America moved on, abandoning military dictatorships, democratically voting governments in and out, refraining from revolution and finding ways of advancing their economies without selling out to foreigners. The present-day leaders of Chile, Uruguay and Brazil were themselves persecuted by military dictatorships, but they put the past behind them, and managed to free their peoples from political oppression without resorting to turmoil and violence.

After intestinal surgery, Fidel Castro withdrew from government in 2008 at the age of 82 and handed over to his brother Raúl. The passage of powers could be seen as a sign of sclerosis in the revolution; nobody else was trusted to carry on the fight, or perhaps no one had the heart to. It was obvious that the revolutionaries who rid Cuba of its tyrant had proved unable to build a viable new society. The economy stagnated at a desolate level, strangled by rigid central planning, and the state allowed no free elections, no free speech and no freedom of the press.

The decision of U.S. President Barack Obama in 2014 to resume diplomatic relations and progressively liberalise trade and travel has cleared the way for Cuba eventually to take leave of its past too. With the revolution clearly having run its course, the opening to the United States can hardly fail to bring significant new liberties. A liberal-minded American president has found common ground with ageing autocrats who know change must come.

Some Cubans remain proud that they could chart their own way for half a century independently of the great power to the north, and they worry that this autonomy will now dissipate. Foreign tourists love the authentic, unforgettable, unique Cuba, with its derelict colonial buildings and its 1950s American cars, and regret that this too will probably disappear.

However, many of the islanders greeted news of the 2014 breakthrough euphorically. Church bells rang out in the capital of Havana, American flags appeared on the streets, and a foreign journalist saw smiling people come out on to the streets to beep their horns and even cry with happiness.[66] The rapprochement with America brought hope to Cubans that they will be able to live much as other liberated people do. It may take time, but they are free to hope, to dream and to plan for a brighter future.[67]

CHAPTER 10

AFRICA – TO HELL AND BACK

Liberty has never come from Government. Liberty has always come from the subjects of it.
– Woodrow Wilson

Freedom Squandered

Castro's revolution may not have worked as planned, but at least he was sincere. That can scarcely be said of the African liberation movement leaders with whom the Cuban leader consorted. They signally failed to make good use of their emancipation; the 30 to 40 years following independence were a nightmare for most of the African continent.

When African leaders took over, the road ahead looked fairly smooth: commodity prices were booming, there was a mood of euphoria, and visionaries such as Ghana's Nkrumah spoke of a forthcoming African paradise of abundance. The British set up a Commonwealth as a forum for continuing relations with its former colonies; as did France for its former francophone territories, also providing them with a special currency linked to the French franc. A number of the new leaders were familiar with notions of individual freedom prevalent in the west, and with some of the positive precedents of freedom fighting elsewhere. It was thus no foregone conclusion that the continent would turn against liberal democracy.

The outlook was, however, not as promising as it may have originally seemed. Poverty and disease kept life expectancy below 40, populations were growing rapidly and few people were educated or skilled. After the end of colonial rule, there was a vacuum of authority, and past experience showed that the immediate aftermath of a breakthrough to freedom could be a dangerous period. Moreover, the new leaders inherited territories created arbitrarily by European colonialists, encompassing a mix of ethnic and linguistic groups which could be toxic. The transition was never likely to be easy.

The main priority of the new leaders was, therefore, to stamp their authority over the states that they inherited. The Ghanaian leader proclaimed "Nkrumahism" as a new ideology, drawing its strength from the "belief that the free development of each is conditioned by the free development of all".[68] In other words, individual liberty was to be subordinated to the collective, which in Ghana meant Nkrumah's own decisions. Other African leaders followed suit, and the continent reverted to the pre-colonial system of powerful chiefs who brooked no opposition. From independence until 1989, nearly all the 50 countries of Africa had one-party governments and personality cults flourished.

In former French Guinea, Sékou Touré called himself "The Great Son of Africa", and students were required to read his 20 volumes of personal deliberations and learn his poems by heart. He ruled by personal decree, as did Hastings Banda in Malawi, who dismissed ministers who disagreed with him and in 1971 declared himself president for life. Banda decided everything down to the smallest detail.

"Everything is my business, everything… anything I say is law. Literally law. It is a fact in this country."

In Ivory Coast, Félix Houphouët-Boigny declared: "Democracy is a system of government for virtuous people. In young countries such as our own, we need a chief who is all-powerful for a specific period of time." Tunisia's president, Habib Bourguiba, when asked about his country's political system, asked: "System? What system? I am the system";[69] while Egypt was subjected to "Nasserism", reflecting the all-pervading influence of its leader Gamal Abdel Nasser. So instead of enjoying democracy, citizens of all these states were exposed to the unlimited power of autocrats.

Competition between the two superpowers, the United States and the Soviet Union, only made matters worse. The Soviet Union saw Africa as a prime area to extend its influence, and tried to position itself strategically as the defender of the people against colonialists. The Americans, on the other hand, sought to contain the Soviets and find their own allies. Both were happy to back strongmen and prop up oppressive regimes in order to promote their own interests, regardless of the wishes of the people.

This superpower struggle over Africa was often disastrous. In Somalia, for example, General Mohammed Siad Barre launched so-called "Scientific Socialism", nationalised businesses, brought in large quantities of Soviet weapons and imposed a draconian personality cult. When the Soviet Union broke with Barre at the end of the 1970s, he turned to the United States for aid, but the economy disintegrated and he lost control over rival clans. Barre fled into exile in 1991, when his regime was toppled in a civil war, and thereafter local warlords made the country ungovernable.

In Ethiopia, Colonel Mengistu Haile Mariam set up a Communist dictatorship that led to a humanitarian catastrophe. The creation of state farms and collectivisation of farmers' smallholdings caused a steep drop in food production. He aggravated this by waging military campaigns against rebels, and when drought struck in 1984-85, it led to a famine which Mengistu refused to acknowledge. For months he barred aid charities from travelling to places where vast numbers of his people were dying of starvation, and instead lavished tens of millions of dollars on celebrations of the 10th anniversary of independence.

Eventually, BBC cameraman Mohammed Amin came across "a tremendous mass of people, groaning, weeping, scattered across the ground in the dawn mist".[70] He made a news film that was broadcast across the world, with a memorable commentary by Michael Buerk: "Dawn, and as the sun breaks through the piercing chill of night on the plain outside Korem, it lights up a biblical famine, now, in the 20th century. This place, say workers here, is the closest thing to hell on earth. Thousands of wasted people are coming here for help. Many find death."

Several hundred thousand people perished and millions of others were displaced. Irish pop singer Bob Geldof staged a "Band Aid" televised rock concert which raised more than $100 million for relief, and other charity aid began to pour in as the world's conscience was pricked. But it was not nature that had brought on the disaster, nor western indifference. The principal cause was the cruel manoeuvring of Mengistu.

Africa's liberation leaders used Marxist-Leninist doctrine not only to justify ruling as dictators, but also to seize assets on behalf of the state, which they and their cronies controlled. After independence, they pocketed much of the revenues earned from exporting cocoa, coffee, diamonds, oil and other valuable natural resources. The new leaders effectively treated power as a licence to steal from the people for whom they were responsible, with many stashing away ill-gotten gains in accounts in Switzerland. Their people may have expected to reap the benefits of liberation from colonial powers, but were instead subjected to tyranny, theft and neglect on a grand scale.

This, however, was not a fault limited to regimes inspired by Marxist-Leninism. In the Congo (renamed Zaire),[71] the depredations of President Mobutu, who was supported by the U.S., deprived the state of one of its main sources of income: annual copper production shrank from 450,000 tonnes in the 1970s to 30.6 tonnes by 1994. The Ivory Coast's president, Houphouët-Boigny, backed by France, conducted foreign commerce for his own profit, spent extravagantly on a luxurious palace, and ran up large debts – on the country's account, not his own.[72]

In Nigeria, political parties controlled state resources – it had huge reserves of oil – and plundered them to reward themselves and their supporters. People voted for a party according to its ability to steal state assets. Even Ghana's Nkrumah, the champion of African emancipation, enriched himself by organising bribes through a National Development Corporation. In all these countries, free enterprise was open to the leader and his associates, but scarcely at all to the ordinary people.

In some countries, the post-colonial tyranny was bizarre, and often gruesome. When a 27-year-old officer named Muammar Gaddafi came to power in a coup in Libya in 1969, the freedom from foreign influence that he gained for his people soon gave way to arbitrary impositions. He banned nightclubs, alcohol and Christian churches, and indoctrinated his people with fanciful ideas formulated in a "Green Book", which children were forced to study at school. He himself is said to have raped kidnapped teenage girls in specially built dungeons, and kept murdered enemies in freezers.[73]

In Uganda, Idi Amin ordered all Indians with British passports out of the country, so that their businesses and property could be taken over by his comrades. He terrorised any challengers to his regime, and is reputed to have made blood rituals over the bodies of enemies; one of his wives was found in a car with her limbs dismembered.

Jean-Bédel Bokassa, who ruled the Central African Republic in similar style, shocked a visiting French minister at a banquet by remarking that they had just eaten human flesh. He crowned himself Emperor in a coronation styled on Napoleon's, ordering from France a crown of diamonds, a red cloak trimmed with ermine, a throne in the shape of an eagle, a coach and horses, and 60 Mercedes Benz cars. Meanwhile, the rest of his country languished in poverty.[74]

Amid this terrible litany, one leader was a more honourable exception, if only in his intentions. In Tanganyika (later Tanzania), Julius Nyerere experimented with an idealistic system of grass-roots government, harking back to pre-colonial Africa. He was a sincere socialist and genuinely sought to respond to the people's wishes. His main idea was to relocate farmers into communal villages run on socialist principles. However, when farmers held back, he uprooted 11 million of them in a forced resettlement. Instead of working on their farms, the rural population was then stranded in artificial settlements offering no sustenance, resulting in a collapse of agricultural production.

Nyerere nationalised much of Tanzania's productive capacity, but the new enterprises were wasteful, and by the 1980s only a continual flow of foreign aid saved the country from famine and bankruptcy. Yet nobody inside the country questioned his policies, since, ironically, even a leader as intelligent and well-meaning as Nyerere considered it right to stifle free debate. He created a one-party state, arguing that African society was classless and thus needed no democratic interplay between government and opposition.

Nyerere impressed people with his modest way of life and personal honesty, gaining many admirers among socialist circles in the west, who earnestly hoped that his experiment would succeed. Alas, it was nothing short of a disaster: the imposition of rigidly planned socialism deprived his people of the freedom to earn their livings, and they paid a terrible price.

When it was clear the undertaking had failed, Nyerere resigned in 1985. He was one of only six African leaders to voluntarily leave office in the 30 years of post-colonial independence. All six had ruled for more than 20 years, hardly testifying to the free play of democratic choice.

The Old Guard Goes, New Wars Start

The death knell for the old guard of independence leaders came in 1989-90, with the demise of the Soviet Union. Moscow could no longer sustain African client states which sucked out resources it could ill afford to provide. As the Soviets withdrew, the United States lost interest in propping up tyrants such a Zaire's Mobutu to counter Moscow's influence. In Africa, students and young professionals, tired of being exploited, began to agitate for change. With the

new generation, the notions of democracy and freedom
tentatively re-surfaced, inspiring populations who had never
quite forgotten what they meant.

By 1994, nearly all the leaders who had imposed
one-party rule for decades were gone. But a number of
countries were still subjected to unremitting violence,
which made it impossible for people to lead free lives.
Warlord Charles Taylor laid waste to Liberia and Sierra
Leone in order to take over their diamond mining. The
United Nations and the United States tried to restore
order in Somalia, but it was beyond them; the looting,
anarchy and killings continued unimpeded, and Somalia
came to epitomise the concept of a failed state. In Angola,
the civil war dragged on until 2002, resulting in some
200,000 deaths and four million displaced persons. As for
Zaire, Mobutu was ousted from power in 1997, but it too
slid into civil war.

In Algeria, the leftist military leaders who fought
for independence forfeited popular support by
concentrating wealth within their own elite. Meanwhile,
the nationalised economy stagnated, unemployment
soared and impoverished citizens huddled in slums. As
a consequence, a newly formed Islamic Salvation Front
(FIS) won a landslide victory over the ruling National
Liberation Front (FLN) in the first round of elections in
1991. The FLN, dominated by the military that fought
against French colonialism, cancelled the second round
of the vote and thereafter ruled by its own diktat. The
Islamists were banned from political life and, as the
army tried to crush them, they resorted to widespread
assassinations and terror. In eight years of carnage, some
100,000 people are estimated to have died.

The slaughter eventually petered out in 1999, with both sides exhausted. But a rump of radical Islamists reformed under allegiance to Al-Qaeda, the movement behind the 9/11 attacks on America in 2001. Similar fundamentalist Islamic movements emerged in Nigeria, Somalia, Kenya, Sudan, Libya and Tunisia, trying to undermine any democratic order that would allow freedom to develop.

One of the biggest outrages of post-colonial Africa occurred in Rwanda, where the Hutu population massacred some 800,000 ethnic Tutsis in 1994. Tensions had been rising because the majority Hutus felt they were underdogs to the minority Tutsis. After the Hutu president was assassinated, Hutus took this as a pretext to launch a campaign of extermination against Tutsis – in homes, schools, hospitals, foreign aid camps and at roadblocks across the country. Villagers killed their neighbours and teachers their schoolchildren; entire families were massacred together, and women were systematically raped.[75]

The genocide came to an end after three months when a Tutsi rebel group fought its way from neighbouring Uganda to take control of the capital. At which point, a million Hutus crossed into Zaire as refugees, and pictures of the exodus broadcast around the world prompted international relief agencies to rush in aid. Only after a few weeks did some of them uneasily realise they were succouring mass killers.

The international community did nothing to prevent the massacres. The U.N. had a military force in the country, but did not intervene. The Belgians, who were the former colonial rulers of Rwanda, pulled out when the killing of 15 of their soldiers raised a public outcry at home. France's president, François Mitterrand, sent 2,500 French troops, but they achieved nothing and also withdrew, while the U.S. held back, traumatised by its failed intervention in Somalia the year before.

Turning the Corner

In Rwanda, as elsewhere, death and fear crushed any hope the people may have had of fundamental liberties. Africa came to be seen as a disaster, destined to endless wars, killings and economic devastation; forever ruled by scoundrels with no respect for liberty, rights or law. Cynics questioned whether Africans had been better off under colonial rule. However, liberty consists not just of freedom from tyranny; it is also freedom to guide one's own destiny, for better or for worse. That liberty Africans have indeed gained, and none of them would want to return responsibility to foreign colonialists.

Africa is also becoming less oppressive, as gradually an undercurrent of reconstruction, reform, enterprise and, yes, freedom has begun to make itself felt. The British helped restore order in Sierra Leone in 2002, and wars elsewhere have been resolved, died away or become shorter and less destructive. The exceptions have begun to prove a tentative new rule – that war is no longer a major threat to the lives and liberties of Africa's long-suffering people.

The benefits of this are showing up in U.N. development statistics. When the U.N. set Millennium Development Goals (MDGs) in 2005 aimed at diminishing poverty, hunger, disease and discrimination, few people believed Africa would get anywhere near them. However, the 2013 update reported: "Africa... is on track to achieve the targets of universal primary education; gender parity at all levels of education; lower HIV/AIDS prevalence among 15-24 year olds; increased proportion of the population with access to antiretroviral drugs; and increased proportion of seats held by women in national parliaments by 2015."[76] During this period, malaria deaths in some of the worst affected countries declined by 30 per cent, and child mortality rates fell steeply.[77] All of these advances enable Africans to live their lives with fewer constraints than before.

One particular liberty has played a great role in making Africans better off: that is the freedom Africans have gained to earn a living, do business and trade as they wish. Over the past 20 years, Africans have increasingly been running their economies according to free-market principles, rather than the Marxist methods that failed them so disastrously. Economic statistics show that between 2003 and 2013, Africa's real income per person increased by more than 30 per cent, making it the fastest-growing continent in the world. In Mozambique alone, the economy grew by nearly two-thirds in just seven years.

New communication technologies such as the mobile phone have also helped Africa join the globalised economy. Whereas 20 years ago, a telephone would have been a rare occurrence outside a few large cities, an *Economist* correspondent travelling for 112 days through Africa in 2013 accessed emails on his smartphone on all but nine days. Most importantly, the liberating effect of proliferating mobile phones extends to the very poor people in rural areas. As a result, they are able to use their phones for small-scale trade and financial transactions, gaining access to the world of free enterprise.

Positions at the pinnacle of the global economy are now open to African-born businessmen. When Tidjane Thiam, a native of the Ivory Coast, was nominated to head the global bank Credit Suisse in 2015 – having previously presided over the Prudential insurance giant – his strong track record caused a jump in the bank's share price.

Africa has also become better governed politically. In 1990, just three African countries had multiparty political systems, universal suffrage, regular fraud-free elections and secret ballots. Now Eritrea is the only state not to hold elections at all. Elsewhere, democratic procedures may not be entirely regular, but opposition parties are better organised and governments change peacefully as a result of elections (as in 2015 in Nigeria, which has a population of 178 million). Although democracy can release pent-up ethnic animosities, it has progressively freed people from Africa's long succession of tyrants. Africans are increasingly able to live unhindered by oppression.

However, Africa still scores poorly in global calculations of freedom. A survey by Freedom House, an American watchdog organisation, showed that countries in Africa in 2014 still registered much lower scores than countries in the west. Forty per cent of people in sub-Saharan Africa were qualified as "not free", 48 per cent as "partly free" and only 12 per cent as "free". Among countries with declining scores were Nigeria, Uganda, Burundi, Rwanda, Madagascar, Lesotho, Swaziland, Burkina Faso, South Sudan and Gambia. As far as liberty of the press was concerned, only three per cent were considered to be free, compared with 66 per cent in Europe.[78]

Despite improvements overall, famine and massacres still afflict South Sudan, and Libya remains in disarray after the overthrow of Gaddafi in 2011 (see Chapter 15). Islamic fundamentalists opposed to the notion of freedom have also destabilised a number of other countries through persistent attacks. Some African leaders backed by repressive security regimes continue to cling to office: in Angola since 1979, in Cameroon since 1982, in Uganda since 1986, in Chad since 1990, and in Congo-Brazzaville since 1997. In reaction to these failings, thousands of Africans each year vote with their feet, migrating illicitly to Europe.

Africa is no longer the Dark Continent, but its cup of freedom is no more than half full. The ideas of democracy, freedom of speech, freedom of religion and freedom of enterprise are burgeoning, but are not yet firmly anchored in African society. African people may still be given short shrift by their rulers, but the late American president, Woodrow Wilson, asserted that governments do not give liberty; rather, it comes from the people they rule. If that is so, freedom is there for the Africans to seize.

CHAPTER 11

WE ARE THE PEOPLE

In the name of Communism we abandoned basic human values. So when I came to power in Russia I started to restore those values; values of openness and freedom.
– Mikhail Gorbachev

First Uprisings

While the Soviet Union was welcomed in Africa as an ally of liberation movements, in eastern Europe it was constantly challenged by people fighting to break from its steely grasp. In the initial years after World War II, many Europeans gave the Soviets credit for fighting to liberate the continent from the Nazis, but it soon became clear that the Red Army was set on extending the Soviet Union's dominion. An "Iron Curtain" came down across Europe, as the new masters forced the people of the occupied countries to accept Communist diktat and isolated them from the west.

This absolute rule only stimulated the desire of people to fight against it. The first challenge came in 1953, in the heart of the German capital, which the Soviet soldiers had conquered only eight years earlier. Construction workers in Communist East Berlin, angered at being forced to work longer for the same pay, swarmed out on to the city's central

Stalinallee to vent their rage. The East German *Volkspolizei* (People's Police) could not cope and retreated from the streets, while the East German Communist leadership took refuge in Soviet headquarters.

What began as a protest against working conditions turned into a mass insurrection, threatening the very existence of the regime. To reassert Communist authority, the Soviet Red Army sent in tanks and declared martial law. It was all over within a few days, leaving 55 people dead, and along with them died any lingering hope the Soviets may have had of achieving popularity – even among the working classes. Over the next 15 years, images of Soviet tanks rumbling over the cobbles of great European cities would become familiar the world over.

However, 1953 also opened the way for the Soviet leadership to experiment in relaxing its dictatorship. In that year, Stalin's death removed a despot who had struck terror into millions of people, including his most senior comrades. The new leader, Nikita Khrushchev, rehabilitated some of Stalin's victims, released several million prisoners from the Gulag and eased censorship. Then, at a Congress of the Communist Party in 1956, he daringly denounced Stalin as a tyrant responsible for millions of deaths.

That was a risky step, since it could have been construed as an attack on the Communist Party itself, which Stalin had headed until three years earlier. It unsettled Communist leaders in the east European satellite countries: Khrushchev seemed to be promising his own people more freedom, so why could people in other nations not have it too? He did not foresee these consequences at the time, but trouble soon erupted in Poland, which had a long, unhappy history of domination by Russia.

Workers in the Polish city of Poznan rioted in 1956, seizing arms and official buildings, but troops and tanks under Soviet command put them down with more than 50 fatalities. The local Communist Party then appointed a nationalist-minded leader, Władsysław Gomułka, who started talking about a "Polish road to socialism". A furious but dithering Khrushchev came within hours of ordering an invasion, put off only by Gomułka's assurances that he would not jeopardise Communist rule.

Hungarian Uprising, 1956

Barely was that crisis over, when uproar broke out in the Hungarian capital, Budapest. In October 1956, students fired up by the protests in Poland demonstrated for multiparty democracy and the departure of the Red Army, which had been occupying Hungary since 1945. The local Communist leadership back-pedalled and appointed a reformist, Imre Nagy, as Prime Minister. But the students were not so easily swayed, and they booed him down when he tried to calm them.

Suddenly, thousands of people poured out on to the streets in rebellious elation, sensing that the moment had come to seize their freedom. A woman who was 13 at the time, remembers her mother telling her: "Don't go to school today. Come down to the square... you will never forget this all your life. Today is revolution."[79]

At the foot of a statue, an actor declaimed a patriotic poem of Sándor Petőfi, a hero of Hungary's failed uprising of 1848:

> *Rise up, Magyar, the country calls!*
> *It's 'now or never' what fate befalls...*

Shall we live as slaves or free men?
That's the question – choose your 'Amen'!
God of Hungarians, we swear unto Thee,
We swear unto Thee – that slaves we shall no longer be![80]

Crowds threw down Communist Red Stars from rooftops, cut Communist insignia out of national flags, and filled the square outside Parliament, chanting "Out with the Ruskies" and "Freedom for Hungary". Men sawed at the legs of a massive statue of Stalin and, with the help of cables and heavy trucks, brought it crashing to the ground, where they swarmed over it to spit and urinate.

When a milling crowd surrounded the State Radio station, firing broke out from within, killing dozens of people. Then Soviet tanks rumbled out over cobbles and tramlines, shooting up buildings and firing red-hot tracer streams down the thoroughfares. Armed Hungarian freedom fighters took to the streets, fighting back with Molotov cocktails and weapons seized from armouries, and slipping away into narrow alleyways where the tanks could not penetrate. Within a few days, the Soviets pulled back and the uprising was victorious – or so it seemed.

Khrushchev tried concessions: he agreed to disband the Hungarian Communist secret police and withdraw Soviet troops from any country which did not ask for them. But events were careering out of control. Strikers refused to go back to work, non-Communist parties began operating again, and Prime Minister Nagy announced Hungary was leaving the Soviet's military alliance. Insurgents hunted down secret police and hanged them from lamp posts.

Alarm bells began ringing among the Communist leaderships in other parts of eastern Europe and even in

China. In a totalitarian state, once a crack had been opened up to freedom, the whole system came under threat. Khrushchev had miscalculated in thinking that he could head a Communist regime and also allow people some freedom. Years later Khrushchev told of a sleepless night he spent tossing and turning as he tried to make up his mind what to do.

By the morning he decided to crack down, and flew around eastern Europe to inform his fellow-Communist leaders. To Yugoslavia's President Tito, he declared: "What is there left for us to do? If we let things take their course the west would say we are either stupid or weak, and that's one and the same thing. We cannot possibly permit it, either as Communists and internationalists, or as the Soviet Union. We would have capitalists on the frontiers of the Soviet Union."[81]

A few days later, Soviet tanks and troops swarmed back into the Hungarian capital in great force, and by 6th November the uprising was crushed, leaving 3,000 Hungarians dead. Prime Minister Nagy fled to the Yugoslav embassy, but was tricked into leaving and executed. Some 200,000 Hungarians escaped to freedom in the west, stumbling by night over fields into Austria. But for those back at home, the liberty they had tasted in the heady days of the uprising was gone.

Other east Europeans looked on fearfully and silently drew the only possible conclusion: forcible resistance to Soviet might was doomed to failure. The Hungarians, isolated behind the Iron Curtain from accurate news, had miscalculated. No western power was going to send hundreds of thousands of troops in to drive the Soviet Red Army out, since that would almost certainly have led to nuclear war. Cruel though it was to acknowledge, the Hungarian uprising of 1956 never had a chance. One way or another, there were no more armed insurrections in eastern Europe.

Prague Spring – Polish Solidarity

There was, however, one more attempt to grant liberty to those under Soviet domination. This took place in Czechoslovakia in 1968, and was led by the Communists themselves, who hoped it would make them more popular. Party leader Alexander Dubček and other reformists declared they would create "socialism with a human face", abolishing press censorship and allowing freedom of speech. This so-called Prague Spring led to an astonishing flourishing of new ideas and hope, which enthralled people around the world. It quickly escaped the control of the Party, however: in political debates, the media, the arts, and in ordinary conversations around the country, people acted as if all constraints were gone.

Inevitably, the Kremlin leaders in Moscow got cold feet. They too wanted to popularise Communism, but Czechs and Slovaks were questioning the Communists' right to rule exclusively, and this raised Soviet fears that they would lose part of their empire. The Soviet leader Leonid Brezhnev, like Khrushchev in 1956, agonised over what to do. He knew Alexander Dubček well and liked him – they had been at a Communist college together. Brezhnev spent hours on the telephone pleading with his buddy "Sasha" to rein in the press and curb public dissent, but it was no use.

Events raced out of control and on 21st August 1968, Soviet tanks again poured into an allied country to restore it by force to the Soviet fold. Czechs and Slovaks remembered what happened to the Hungarians only 12 years earlier, and offered only passive resistance to the assault. Dubček was dragged off to Moscow in chains and then relegated to a distant forestry job in Slovakia. Once more, freedom was trampled into the dust.

Brezhnev knew this would harm the standing of the Soviet Union in public opinion around the world. However, like Dubček, he could not get around the unfortunate truth that Communism and freedom were incompatible. For if people were free, it was clear they would not choose Communism. Unsurprisingly, Brezhnev resorted to repression, ending any wishful thinking that Communists could act democratically or have "a human face".

All was not lost, however, as freedom fighters soon found new chinks in the Soviet armour. In 1975, after years of negotiations, the U.S., the Soviet Union and the countries of Europe signed the Helsinki Accords on European Security and Cooperation. Political dissidents in eastern Europe picked on one article, which enshrined "respect for human rights and fundamental freedoms, including the freedom of thought, conscience, religion or belief". It was far from a guarantee – the Accords did not have the force of a treaty – but the dissidents promptly set up groups championing this part of the agreement. As all the Communist governments in eastern Europe were signatories, they could hardly outlaw people campaigning for implementation (though they did try). The dissidents were thus able to establish precarious footholds in society and renew their fight for freedom.

Just three years later, the election of a Polish Pope dealt another blow against Communist domination of eastern Europe. John Paul II set straight off to visit his home country, and no sooner had he arrived than three million people turned out in a Warsaw square to celebrate a Catholic Mass with him. This was a direct challenge to the Polish Communist

Party, which tried to enforce atheism. But in a nation that had remained stubbornly Christian, the Communists could not stop several million people. They were obviously helpless, and their authority began to crumble. Although it was not evident immediately, from that day onwards the Polish people had freedom within their grasp. To fight for it they had turned out to pray and celebrate Mass, just as early Christians did under the Roman Empire.

Two years later, workers at the port of Gdańsk went on strike over working conditions and occupied the shipyard. They were led by Lech Wałęsa, an electrician and devout Catholic. Communists claimed to be the vanguard of the working class, so shipyard workers were supposed to be on their side. Now, the workers wanted to be free of Communist interference, and a Catholic was at their head. The strikes spread to other shipyards and to coal mines and, as the economy ground to a halt, the government conceded the demands of the protesters – including the right to strike, which had never before been permitted under Communism.

The rebellious workers then set up a nationwide labour union movement named Solidarity. It was the first independent labour organisation in the Soviet bloc, and within 18 months nearly 10 million Polish citizens had joined, representing 80 per cent of the workforce. Karl Marx's prediction in 1848 that workers would lose their chains if they embraced Communism was now turned on its head: the workers were leaving the Communist system in order to free themselves from its oppression.

Predictably, the Soviet leaders became alarmed at losing control, and in 1981 they engineered the appointment of a general in dark glasses, Wojciech Jaruzelski, to head the Polish Communist Party. Jaruzelski declared martial law, arrested over 5,000 Solidarity members and riot police crushed ensuing strikes. That brought order again, but meanwhile the rigidly planned Polish economy was falling apart.

The Berlin Wall Falls

At that point, eastern Europe's freedom fighters found an ally in a totally unexpected quarter. The Soviet economy was suffering from the same sclerosis as Poland's, prompting the new head of the Communist Party, Mikhail Gorbachev, to launch a restructuring programme in 1985. In order to stimulate change, he encouraged freedom of speech and, in order to lighten the burden of military spending, he decided to make peace with the west.

It took a while for the Gorbachev effect to feed through to the satellite countries of eastern Europe. Yet the implications were clear: freedom of speech should apply there too, and peace with the west would remove the need to station Soviet troops there. Gorbachev made clear that Soviet tanks would no longer prop up unpopular Communist regimes, and without Soviet armed might behind them, the local Communist rulers had no means of enforcing their dictatorships. They were marionettes, and Gorbachev had let go of the strings.

By 1989, the people realised the doors to freedom were half open, but the Tiananmen massacre in China that same summer was an ominous warning that the Communists still had well-armed police ready to crack down. So, East German protesters adopted the same tactic that had brought Gandhi victory in India: nonviolent opposition. The demonstrators paraded peacefully, chanting "no violence", first in Leipzig, followed by East Berlin, and then in other cities across East Germany.

When the *Volkspolizei* (People's Police) waded in with beatings and arrests, the people to shouted back: "We are the people".

In early October, rumours spread that the police would fire on the next big demonstration in Leipzig, and hospitals were told to prepare for casualties. A bloodbath loomed, but an unlikely local hero saved the day. Kurt Masur, a world-famous orchestra conductor, called talks between the demonstrators, the police and the local Soviet commanders, and mediated an agreement for the march to go ahead without hindrance. For a few brief days in autumn 1989, Masur was a hero in the fight for freedom. Without his moral authority and humane spirit, blood would undoubtedly have been spilt.

At the next demonstration on 9th October 1989, 70,000 protesters again flooded on to the streets in the early evening, and walked through the city centre holding banners and burning candles. Helmeted riot police were out en masse, but made no attempt to stop them. The critical moment passed, the police forfeited control of the streets, and from then onwards the demonstrators were free to parade whenever they wanted. Within two weeks, their numbers reached over 300,000 and nobody hindered them. Victory was at hand.

The East German Communists dismissed their ageing and ailing leader, Erich Honecker, and came out with a flurry of liberalising reforms. But they had no credibility as reformers and their hold on power wavered. In desperation, the Party spokesman announced at a press conference on 9th November 1989 that East Germans could travel to the west without exit visas.

"When?" shouted a journalist. Spokesman Günter Schabowski was unsure, but stuttered: "As far as I know... as of now."

Neither he nor his colleagues realised, in the heat of the moment, that letting East Germans travel freely meant opening up the Berlin Wall. East Berliners understood straightaway and threaded their way through the dark, grimy streets of the east towards a checkpoint. The border guards had no orders. What were they supposed to do with the pressing throng? Shoot at them, or let them through? As they hesitated, Communist dictatorship collapsed in the space of a few minutes. A few people seized hold of the red-and-white border barrier, manhandled it into the air with the help of a couple of guards, and East Berliners were free – all of them!

They swarmed through the Berlin Wall to ecstatic welcomes from West Berliners gathered on the other side. Strangers embraced and toasted each other with celebratory drinks and flowers. Easterners roamed through West Berlin, where they had been forbidden to set foot in their lifetimes. Currency booths opened to offer them a few West German marks to spend – free, for nothing. The future German Chancellor, Angela Merkel, went through to have drinks in a West Berlin pub, returning to her home in East Berlin in the early hours of the morning.

This time the fight for freedom had been waged not by a charismatic leader, striking workers or a bunch of guerrillas, but by the people as a whole. Peacefully, in joy and goodwill, a whole population had taken their fates into their hands and walked free. This surely was a highpoint in the whole history of the fight for freedom.

Freedom in Czechoslovakia, Poland and Hungary

Less than a fortnight later, Prague was in tumult. Since 1968, Czechs had been held down by intimidation, imprisonment and the presence of tens of thousands of Soviet troops. Now the Berlin Wall had been breached, who would stop the Czechs from seizing their freedom as well? Czech police waded in with truncheons, in vain attempts to drive swelling crowds out of Prague's Wenceslas Square. "Jakeš, it's finished," cried the demonstrators, taunting the last leader of the Czechoslovak Communist Party hanging on to the vestiges of power. When the police lashed out, the people refrained from fighting back and chanted "no violence".

The most prominent leader of the protest movement, Václav Havel, considered that the Communist system was intrinsically violent, since it arbitrarily repressed its citizens – for much of the preceding two decades he himself had been in and out of prison. As far as he was concerned, nonviolence represented the essential difference between the people and the regime.

By mid-December 1989, Prague's "Velvet Revolution" had triumphed. The police withdrew, the regime collapsed and power passed to hundreds of thousands of ordinary citizens, jubilantly celebrating the freedom that they had peacefully seized after 40 years of repression. Alexander Dubček returned from his anonymous provincial job to join Havel on a balcony, hailing the exalted throng. By the year-end, Havel was ensconced as president in Prague's castle, and Dubček presided over a freely elected Parliament.

The Polish people had meanwhile been paving the way with a low-key approach. In February 1989, six years after the lifting of martial law, the opposition Solidarity movement started Round Table talks with the ruling Communists. There too, they were careful to avoid open confrontation, remembering that in 1981 Lech Wałęsa and other Solidarity leaders had landed in jail. But now the Communists were losing their will to hold on, and they engaged in dialogue with the opposition. The Round Table formula implied that it was a discussion between equals.

The authorities agreed to hold free elections, but only if a certain number of seats in Parliament were reserved for the Communists. Solidarity leaders reluctantly agreed and, fortunately for them, voters scotched the attempt to fix the result by scratching out the names of the regime's candidates. As a result, no leading Communists were elected, and Solidarity and its allies won an overwhelming majority. That completed the demoralisation of the Communists, and by the time the rest of eastern Europe rose up, the Polish were already living under a free and democratic government.

Poland had achieved its freedom in its own way; there were no street fights, no massed crowds on squares, no pacifist candle-bearers, just citizens sitting together and negotiating a way forward. Along with the Communists and the dockyard strike leader were two prominent intellectuals and a Catholic journalist. The forum thus brought together a heterogeneous group, which could easily have turned into an ineffective talking shop. It is to the credit of the participants that within a short time it led to freedom for all the country's people, with no unrest, no bloodshed and no civil war. In August 1989, the Catholic Tadeusz Mazowiecki became the newly liberated Poland's first Prime Minister.

It had all started earlier in the same year with an apparently innocuous move by Hungary. Hungarians had learned the hard way that armed insurrection was hopeless. But under János Kádár, Communist rule became gradually more relaxed. The Hungarians called it "goulash Communism" – meaning you could enjoy some of the individual pleasures of life if you did not directly cross the Communists. Hungarians even boasted sourly that theirs was "the jolliest barrack in the socialist camp".

By the mid-1980s, the Hungarian Communists allowed part of the economy to be run by private enterprise, and at the beginning of 1989 they began cutting down the 150 miles of barbed wire fence on their frontier with Austria. At first this seemed no more than a local gesture to improve neighbourly relations, but the wider implications soon became apparent. Not only could Hungarians cross freely, but soon thousands of East Germans headed that way too. They were allowed to go to Hungary as part of the Soviet bloc, and now they could travel from there on to Austria and West Germany. One thing rapidly led to another and, within months, freedom fighters were chipping the first blocks away from the Berlin Wall.

So the wheel came full circle. After the defeat of 1956, the Hungarians seemed most unlikely to make the first move towards allowing the captive peoples to walk free. As it turned out, their dismantling of the wire fence helped seal the fate of dictatorships all over eastern Europe. The whole process was a victory for the nonviolent path to freedom, and those who participated felt tremendous satisfaction that they had seized liberty without harming others. Without Gorbachev, however, this would scarcely have been possible. Only when he pulled the rug from under the feet of the east European Communist leaders did a peaceful transition to liberty become possible.

The Soviet Union Collapses

Liberty proved fatal to the Soviet Union itself, which fell apart at the end of 1991. In hindsight, its collapse was inevitable, but only a couple of years earlier the possibility seemed inconceivable. It was ruled by a Communist Party which rejected all opposition, and it possessed a mighty nuclear arsenal, capable of annihilating a large part of the world's population. However, the rigid Soviet economy was unable to withstand Gorbachev's shake-up, and his encouragement of free discussion undermined the Communists' hold on power.

When Communist authority broke down, there was no other force to hold the Soviet Union together. The internal republics, Estonia, Latvia, Lithuania, Ukraine, Georgia, Armenia, Kazakhstan, Kyrgystan, and Turkmenistan – annexed many years earlier by Communist Russia – chose to leave the Union and became independent. That left only one internal republic – Russia itself.

As 1991 drew to an end, hardline Communists and military officers hoping to wind back the clock staged a putsch against Gorbachev. It was the classic Soviet response to an outburst of freedom, but this time it did not work. Huge crowds turned out in Moscow in protest and soldiers refused orders to shoot. Russia's Igor Yeltsin climbed on top of an armoured car and summoned the rebels to surrender. As the putsch collapsed, Yeltsin took Russia out of what was left of the Soviet Union, which at that point ceased to exist.

Gorbachev brought lasting peace and freedom to millions of people. The people of eastern Europe whom the Soviet Communists had oppressed won independence and control over their own lives; while in the west, people were liberated from the threat of Soviet nuclear missiles. In his own country, he released imprisoned dissidents, ended censorship, tolerated religion and allowed free political debate. Gorbachev never intended to cause the collapse of the Soviet Union, nor give up Communism, but he was heading a totalitarian system that could not be reconciled with liberty, and that contradiction brought the Soviet Union down.

After Russia emerged from the ruins of the old order, the floodgates opened to a fresh wave of liberalisation in politics, the media and the economy. Free elections brought opposition parties into Parliament; the media broadcast without censorship; and most of the old Soviet industry, including its plentiful oil resources, were privatised and passed into the hands of newly minted capitalist businessmen.

To many ordinary Russians, the collapse of the old order seemed a disaster. De-controlled prices soared, wages and pensions could not keep up and schools came close to collapse. Russians were aghast at the turmoil accompanying liberalisation, and became increasingly disenchanted by Yeltsin's drinking habits and lack of focus. When Yeltsin gave way to Vladimir Putin in 1999, Russians once again had a strong leader in charge, and they confirmed him as president in an election a year later.

The east European states which had been on the Soviet side of the Iron Curtain meanwhile turned towards the liberal west. In 2004, Estonia, Latvia, Lithuania, Poland, the Czech Republic, Slovakia, Hungary and Slovenia joined the European Union (EU), followed by Romania and Bulgaria in 2007, and Croatia in 2013. To accede, they had to comply with the EU's standards on rule of law, political freedoms, freedom of movement, free-market economy and protection for minorities. As a result, east Europeans could travel, emigrate and work all over Europe. They could do business freely, vote freely for a choice of parties, and enjoy the individual liberties that the rule of law protected.

Germany was a special case; with reunification in 1990 bringing together the democratic west with the Communist east, the East Germans gained liberty politically, but less so economically. Indeed the first change that many of them noticed when the Berlin Wall fell was that they lost their jobs. Within a year the number of East Germans employed fell from nine to seven million, and a third of those laid off never found another job. Their worn-out, dirty industry produced outdated goods that nobody wanted, and East Germans had no experience in free, globalised markets. The West Germans did, and they bought up collapsing state-owned businesses for a song. The East Germans perceived that whatever value they had created passed into the hands of West Germans, and they were disappointed to move from submission to the Soviet Union to dependency on West Germany.

In other ex-Communist states, the transition to a free-market economy also caused initial hardship in terms of unemployment and disruption, but people there could at least feel they had achieved independence from foreign domination and taken their fates into their own hands.

Conflict in Romania and Yugoslavia

Only in two countries did Communism end in bloodshed. One was Romania, where Nicolae Ceaușescu ruled with the cruel extravagance of a Byzantine despot. He forced women to have babies by ordering secret police to monitor their most intimate functions; he persecuted the Hungarian minority in Romania; and pursued a reckless industrialisation which produced little of value. He also racked up enormous foreign debts, and sold much of Romania's food and goods abroad to pay them back, resulting in fearful suffering among the people.

In 1989, the country was on its knees, yet he and his wife Elena, who had been co-opted into the government, persisted nonchalantly as if nothing was wrong. When protests broke out in the Hungarian-minority town of Timoşoara (Temesvar) on 17th December, Ceauşescu sent riot police to put them down by force. Five days later, he was haranguing a crowd from a balcony in Bucharest, as he had done so often before, but this time a groundswell of boos and catcalls arose. He paused, tried to continue, then left the balcony. In that moment, he lost the power he had wielded for 24 years. A helicopter fluttered overhead and carried the tyrant and his wife off into the countryside. There, turncoat soldiers arrested them and put them before an improvised military tribunal. Within minutes they were condemned, put up against a wall and summarily shot, which was filmed for posterity so that people could see them falling dead.

It was Christmas Day 1989. People around the world who switched on their televisions on this festive day saw the grisly images of this squalid execution. The last of the great dictators of the Soviet period was no more. Several thousand people were killed in a few weeks in fighting involving the Securitate secret police, but Communism was finished, and from then onwards Romania allowed other political parties and held freer elections.

The biggest catastrophe resulting from the end of Communism, however, was the war in Yugoslavia (1991-2001). There the collapse of the old order was exploited by Serbs trying to gain the upper hand over the other ethnic groups which made up the state. The ex-Communist leader of Serbia, Slobodan Milošević, transformed into a nationalist seeking to create Greater Serbia. Slovenia and Croatia quickly declared independence, but Milošević started a war to "liberate" fellow-Serbs in Bosnia-Herzegovina, Croatia and Kosovo.

Still marked by memories of two World Wars, Europe felt helpless in the face of this assault on the spirit of fraternity, carefully built up since 1945. The war, which inflicted mass killings, rape and destruction on the population, reached a peak in 1995 when Serb forces massacred 8,000 males in the Bosnian town of Srebrenica. A Dutch contingent of 110 peace-keeping troops withdrew from the town without offering resistance, while British and French troops elsewhere in Bosnia intervened only to protect the flow of humanitarian aid.

Srebenica was the worst massacre in Europe since the months following World War II, and it shocked the United States and Europe into acting decisively to end the conflict. The U.S. bombed Serb positions in Bosnia, and engineered a power-sharing arrangement between the three ethnic groups living there. In 1999, Europe joined the United States in evicting Serbs from Kosovo, following Serb massacres among the Albanian majority there. This reined back Serbia's overweening ambitions, and eventually all the component parts of ex-Yugoslavia were free to become independent states.

Back in Serbia, the population became disenchanted with Milošević's failed chauvinism, and resented that he still tried to dominate their state as in the Communist era. After he contested his defeat in a presidential election in 2000, several hundred thousand people demonstrating for freedom, democracy and rapprochement with Europe converged on Belgrade and stormed Parliament. Milošević was forced to resign, and a year later he was put on trial at the International War Crimes Tribunal in The Hague (he died before it was complete).

The liberation of eastern Europe had started with peaceful East Germans chanting "we are the people", a Velvet Revolution in Prague, and a freely debated passage of powers at a round table in Poland. But ex-Yugoslavia's emancipation had been achieved at a cruel cost. Its break-up was a salutary lesson of how a fight for freedom can be disastrously abused by people of bad will.

All over eastern Europe, people have gained significant new liberties in their everyday lives. No longer do they need to close windows when they talk about anything sensitive: they are free from the fear of secret police informers. If they have a religious faith, they no longer have to conceal their church-going for fear of discrimination. They are free from the oppressive supervision of a foreign state, the Soviet Union. Citizens can choose between multiple political parties and debate their merits openly. They are free to try to make profit and accumulate personal property. They are free from indoctrination in schools and from the oppression of lies and thought control. The liberation of eastern Europe thus counts as one of the great successes in the fight for freedom.

CHAPTER 12

FREEDOM FOR WOMEN

I don't want to be remembered as the girl who was shot.
I want to be remembered as the girl who stood up.
– Malala Yousafzai

The First Struggles

In their fight to be free, women have encountered deprivation, humiliation, enslavement, religious bigotry, ignorance and, at times, almost unimaginably sadistic violence. The struggle concerns half the planet's population and it is one of the most agonising stories of all. The oppression women have faced has been colossal, and their ongoing subjugation in many parts of the world has impoverished society.

This desolate picture may not fit today's egalitarian Scandinavian countries, where women have long filled important political and business positions, enjoy ample state-supported opportunities to combine careers with childcare, and share family duties with men. Nor does it reflect many other developed parts of the world, but millions of women elsewhere are still forced into a subordination which is unfair, inhuman and at times downright cruel.

Since earliest civilizations, the role of women has been mainly to give birth, bring up children, provide sexual companionship, tend the family hearth and cultivate a nearby field. The idea that they should do something beyond this was scarcely considered. Men often treated their women as belongings, restricted their movements and their dress, forced them into sex and childbirth, arranged their marriages, and prevented them from learning, exercising professions, owning property and voting. This has been the custom since time immemorial, rooted in the patriarchal order that has governed most primitive rural societies, depriving women of many of the fundamental liberties available to men.

This suppression has never been total. Behind many a strong man has stood an equally strong woman, not just providing support and encouragement, but as a powerful thinker in her own right; and even in the most ancient times there were sporadic examples of women freely exercising responsibilities on their own. Cleopatra and Nefertiti became rulers of ancient Egypt, Artemisia commanded a Persian warship at Salamis, and in ancient Sparta women managed family estates while their menfolk fought. Women of ancient Rome could become citizens, own property, do business and make wills. Boadicea ruled as queen of an English tribe, and in the early Christian church women were priests and bishops.

However, these were exceptions rather than the rule. Even in ancient Athens, where liberty first flourished, women had to submit to their fathers or husbands, and were ineligible for full citizenship. They could not bring legal proceedings and their property was at the disposal of their husbands. From the 4th century onwards, the Christian Church discriminated against women on the grounds that Eve led Adam into sin in the Garden of Eden, and medieval law in Europe was weighted in favour of men. Any urge women may have had for liberty, in the sense of equal rights with men, had to be sublimated. They could not choose to do what they wanted with their lives, they were constrained by social norms that they had not set themselves, and laws did little or nothing to protect them against oppression.

Such attitudes prevailed even in the European societies that pioneered democracy, freedom of speech, freedom of learning and freedom from arbitrary imprisonment. Only in the last 150 years did the exclusion of women from this liberalising process diminish – and the first breakthroughs were made in Britain.

One of the first liberties to be won by British women was the right to be educated. Even though many of the great 18th and 19th century novels were written by women, education was still out of the reach of most females and that excluded them from most professions. Women campaigners set out to change that – and they did not care if they offended the stuffy, conservative establishment in doing so.

One such character was Mary Wollstonecraft (1759-97), mother of an illegitimate daughter and wife of one of England's first anarchists. Inspired by the liberal ideas of the Enlightenment, she wrote a path-finding work, *A Vindication of the Rights of Woman,* arguing that women were brought up to have limited expectations because they had little education. An equally unorthodox champion rose to the challenge: Elizabeth Jesser Reid (1789-1866), a campaigner against slavery and friend of French and German revolutionaries, founded Bedford College in London to provide England's first liberal higher education to female students. Among its graduates was the novelist George Eliot, who likewise courted controversy by living with a married man for two decades and then marrying a man 20 years her younger. Polite society was scandalised, but loved her books – Queen Victoria was an avid reader.

Women's colleges followed at Cambridge and Oxford universities, attracting talented female students who excelled academically, but often had to overcome obstruction by their own families. Britain opened up education to women, but well into the 20th century many women graduates were ostracised in society as "bluestockings", unfit for regular family life.[82] If a woman thought originally, campaigned for radical social issues or promoted female education, she was suspect in Victorian England. But these pioneering women did not care. They were fighters in spirit, and their next struggle was to gain for women the same legal rights as men.

A group popularly known as the Langham Place Ladies campaigned for married women to be entitled to their own legal identity, property and inherited wealth. As it was, once women were married they had to share the identity of their husbands and lost their right to property. They were supposed to consent to sex and mothering children, and the husband had control over the children and finances. In divorce, the provisions were weighted in favour of the man, and if the wife ran away, the police could be sent to find her. Any inheritances passed almost exclusively to the male line of a family.

Apart from the humblest of paid occupations, marriage was the only status that females in England – or indeed anywhere else in Europe – could aspire to in the 19th century. If a woman remained unmarried, she could earn her living only as a governess, domestic help, a seamstress, an unskilled factory-worker or an agricultural labourer. Under such circumstances, women were clearly not free to realise their potential.

This injustice jarred in a country which had pioneered so many liberties for men, and feminists received support from one of the pace-setting male thinkers of the time, John Stuart Mill, author of the influential book *On Liberty,* published in 1859. He campaigned for their rights in Parliament and argued that women were just as capable as men, so should not be barred from any activities. He himself treated his wife as an equal, and said his book belonged as much to her as to him, since she had contributed her "exalted sense of truth and right" and her "all but unrivalled wisdom".[83]

The struggle eventually bore fruit. Successive Acts of Parliament in 1870, 1882, 1922, and 1936 enabled married women to retain their earnings, own property and inherit on the same terms as men.

There was scarcely any parallel evolution in France, despite the liberating impulses of the Enlightenment. Only a few years before England's Mary Wollstonecraft called for women to be liberated through education, France's Jean-Jacques Rousseau declared that it was in the order of nature for women to obey men, and wrote: "When she tries to usurp our rights, she is our inferior." The French Revolution of 1789-92 proclaimed liberty and equality for all, but it discriminated against women in that its Declaration on the Rights of Man and the Citizen reserved "active citizenship" to property-owning males and restricted women to "passive citizenship".

This bias prompted Olympe de Gouges to launch a protest movement and publish her own Declaration of the Rights of Woman and the Female Citizen. Like a number of other feminist pioneers, she had a controversial background: born illegitimate, she had a loveless marriage, was widowed, and cohabited with several men who financed her campaigns.

Her protest was brushed aside and, as the Revolution reached its violent climax, she was guillotined at the age of 45.

All over continental Europe, it was the same story. Leo Tolstoy's novel *Anna Karenina* and Gustave Flaubert's *Madame Bovary* portrayed the tragic destinies of women stifled by rigid male society in 19th century Russia and France. While in Germany, it was taken for granted that women would confine themselves to *Kinder, Kirche, Küche* – children, church, kitchen.

In America too, women encountered dismaying setbacks as they pressed for more freedom. In pre-independence colonial America, women had earned their own living as seamstresses or keeping boarding houses, but also as doctors, lawyers, preachers, teachers, writers and singers. When America became independent, introducing wide-ranging new liberties for men, women paradoxically found their opportunities to realise themselves were diminished.

By the early 19th century, American women were excluded from all professions except writing and teaching, and were otherwise limited to factory or domestic labour. On its foundation in 1846, the American Medical Association specifically barred women from becoming members. By 1890, only one American doctor in 20 was female, compared with one in five in France and Germany.

Female activists such as Abby Kelley Foster and Lucy Stone, who campaigned to free black slaves, came to the painful realisation that they were hardly better off themselves. "In striving to strike off his chains, we found most surely we were chained ourselves," wrote Foster. Their male fellow-abolitionists were unsympathetic. Foster was barred as a woman from speaking at a World Anti-Slavery Convention in London in 1840, and was made to sit in a special area for women. A male chairman of the meeting ruled: "No woman shall speak or vote where I am moderator. I will not countenance such an outrage on decency. I will not consent to have women lord it over men in public assemblies. It is enough for women to rule at home".

The Vote

Increasingly, the early feminists realised that women could never be as free as men, unless they could participate on equal terms in deciding their political destinies. The exclusion of women from voting thus became the key issue to be contested. In America, women began campaigning for this right at a convention in Seneca Falls, New York, as early as 1848. In demanding the vote, their final declaration adopted the same language as the Preamble of the American Declaration of Independence, with one pointed difference. Written by Elizabeth Cady Stanton, it asserted: "We hold these truths to be self-evident: that all men *and women* are created equal."[84]

However, American women faced determined opposition. Their movement was labelled immoral, and they were attacked and verbally abused. The alcohol industry lobbied hard against female suffrage, fearing that empowered women would legislate against alcohol consumption to stop drunken men ruining families. In the late 1800s, four sparsely populated states in the far west gave women the vote, but Congress repeatedly rejected attempts to extend this nationwide.

Back in Britain, Millicent Fawcett, who was well established in society, created a movement in 1897 to lobby for the right of women to vote in Parliamentary elections. As a follower of John Stuart Mill, she helped found a women's college at Cambridge University and, until she was widowed at 38, was married to a Liberal Member of Parliament and government minister. When another Liberal, H.H. Asquith, became Prime Minister in 1908, she hoped his commitment to political reform would prove decisive for the women's vote. However, Asquith refused to lend support because he feared women would favour the conservative opposition.

As nonviolence was not working, women began fighting for the vote by more aggressive means. In 1903, Emmeline Pankhurst and her two daughters, Sylvia and Christabel, founded a Women's Social and Political Union known as the Suffragettes. The leaders were well-brought up ladies who shocked society with their brash provocations. Instead of rational arguments and well-intentioned resolutions, the British establishment was confronted by militant women who broke the law, damaged property, risked lives and rampaged in public. The Suffragettes disrupted political meetings, were roughed up by police, refused to pay fines and were regularly sent to prison.

When even the Church of England came out against them, the Suffragettes responded by burning down some of its churches. They chained themselves to the railings of Buckingham Palace, broke shop windows in Oxford Street, slashed paintings in the National Gallery and set fire to letter boxes. They attacked politicians and firebombed their homes, and once in prison they staged hunger strikes that led to them being painfully force-fed. It was to little avail: being thrown into jail like common criminals brought public attention, but still no vote.

In the most dramatic action in 1913, Suffragette Emily Davison ran on to the Derby race course in front of the

King's horse and was trampled to death. Men and women alike were shocked at her reckless gesture. The Suffragettes had a martyr, but it was not clear that the public would support such extremism.

The movement could well have ground to a halt had World War I not broken out, prompting the British people, rich and poor, men and women, to come together against a common enemy. Emmeline and Christabel Pankhurst suspended their campaign to join the war effort, which brought more than a million women into the workforce, in dockyards, transport, banks, the civil service and agriculture.

Wartime solidarity reinforced the idea of social equality, and thus the campaigning women could make a breakthrough at the end of the war without resorting to further disorders. In 1918, the British Parliament passed an Act granting them voting rights, although they were still confined to women over 30 who owned or occupied property over a certain value, or who were university educated. While this was undoubtedly a historic victory for women, they could not yet vote on the same terms as men.

With the Bolshevik insurrection tearing Russia apart, the government worried about the danger of revolution by British soldiers returning from the forces. Under the existing property-ownership restrictions, millions of young men who fought for their country would have been excluded from voting in the 1918 election. So, in that year, the government changed the law to open up suffrage to all men over 21.

Thus, class no longer restrained this basic liberty, but gender still did. If women had been given the same voting rights as men, they would have been in the majority – as it was, they represented 43 per cent of the electorate. Ironically, most of the women who volunteered for war work were disqualified because they were below the minimum age of 30.[85]

Now women cast off the stuffy constraints of the past. They abandoned long dresses and tight bodices for skimpy lightweight dresses, ideal for moving around freely. Society had changed forever and, in 1928, all British women over 21 were given the vote, finally putting them on an equal standing with men. The goal had been reached, but by then women in New Zealand, Australia, Russia and Scandinavia had beaten the British to it.

In the United States, the female suffrage movement launched by Elizabeth Cady Stanton and Susan B. Anthony in the mid-19th century likewise exploited the social cohesion inspired by World War I. Two new activists, Alice Paul and Lucy Burns, organised picketing of President Woodrow Wilson outside the White House. Known as the "Silent Sentinels", the women held banners denouncing the president as "Kaiser Wilson". When Alice Paul was arrested, amongst hundreds of other women, she went on hunger strike. In 1918 Wilson relented, and in 1920 a constitutional amendment outlawed sex-based restrictions on voting.

Germany, Austria, Poland, Czechoslovakia and the Netherlands followed suit, while France, Italy and Belgium delayed female suffrage until after World War II. Switzerland granted full voting rights for women only in 1971. Even then, Swiss women depended on men for this democratic freedom: it was approved in a referendum in which only men could take part.

Contraception and Equality at Work

Winning the vote was a major step forward, but women soon gained a liberty just as important – that of preventing unwanted pregnancy. Marie Stopes opened the first birth-control clinics in Britain in the 1920s and 1930s, and they soon proliferated elsewhere. Subsequently women were liberated further by invention of the contraceptive pill and legalisation of abortion.

As at other stages in women's emancipation, these gains were made in the face of constant opposition from conservatives; Marie Stopes and other birth-control advocates were accused of immorality and obscenity. Even today, pro-life movements in America try to stop abortions, while the Catholic Church (governed by men) forbids its followers to practise nearly all forms of contraception.

In developed countries, society also liberated women from the shame of bearing illegitimate children. Only two generations ago, mothers were often forced to give away children born out of wedlock immediately after giving birth, causing deep grief. Now, more British children are born to unmarried parents than to married ones – and largely by choice.[86] In America, about four children in 10 are born out of wedlock.

After winning one liberty after another, many women felt they should also be free to work and hold positions of responsibility. Ironically, it was 20th century Communist regimes which were the first to remove obstacles to that ambition; women on the eastern side of Europe's Iron Curtain could participate fully in the economy – indeed, they were expected to. Long before it became common in the west, women there were fighting as combat troops, driving trams and trucks, working in factories – and earning their own money.

Nowhere was the divergence more evident than in post-war Germany during the Cold War. In West Germany, women were still expected to confine themselves largely to "children, church and kitchen". Communist East Germany, however, legislated for women to engage actively in the workplace, and 90 per cent had jobs. Abortion was permitted, nursery schools were abundant, and women had equal opportunities to be educated and play a role in politics.

When Germany was reunified in 1990, many of those hard-working East German women lost their jobs, and they were disappointed that the democratic west provided working women with less social support. With the fall of the Berlin Wall, these women won freedom from political oppression, but lost some of their scope to evolve as individuals.

Unified Germany is, nevertheless, among the many countries where women have been able to assume positions of high responsibility. Angela Merkel has been Chancellor since 2005 and has become one of the world's most influential politicians, while Denmark had a woman Prime Minister (Helle Thorning-Schmidt) from 2011 to 2015. In business, women hold 41 per cent of Norwegian board positions,[87] and in America, women head leading manufacturers of automobiles, aircraft, computers, online portals, synthetic fibres and soft drinks.

These societies have enabled women both to pursue a career and rear families, providing paid childbirth leave for both sexes, and the right to return to jobs after maternity leave. Research shows that countries providing readily accessible childcare have both strong levels of fertility and high rates of women at work: Scandinavia, France, and the United States are examples of this.[88]

Women in developed countries have thus won rights to be educated on equal terms, to own property, to do the same jobs as men, to rise to positions of influence in all walks of life, to have their entitlements protected in divorce, to control contraception and combine work with family. Sexual harassment has not entirely ceased, and equal pay and job opportunities are far from being universally applied, but overall these are gains which have made women significantly freer.

Outside the Developed World

Beyond the established democracies, it is quite a different story. In those parts of the world, repression of women is often systematic, cruel and demeaning; their fight to liberate themselves has only just begun. Women fall foul of patriarchal traditions, religious zealotry, commercial exploitation, neglect and downright misogyny. In these societies, rigid customs overwhelm the concept of freedom, and violence towards women is endemic.

The catalogue of horrors is sickening. In Thailand, Cambodia, Malaysia, India and Nepal, human traffickers kidnap hundreds of thousands of teenage girls and force them into brothels in Asia and the Middle East, where they are kept as slaves. Retribution for those who escape or complain is beating, rape or even murder. More women and girls are shipped annually to brothels than African slaves were sent each year across the Atlantic in the 18th and 19th centuries.[89]

In parts of the Middle East and Pakistan, society condones men who kidnap teenage girls and force them into marriage. Husbands beat their wives with impunity and can prevent them from leaving home. After rape, the woman is likely to be punished on the supposition she must have enticed the man. Kinfolk may even insist that a raped or kidnapped woman be killed on the grounds that their honour has been damaged by her "submission". A woman who fails to produce a bloodstained sheet after her wedding night – to prove she was a virgin – may also suffer the same fate.

Feuds between clans may be settled by a village assembly, condemning a young woman to be gang-raped by the winning side.[90] Judges, lawyers, officials, and village elders do little or nothing to protect women from such arbitrary violence, and police habitually pressure rape victims to refrain from bringing charges.

In one episode in 2014, a young pregnant woman was stoned to death by her family in the Pakistani city of Lahore, outside a courthouse where she had married against the wishes of her family. The marriage was legal, but police, lawyers, members of her own family and bystanders watched passively, and nobody intervened.[91] A similar event took place in March 2015 in Afghanistan: a crowd lynched a 27-year-old woman wrongly accused of burning the Qur'an, the sacred book of Islam. There also, 19 on-looking policemen did nothing to protect her.[92]

In many Muslim countries, a further common restriction is that women are forced to cover their bodies and hair entirely in public, and sometimes their faces too, leaving just a slit for contact with the outside world. Of course, there are many women in all cultures who dress modestly by their own choice, and some Muslim women wear headscarves as an expression of cultural identity. In many other cases, however, women are forced to adopt all-enveloping dress codes in order to protect themselves from rape or violence by men, and that deprives women of a freedom that is afforded to males.

Worse still, a swathe of societies in west Africa, and to a lesser extent east Africa, the Middle East and Pakistan, force girls approaching puberty to undergo female genital cutting. This involves severing of the clitoris and genital lips, hindering females from experiencing sexual pleasure. In some instances, the genital lips are also stitched together, ensuring virginity until matrimony. In most cases, the cutting is done without anaesthetic or sanitary tools, leading to the death of some of the young girls. Remarkably, this mutilation is perpetrated not by men, but by female elders who cling to established tradition, cost what it may to their fellow-women.

In areas of constant civil war, such as Congo in Central Africa, women are among the principal victims. Indisciplined bands of soldiers gang-rape women and insert sticks and knives into their genitals, crippling some of them for life. In South Sudan, militias are reported to have chopped the noses or ears off women they violated. During the 14 years of civil war in Liberia until 2003, a U.N. report claimed that 90 per cent of girls and women over the age of three were sexually abused.[93]

The dreadful litany goes on. Societies with very conservative traditions forbid girls to be educated. In west Africa, an extremist Islamic militia even uses the name Boko Haram, which means "western education is prohibited". Women account for nearly two-thirds of the world's 780 million people who cannot read, and this discrepancy ensures that they remain forever inferior to men.

Many women in such traditionalist societies are not allowed to go out to work for their own money, depriving them of financial independence and the chance to realise themselves professionally. In Yemen, women make up only six per cent of the non-agricultural workforce, and in Pakistan nine per cent – compared with 50 per cent in the

U.S.[94] As a consequence, women earn only 10 per cent of global income.[95] By excluding half their population from nearly all but subsistence farming, these societies hold back their economic potential and condemn themselves to perpetual poverty.

By contrast, allowing women to do paid work has brought some dramatic benefits, not only by increasing the prosperity of a society, but in improving personal lives. A mother of six children in Burundi described how for years she was allowed out of the home only to accompany her husband to the market, where he spent his money on goods that she then had to carry home. Once she started earning her own money with the help of a micro-credit, her husband began to respect her, stopped beating her and no longer tried to control her movements. Thereafter, she told him when she was going out, but no longer asked his permission.[96]

There are other benefits too. In those parts of Africa where men tend to spend their earnings on beer and prostitutes, allocation of family income changes when women have money to dispose of: the women insist on spending more of it on better healthcare and family nutrition. A similar re-allocation also occurred in the 1920s in America, where maternal mortality dropped significantly as soon as women gained the vote and could influence spending. Empowering females also strengthens the restraining influence that they can exert on violent young males.

It is difficult to ignore that some of the worst oppression of women takes place in the Muslim world. Militant fundamentalist movements such as the self-styled Islamic State openly flaunt their ruthless enslavement of girls and women. The Grand Mufti of Saudi Arabia, Sheikh Abdulaziz, declared in 2004: "Allowing women to mix with men is the root of evil and catastrophe," by which he implied that women should be excluded from men's activities.[97]

Islam itself does not systematically discriminate against women, and Islamic civilisation at one time freely acknowledged erotic love. The Arab Abbasid empire (8th to 13th century) encouraged open discussion of ideas, including sexuality, and a book published in the 10th century contained more than a thousand words for sexual intercourse.[98] Egypt took a relaxed attitude to sexuality well into the early years of the 20th century, when the country also had an active feminist movement. In Turkey, the moderniser Kemal Atatürk accorded women a wide range of basic rights in the 1920s.

Islam's sacred Qur'an text contains passages that both support and belittle women. On the one hand, it rules that a married Muslim woman can keep her property and the money she earns from work. Men are urged to treat women with kindness and equity, and women are declared to be equal with men before God. On the other hand, it articulates the discriminatory tenets of patriarchal societies, for example: "Men are in charge of women... so good women are the obedient." Women have similar rights to men but "men are a degree above them". In court, a man's testimony is worth twice as much as a woman's, and in inheritance "the share of the male shall be twice that of a female". Men are allowed to marry several wives, but not vice versa.[99]

The Old Testament, sacred to Jews and Christians, makes a few assertions in a similar vein: in one place sanctioning the stoning of a woman who fails a virginity test.[100] Some early Christian leaders went so far as to speak of women as intrinsically wicked. In modern times, however, western societies have moved away from such extreme religious strictures, and instead give precedence to more liberal secular laws.

Muslims, by contrast, hold that the Qur'an is God's final and comprehensive revelation, containing all the guidance that people need in public and private life. Its inconsistencies nevertheless offer scope for differing interpretations. Many of the current restraints and persecutions of women are enforced by the rulings of particularly conservative Islamic experts who have gained the upper hand by forming repressive alliances with patriarchal families, and in some countries also with authoritarian governments.

Resistance

The oppression visited on women in these less-developed parts of the world is so formidable that prospects of change seem hopeless. Thankfully, this is not the case; in practically every country where women are persecuted or held back, activists are fighting to break their chains.

The combatants include brave local women who have been victims of violence, expatriates who return after successful careers in the west, liberalisers in governments and fund-raising sympathisers in the west. They set up women's hospitals and schools, pay school fees for peasant girls, teach women about contraception and AIDS prevention, organise micro-credits to launch women in business, rescue girls from enslavement in brothels, mobilise help in rich countries, flout dress prohibitions and pressure police to enforce laws against rape. Above all, they give courage to their fellow-women to resist.

In Muslim countries, women militants dispute the right of the conservative clergy to enforce their repressive interpretations of Islam. They insist on the more liberal affirmations of the Qur'an, and point to the Prophet Muhammad's wife, Aisha, as a woman of independent intellect and a brave leader of soldiers. They protest against women's exclusion from Islamic scholarship and wage lonely campaigns in parliaments for female rights.

Among the many individuals standing up to fight is a young Pakistani girl, Malala Yousafzai who in 2009 defied Taliban Islamic fundamentalists preventing girls from going to school. At the age of 11, she began blogging on behalf of girls' education on a BBC website in the local Urdu language, using the pseudonym "Cornflower". She attracted a wide following and eventually her true identity became known, which earned her Pakistan's first National Youth Peace Prize in 2011, but also death threats from the Taliban.

The following year, armed Taliban boarded her school bus and tried to murder her by shooting her in the head. A bullet entered her face, ricocheted off her skull and lodged deep in her shoulder next to her spine. Critically injured, Malala was airlifted to Britain, where she recovered and subsequently headed a United Nations campaign called "I am Malala" to make education available for all.

"All I want is an education, and I am afraid of no one," Malala told an audience. "The terrorists thought they would change my aims and stop my ambitions, but nothing changed in my life except this: weakness, fear and hopelessness died. Strength, power and courage were born."

As the campaign spread virally around the world, she transformed from a victim of brutal crime in a remote valley into a global spokesperson for women's freedom. In 2014, she was awarded the Nobel Peace Prize (jointly with Indian child rights activist Kailash Satyarthi), making her, at age 17, the youngest-ever Nobel laureate. Instead of destroying Malala, the Taliban succeeded only in enhancing her stature.[101]

In Malala, the Taliban had picked on a girl who was brainy, devoted to education and a talented communicator. Importantly, she also had family backing; she was emboldened on her path by her father, a poet and owner of a school for both boys and girls. When other families refused to let their children participate in the blogging, Malala's father encouraged her to go ahead. He too had to resist clerics trying to rid his school of girls. Courage ran in the family.

In neighbouring Afghanistan, when the Taliban were in power in the 1990s, they also forbade education for girls. In response, Sakena Yacoobi, who had been prevented from taking up a place at Kabul University, organised secret schools for some 3,800 girls, who would arrive for lessons in small groups while helpers kept lookout. Now that the Taliban are no longer in government, Sakena provides education for 350,000 women and children through her Afghan Institute of Learning.[102]

Some of the victories in emancipating women are of even greater scope. In Rwanda in central Africa, women were raped en masse in the 1994 massacres, but far more men were killed. With men in short supply, the government actively furthers women's participation in politics and the economy. Women hold high government posts and a greater proportion of seats in parliament than any other country – 55 per cent (compared with 17 per cent in the U.S. House of Representatives). With women engaged fully in the economy, Rwanda's growth is among the strongest in Africa.[103]

Botswana, Mozambique, Tunisia, Morocco, and Sri Lanka have made strides in the same direction. So too has predominantly Muslim Bangladesh, which is led by a female

Prime Minister, Sheikh Hasina. There girls and women have been enabled to participate freely in society, and move from poor rural work to employment in a dynamic garment export industry. Their workplaces are criticised in the west as sweatshops, but the women employees are empowered to earn their own wages for the first time, and for many, conditions are better than scratching a living from the soil. Until 1971, Bangladesh was part of Pakistan, but today far more of its females are educated and hold jobs than in Pakistan.

The other big, and surprising, success story in Asia has been China. Imperial China had a particularly terrible way of handicapping girls – foot binding. The toes and arches of a girl's feet were broken, folded under the soles and bound tightly with cloth soaked in a blood and herbs. As a result, her feet were stunted, and she could only wobble around awkwardly. The purpose was to make the feet look dainty, which Chinese men considered attractive, but it prevented the women from taking part in public life. They could walk only short distances from their homes, and were dependent on their families, especially their men. The practice affected some 45 per cent of Chinese women in the 19th century.

Foot-binding was outlawed in 1912, but the greatest advances came after Mao Zedong seized power in 1949. Although the Communist leader caused his people immense suffering through his madcap revolutionary schemes, he acted decisively to liberate women from the shackles of conservative tradition. He granted women rights to vote (1953), seek divorce and have legal abortions. He abolished child marriage, prostitution and concubinage, and opened the way for women to take part in political life and the official economy. It remains one of the great paradoxes of history that a Communist who suppressed so many other liberties did so much to emancipate women. In this, he was implementing the original Communist ideal of social justice.

Women are not totally free of discrimination in modern China; they are still harassed sexually, and the predominance of males over females (107 to 100) indicates that many girls are aborted. In part this is due to a government regulation applied between 1979 and 2015 that couples should have only one child, in order to slow population growth.

That said, the unleashing of the potential of women is unmistakable. Today, some 80 per cent of employees in factories in east China are females. As a result of this, China's workforce has grown dramatically over the past half century, and this has helped fuel the tremendous growth in its economy. In 2010, six of the 10 richest self-made women in the world were Chinese.[104]

New Strategies, New Benefits

It is not always clear which approaches work best. Education is acclaimed as a great liberator, but curiously in certain parts of the world its effect is disappointing. Micro-credits for women work well in Asia, but only patchily in Africa. Initiatives taken by locals on the spot do better than projects run from the west, while some successes are totally unexpected. In Brazil, the introduction of television to remote villages where women were burdened with too many children brought the birth rate down – simply because the women decided to emulate TV soap opera heroines who had fewer children.[105]

Social media can help women to free themselves from the prying eyes of relatives, neighbours and religious police. In Saudi Arabia, where restrictions on women are particularly severe, young women flirt over Facebook and WhatsApp, watch forbidden films streamed over YouTube, freely debate ideas on Twitter, order transport through Uber, and sell jewellery through Instagram.[106] In 2018, they still had to submit to male "guardians" in arranging travel, obtaining a passport, getting married or divorced and signing contracts, and were largely segregated from men in public places. But in 2012 Saudi women for the first time could participate in Olympic Games, in 2015 they won the right to vote (if only in local elections) and in 2018 they were permitted to drive cars (Saudi Arabia was the last country in the world to lift the driving ban). In Iran, where women are obliged to wear a hijab (close-fitting veil) on pain of fine or imprisonment, more than a million people follow a Facebook page called *My Stealthy Freedom*, in which young women show themselves photographed in the countryside freely shaking their hair.

These women who turn to social media are acting spontaneously to liberate themselves, rather than relying on legislation, foreign aid or organised political movements. At this grass-roots level, women fight for freedom not just in what they do, but also in what they avoid doing. Large numbers of Muslim women discreetly find their way around the constrictions of their religious teachers, as do Catholic women who privately ignore their Church's prohibition of contraception.

Despite these new strategies and advances, it is clear that in the fight for women's freedom disparities still exist between the democracies of the developed world and the more repressive societies of the developing world. However, generalisations can be misleading, as not all Muslim women are oppressed: many are well educated, lead successful professional lives and assert themselves equally towards men.

Evidence from India and Africa also shows that oppression is not confined to areas where Islamic fundamentalists hold sway. As for the societies of Europe and North America, women have come far in their fight for liberation, but that has happened only in the last 150 years or so. The divergence may therefore be largely a matter of time.

The dreadful violence and discrimination that still afflict women around the world begs the question: will the battle to free women ever be won? As with all other fights for freedom, a final victory is unlikely, yet progress towards that end is unmistakable. They will surely become better educated, earn more money, gain more influence, achieve greater parity, speak out more boldly, and realise more of their potential. But they are likely to have to fight all the way.

CHAPTER 13

MARTIN LUTHER KING

Let freedom ring.
– March on Washington, 1963

Civil Disobedience

When slavery was outlawed in the United States at the time of the Civil War, millions of black people were able to walk free from the ties that bound them to their owners; but, as they soon found out, they were only partly free. Racial discrimination and denial of voting rights enabled whites to continue dominating them in the south.

At every turn of life, blacks there were the underdogs. Local voting laws set property conditions that for blacks were nigh impossible to fulfil – the whites had kept most of the land. White local governments cut back education spending for blacks and legislated to curb their civil rights. Segregation allotted the worst of schools, accommodation, entertainment and medical treatment to the blacks. Treatment of the former southern slaves made a mockery of America's reputation as the land of the free.

A long constitutional war of attrition developed, between the liberalising Federal government in Washington and local state governments in the south. It was as if the Civil War never really ended. Thus in 1954, when the Federal Supreme Court decreed that all segregation in schools was illegal, white authorities in the south did all they could to obstruct compliance. Matters came to a head in 1957, when nine black students tried to enrol at a high school in Little Rock, Arkansas, only to be turned back by National Guards sent by Governor Orval Faubus.

President Dwight D. Eisenhower responded by placing the National Guard under Federal orders and directing it to escort the black children into the school. This only helped so far: the Little Rock Nine, as the banned students became known, were taunted and physically abused by the white children in the school, and one even had acid thrown in her face. Rather than yield to Eisenhower's pressure, Governor Faubus temporarily closed all public schools and won a referendum among local whites directly challenging Federal authority. For two and a half years, he delayed desegregation, and by the time it did go ahead, relations between the races had hit rock bottom.

By that time, a charismatic leader who would decisively change the fortunes of blacks was on the rise. Martin Luther King Jr. (1929-68) decided in the mid-1950s that black people should fight for the liberties denied to them. The time was ripe for concerted action, and Martin Luther King knew early in life that emancipating America's blacks was his mission. In following this calling, he proved an inspirational leader and achieved much of what he set out to do.

After studying at a seminary, King became a pastor at a Baptist church in Montgomery, Alabama, at the age of 25. Christianity could have inspired him to preach obedience, but King was drawn to Jesus's great liberating message of bringing the Kingdom of God to the downtrodden. From Mahatma Gandhi, whose inspiration he acknowledged, he learned the power of civil disobedience, hailing this as "the most potent weapon available to oppressed people in their struggle for justice and human dignity". He argued against violence on the grounds that it sought to humiliate rather than convert, destroyed community and brotherhood, prevented dialogue and created bitterness and brutality.[107] As time would show, King also knew how to juggle with the threat of bloody revolution. He was a master of brinkmanship.

In 1955, he launched into his first campaign on behalf of the blacks of Montgomery. A young black woman was arrested for refusing to give up her seat to a white man on a bus, as segregationist law required her to. The action was pre-planned, and King and other black community leaders reacted by organising a boycott of the public bus service. The white authorities thought it would peter out after a few days since the blacks had to get to work, but King organised blacks with cars to give lifts to others, with the result that the boycott lasted 385 days.

With tensions running high, the authorities began arresting volunteer drivers on petty pretexts. King himself was detained, but released after black supporters paid bail. Then came death threats. King told a mass meeting: "If one day you find me sprawled out dead, I do not want you to retaliate with a single act of violence. I urge you to continue protesting with the same dignity you have shown so far."[108]

Sure enough, his house was firebombed shortly afterwards while he was away. After his wife and small daughter heard the explosion on the front porch, King rushed back home, only to find an angry crowd of armed blacks confronting the police. Sensing that violence was about to break out, he told them: "We believe in law and order... don't get your weapons. He who lives by the sword will die by the sword. Remember that is what God said. We are not advocating violence."

All the same, Martin Luther King was a fighter. He added: "I want it known the length and breadth of this land that if I am stopped, this movement will not stop. If I am stopped, our work will not stop. For what we are doing is right. What we are doing is just. And God is with us."[109]

The local authorities' next move was to pass an anti-boycott law, and King promptly courted arrest by disobeying it, correctly sensing that the wind was blowing his way. By this time news of the repression and the organised campaigning by the blacks in Montgomery was appearing in media all over the United States, and public opinion began to appreciate that lack of liberty for the black community was a national issue.

King's bold tactics worked: in November 1956, the U.S. Supreme Court declared bus segregation laws unconstitutional. The blacks called off the boycott and, just before Christmas 1956, Martin Luther King was one of the first passengers to ride a desegregated bus.

That victory, however, did not break the stalemate between the races. Consequently, King and other black leaders decided in 1961 to extend their campaign of civil disobedience to the larger city of Birmingham, Alabama. Thousands of blacks systematically broke the segregation laws there by staging sit-ins in spaces reserved for whites. Many were arrested, including, for the 13th time in his life, King himself.

The black campaigners knew that time in jail benefited their cause, because it drew public attention across the nation. With many of the adults in prison, King's movement mobilised children as protestors, and police promptly turned fire hoses and dogs on them. In doing so, the white authorities inadvertently handed victory to their opponents, since television images of the police assaulting children caused outrage around the world. The police chief was forced to resign, segregation signs were taken down and King's reputation soared.

His battle was far from won, however. In a *Letter from Birmingham Jail*, he expressed frustration at white liberals and clergymen: "The Negro's great stumbling block in his stride toward freedom is… the white moderate, who is more devoted to 'order' than to justice; who prefers a negative peace which is the absence of tension to a positive peace which is the presence of justice; who constantly says: 'I agree with you in the goal you seek, but I cannot agree with your methods of direct action'."[110]

For the peace-loving whites, King was fighting too much, but for hard-core black activists he was not militant enough. Malcolm X and Stokely Carmichael scorned King's vision of racial integration as an insult to the Black-American identity. As European empires in Africa had been built by force, so blacks in America should use violence to seize what was due to them. The two militants opposed King's drive for racial harmony, but they did help position him as a black freedom fighter with whom the whites could deal.

March on Washington

The election of John F. Kennedy to the presidency in 1960 brought a breath of fresh air to American politics, and both raised and frustrated the expectations of the black community.

As a Democrat, Kennedy had come to power with the votes of black people but, despite his liberal inclinations, he watched his back in the south. White Democrats dominated politics there, and most were precisely the segregationists who resisted Martin Luther King.

This concern to avoid upsetting the whites drove the Kennedy administration to actions that were none too friendly towards the blacks. The president's brother Robert, the Attorney General, put a wiretap on Martin Luther King's telephone, and the FBI alleged that the black civil rights movement was infiltrated with Communists – a charge that was never substantiated.

On the other hand, Kennedy could not withdraw support from the black freedom movement altogether – they were his electorate too, and they expected action. During the three years of his presidency, Kennedy gingerly backed their cause, though proceeding with great caution. The outcry at the violence against black children in Birmingham finally tipped the balance: Kennedy's administration drafted a long-awaited Civil Rights bill, designed to end racial oppression.

In June 1963, Kennedy faced down Alabama Governor George Wallace, who stood in the door of the University of Alabama, vowing "segregation now, segregation tomorrow, segregation forever", as he blocked two black students trying to enrol. Kennedy thereupon placed the National Guard under Federal orders, its general ordered Wallace to stand aside in the name of the President of the United States of America – and he did.

Even then the stalemate persisted. The blacks had scarcely any more freedom than after the similar confrontation in Arkansas in 1957, and Congress was procrastinating about passing the Civil Rights bill. So, in August 1963, King and the other black leaders decided to organise a "March on Washington". It sounded ominous, and at first the president tried to persuade them to call it off, but once it was clear they would not, Kennedy aimed to make it a success and sway public opinion behind his Civil Rights bill. "Success" meant a large turnout, no violence and no aggressive rhetoric.

Many participants had to take time off work and make long bus journeys they could ill afford, but nevertheless, on 28th August, the organisers succeeded in bringing a crowd of a quarter of a million together before the Lincoln Memorial in Washington. Negotiations continued until the last moment, with Archbishop Patrick O'Boyle refusing to say the opening prayer until one speech was toned down. The government readied tens of thousands of police and troops, jails shifted inmates to other prisons in case of mass arrests, the city banned sales of alcoholic drinks, and hospitals prepared for numerous casualties. Some 1,700 foreign correspondents flew in to report on the event – more than for Kennedy's inauguration two years earlier.

Despite a threat of violence hanging in the air, the gathering passed off entirely peacefully. Although the authorities were fearful of their presence, the blacks exercised their free choice to abjure violence, and in doing so made their will felt. Instead of discord, the gathering attracted solidarity, not only from fellow-blacks in the north, but also from sympathetic whites. Bob Dylan was among the performers who sang in support, the white labour union leader Walter Reuther gave a speech, and there were many other white faces in the crowd. Like the American independence fighters of 1776 and the Vietnamese guerrillas of the 20th century, it helped the Washington marchers to have allies in the other camp – in this case, whites sympathetic to black aspirations.

In planning the march, some of King's co-leaders wanted to focus on jobs for black people. He, however, insisted that it would be a demonstration for freedom, and that is what made it memorable. A few more jobs would not have brought them voting rights or eliminated the demeaning segregation, and nobody today would remember a rally for work.

When it came to his turn to speak, King appealed to the quarter of a million people to share his vision. "I have a dream," he called out. "A dream of blacks and whites joining hands in brotherhood in the red hills of Georgia and in Alabama, of Mississippi becoming an oasis of freedom and justice... of people being judged not by the colour of their skin but by the content of their character." As the crowd thrilled to his oratory, he called on Americans to act:

> "And so let freedom ring from the prodigious hilltops of New Hampshire.
> Let freedom ring from the mighty mountains of New York.
> Let freedom ring from the heightening Alleghenies of Pennsylvania!
> Let freedom ring from the snow-capped Rockies of Colorado.
> Let freedom ring from the curvaceous peaks of California.
> But not only that.
> Let freedom ring from Stone Mountain of Georgia.
> Let freedom ring from Lookout Mountain of Tennessee.
> Let freedom ring from every hill and every molehill of Mississippi, from every mountainside, let freedom ring!
> And when this happens, when we allow freedom to

> *ring, when we let it ring from every village and every
> hamlet, from every state and every city, we will be able
> to speed up that day when all of God's children, black
> men and white men, Jews and Gentiles, Protestants
> and Catholics, will be able to join hands and sing in
> the words of the old Negro spiritual: 'Free at last! Free
> at last! Thank God Almighty, we are free at last!'"*[111]

With these words, Martin Luther King transformed a worthy protest into a soaring demonstration of the power of the free human spirit. Having gathered a crowd that could have brought Washington to its knees, he shared a dream and spoke of friendship and harmony. He focused on the very essence of the blacks' plight – the lack of freedom resulting from chronic inequality. It remains one of the greatest appeals for freedom in the history of mankind.

At the end of the day, the vast throng wended its way home without incident. President Kennedy diplomatically received the black leaders at the White House and the event came to a close. It was a triumph for King's forceful leadership and his principle of nonviolence; determination won over passivity, and a positive vision pushed aside hateful resentment.

Suddenly, all seemed lost when Kennedy was assassinated only a few months later, on 22nd November 1963. In the ensuing turmoil, few believed that the blacks could expect any further progress, but Kennedy's successor, Lyndon B. Johnson, proved to be the man for the task. A candid, hard-talking southerner, he knew how to strike deals with hard-bitten congressmen and senators. He had a common touch and he was intensely committed to the Democrats' tradition of fighting for the underprivileged.

When southern Democrats in Congress swore to resist to the bitter end any measure that would bring about social equality or intermingling among the races, Johnson countered that they should honour the wish of the assassinated president. After a gruelling half year of wrangling and horse-trading, he persuaded Congress to approve the Bill as the 1964 Civil Rights Act.

The Act outlawed racial discrimination in all public places, and obliged employers to provide equal employment opportunities. It decreed uniform standards for establishing the right to vote, thus outlawing discrimination against the blacks. Federal funds could be withheld from any undertaking involving discrimination based on colour, race or national origin.

Finale in Selma

Yet the Federal Act lacked teeth. When 50 blacks sought to register to vote in the city of Selma, Alabama, in July 1964, the local sheriff and his white posse arrested them. A local judge forbade civil rights meetings, and when the blacks tried to go to a movie theatre or eat at a hamburger stand, they were turned away. The whites continued to apply their local practices in defiance of the Federal law.

In the early months of 1965, King joined in further mass attempts at voter registration, which state troopers again prevented by force. Once more he was imprisoned, while the Selma sheriff repeatedly clubbed a black woman leader in front of press photographers. King and his fellow-leaders kept up the pressure relentlessly, but the violence by their oppressors persisted, giving the black community the moral advantage.

On 7th March 1965, some 600 black protestors set out from Selma for the Alabama capital of Montgomery to protest to the state governor, but white state troopers and police attacked them as they left the town. Television reporters filmed the whites as they tear-gassed, beat and whipped the fleeing blacks. Once again the nation was outraged by the brutality.

As the Selma crisis came to a head, King telephoned President Johnson to berate him for his inaction. He sensed the President was on his side, but was hesitant to overrule southern authorities. Two days later, King showed that he too knew how to play the political game. He led another crowd on a march, but when they came to the cordon of white state troopers, King stopped, ordered his followers to kneel down and pray, and then led them all back again. He had made his point, but decided to respect a last-minute Federal injunction for delay.

The respect that the black marchers in Selma showed for the rule of democratic law gave the president the chance to take the offensive. On 17th March, Johnson introduced new voting rights legislation to Congress and five days later the protestors were able start out again for Montgomery, this time protected by hundreds of state troopers whom Johnson had placed under Federal orders. The president pushed the equal voting rights legislation through Congress and, on 6th August 1965, he signed the new Act into force. Voting, said Johnson, was "the most powerful instrument ever devised by man for breaking down injustice and destroying the terrible walls which imprison men because they are different from other men".[112]

Martin Luther King won, not just because nonviolence gave him the moral high ground, but because he bravely sought confrontation until the other side cracked and resorted to brutality. He risked letting nonviolence run out of control several times, but he never overstepped the line. King proved himself a superior tactician, a keen judge of public opinion and an assured politician.

His achievements were considerable. He ended much of the discrimination that flouted the liberties of southern blacks despite the abolition of slavery. For King, freedom was not just a legal formality: it required substance in the form of voting rights, treatment by officialdom, and access to schools, medical care, transport and public gathering places. He bent the president and Congress to his will, and engaged the broad American public on his side. Discrimination would continue, but would not be systematically condoned. Southern whites would no longer feel they could trample on the liberties of blacks with impunity.

As an indirect consequence of his struggle, an African American would finally take office as President of the United States in 2009. Fittingly, Barack Obama invited the Little Rock Nine of 1957 to his inauguration. Beyond whites and blacks, beyond America, Martin Luther King inspired the wider world with his appeal at the "March on Washington" for freedom to create harmony. He articulated a vision to which all could aspire.

King's fight for freedom earned him the Nobel Peace Prize in 1964, but he was able to savour the recognition for only four years. Having been imprisoned 29 times and surviving an attempt on his life by a deranged black woman, he met his end in yet another American political assassination. On the evening of 4th April 1968, he was shot dead as he stood on the balcony of a motel in Memphis, Tennessee. James Earl Ray, a white segregationist on the run from prison, was later convicted for his murder.

The day before, King told a rally that he had seen the promised land. "I may not get there with you. But I want you to know tonight, that we, as a people, will get to the promised land. So I'm happy, tonight. I'm not worried about anything. I'm not fearing any man."[113]

CHAPTER 14

NELSON MANDELA

To be free is not merely to cast off one's chains, but to live in a
way that respects and enhances the freedom of others.
– Nelson Mandela

Freedom for All – The Struggle Begins

Nelson Mandela trod in the footsteps of memorable predecessors – those of black African liberation movement leaders who won freedom for their people, and of Mahatma Gandhi and Martin Luther King, who showed the paradoxical power of nonviolence to defeat tyranny. Now it was to be his turn in the fight for freedom, and he would do it in his own distinctive way.

The South Africa into which Mandela was born in 1918 was beset by rivalry between two sets of white settlers. Sturdy, independent-minded Dutch farmers arrived in the country in the 17th century, while the British took over the southern Cape region a century later. The discovery of gold and diamonds in the Transvaal territory occupied by the Dutch led to wars that the British eventually won (1899-1902), but only after humiliating setbacks.

The victory brought the whole country under British rule, but the British needed good relations with the larger numbers of Dutch in order to exploit the land's mineral riches. The Dutch, or Afrikaaners as they became known, consolidated their influence, and in 1931 Britain granted independence to a government in which Afrikaaners had the upper hand.

In all this, South African blacks such as Nelson Mandela had no say. Their lot was mainly to farm for subsistence or work for meagre wages in the white-owned gold and diamond mines, with no vote and no political representation. The Afrikaaners also introduced an apartheid system segregating the two races. In practice, this enabled the whites to take any land they wanted, control the economy and disrupt African social life. Apartheid not only kept the blacks apart; it kept them down.

Mandela was one of the few blacks to be given an education, since he was the son of a one of the tribal leaders whom the Afrikaaners saw as harmless relics of a bygone society. These traditional chiefs had lost their power to rule, but were steeped in conservative lore, protective of their customary privileges and apprehensive of change. As the child of one such chief, Nelson was schooled to prepare for a respectable profession, and then a leadership role in a fossilised black society.

After the death of his father, Nelson's guardian told the teenager to marry a girl the guardian had selected for him. Neither boy nor girl knew each other or had any inclination to go through with it, so Nelson took off for Johannesburg, the big city. It was there that he realised the trap the whites had set by selecting him for preferential education. He would be a creature of privilege compared with the other blacks, beholden to the whites for his status, and prevented from being his own man. That was not for him: a strapping young male with a genial charm, a way with his words, and a dawning consciousness of his potential. He grasped that his true goal was freedom, rather than acting as the puppet of others.

In Johannesburg's segregated society, he and other blacks were barred from the public places, schools, hospitals and eating places that whites used, and were instead condemned to inferior facilities. This policy attracted criticism overseas after the defeat of racist Nazi Germany in World War II, and so Prime Minister Henrik Verwoerd reformulated it as "separate development".

Blacks were granted "Bantustan" homelands, but they represented only 13 per cent of South Africa's surface. The land was poor, and they were split up haphazardly into pieces, making them impossible to administer effectively. The rest of the country was reserved for the whites, and there blacks could stay only to fulfil the demand for labour. What was dressed up as giving blacks equal rights in fact condemned them to permanent inferiority.

By this time, Mandela was politically active in the African National Congress (ANC), which he joined in 1944. The ANC was formed in 1912 to canvass for the rights of blacks, but when Mandela enrolled, it had only a few thousand members and its polite petitioning had proved fruitless. Together with Walter Sisulu and Oliver Tambo, Mandela set up an ANC Youth League, with the aim of turning the ANC into a mass movement, campaigning against white repression through civil disobedience and non-cooperation.

No longer were they calling just for better treatment, but now also for full citizenship, redistribution of land, trade union rights and free education for all children. Their goal was equal rights for all, irrespective of colour. This would mean freedom for the majority blacks, and as such, it represented a direct challenge to Afrikaaners' supremacy.

The re-modelled ANC in 1952 launched a "Defiance Campaign" calling for non-compliance with racist laws, which led to thousands of arrests – among them Mandela. On his release, as the Afrikaaners engaged in a war of attrition to stifle the resistance, he was served with a legal notice banning him from attending gatherings. In 1956, a long series of arrests and court convictions culminated in Mandela and other ANC leaders being put on trial for "high treason", in a process that the authorities drew out over five years to keep them under intimidating pressure.

Younger blacks disenchanted with the ANC hived off to form a Pan-African Congress (PAC), promoting the interests only of blacks rather than racial harmony. In 1960, both movements staged protests against laws obliging non-whites to carry passbooks showing where they had a right to live. Mandela and thousands of other blacks burned the documents in protest, and others courted arrest by refusing to carry them.

This struggle against the restrictions on freedom of movement led to disaster in 1961, when the PAC demonstrated in the dusty African township of Sharpeville. Ten thousand blacks gathered before the police station, whereupon the police opened fire and killed 69 of them, including eight women and 10 children, many shot in the back. It was a lethal demonstration of the regime's power to crush protest.

The rest of the world reacted in horror at press photos of black bodies lying on the rough ground, shot down by obviously racist police. Protest movements then sprang up in western societies, which began to treat South Africa's apartheid rulers as pariahs. Demonstrations took place worldwide, and the United Nations passed a resolution of condemnation, but as this was the Cold War era, the Afrikaaner government could deflect western anger by alleging that Communists controlled the resistance movements.[114] Western governments, fearful of Soviet influence, did little to pressure the white regime. Big companies went on doing business with South Africa, and banks in London and Zurich continued to sell its gold.

Turning to Violence

The consequences of Sharpeville at home were drastic. The government declared martial law, banned both the ANC and PAC, and imprisoned Mandela and other leading activists without charges. Shortly afterwards, Mandela and the other defendants in the "treason trial" were acquitted, and they could walk free – if only for a time.

Realising that they could no longer campaign legally for the freedom of their people, Mandela and other anti-apartheid leaders went underground, and the ANC set up an armed wing called Umkhonto we Sizwe (Spear of the Nation) to oppose the white regime with physical force. After six months of military training elsewhere in Africa, Mandela returned to participate briefly in a campaign of sabotage of electricity pylons and bombing of public installations, which lasted for 16 years. In these, a few dozen people were killed and several hundred injured. The casualties were not large in number, but the persistent attacks created a pervasive sense of insecurity.

Mandela's participation in the violence has been held against him ever since. Rather than hail him as a hero in the fight for freedom, critics have condemned him as a terrorist. This judgement, however, is unfair. True, he and

his movement did use terror as a tactic, but the casualty toll
over a quarter of a century was no worse than a single bad
day in Iraq or Pakistan in recent years. Secondly, it bore no
comparison with the much greater violence of the regime,
which left the blacks no opportunity to pursue their goals
peacefully. Thirdly, nearly all the violence was carried out
while Mandela was in prison and in no position to participate.
Most importantly, his peaceful activism far outweighed his
involvement in violence.

Mandela admired the nonviolent campaigns of Gandhi
and Martin Luther King, but Gandhi was confronting a
relatively liberal colonial administration, while King had
the tacit support of the U.S. Federal Government. Mandela
and the ANC were on their own against an exceptionally
tough enemy. Without some degree of violence, Mandela
would not be celebrated today as a champion of his people's
freedom, because the blacks would not have won. The idea
that he should have conducted his struggle solely through
nonviolence is thus unjustified. He demonstrated why a
fight for freedom sometimes really must be a fight.

After a short period of clandestine existence – disguised
as a chauffeur and nicknamed the Black Pimpernel –
Mandela was captured on a lonely road at night after a tip-
off. Late in 1962, he was sentenced to five years in jail after
a trial at which he upheld the ANC's goals of freedom, civil
rights and racial harmony. While serving his sentence, he
was put on trial again, this time for sabotage and attempting
to overthrow the state by force. Daringly, he declined to
make a detailed defence, opting instead to make a four-hour
speech to the court, explaining why the ANC had resorted
to resistance. He concluded with these words:

"During my lifetime I have dedicated myself to this struggle of the African people. I have fought against white domination, and I have fought against black domination. I have cherished the ideal of a democratic and free society in which all persons will live together in harmony and with equal opportunities. It is an ideal, which I hope to live for and to achieve. But, My Lord, if it needs be, it is an ideal for which I am prepared to die."

Mandela's eloquence in the face of persecution made a big impact, both at home and abroad. One of the main South African newspapers ignored censorship and printed the speech, vigils were held in St Paul's Cathedral in London, and the University of London Students' Union elected Mandela as its president in absentia. The U.N. Security Council (with abstentions by the U.S. and Britain) urged the South African government to end the trial and grant amnesty to the defendants.

Despite the global support for Mandela and his co-defendants, the trial wound on into 1964, with many expecting them eventually to be sentenced to death. Reactionary though he was, however, the judge disliked having to blindly sanction the regime's roughneck actions. Instead, he sentenced the defendants to life imprisonment, and with that Mandela was dispatched for the next 18 years to Robben Island, located four miles off the Cape in the Atlantic Ocean.

Jailed for Life

That should have been the end of Mandela; he was to be incarcerated until he died, and all the signs suggested he would wither away in oblivion, broken in spirit and health, and the world would move on without him. Instead, isolated though he was on that barren rock, he embarked on what he later called his "Long Walk to Freedom".

Daily life consisted of confinement in a damp concrete cell with a straw sleeping mat and a light bulb burning day and night; hard labour breaking rocks; digging a dusty, white lime quarry; porridge with the occasional root or gristle thrown in; verbal and physical abuse by white prison wardens; and only one letter and one family visit every six months. Censors cut out passages they objected to with razors, so the letters arrived in tatters and were scarcely readable. When his mother and eldest son died, Mandela was refused permission to attend their funerals.

For three years, Mandela's requests for sunglasses were turned down, and as a result his eyesight suffered permanent damage from the glare in the quarry. Although weakened by tuberculosis, he plied the authorities with applications for improvements, such as reading glasses and study facilities – and, above all, long trousers rather than the regulation shorts. He considered long trousers to be a matter of dignity, but the prison chiefs refused. He persisted regardless, and after a visit by the International Red Cross he won this small freedom, with difficulty, but a victory all the same.

Mandela cultivated a relationship with his wardens and when he told them of the ANC's commitment to non-racism, some listened sympathetically. Gradually, Mandela's fellow prisoners and the guards acknowledged him as a leader. Nevertheless, it was not clear there was any point in being a leader, since his sentence precluded any release, and events in his country were unfolding without him. In 1976, blacks in the sprawling township of Soweto mounted an insurrection against a law introducing school teaching in Afrikaans; a language hardly any of them could understand. They were brutally put down, leaving 176 dead in the dust.

By this time, he risked being overtaken by more aggressive militants such as Steve Biko, who advocated a fight for supremacy between blacks and whites. However, Biko's hard-nosed confrontation proved no more successful than Mandela's measured approach. Biko was arrested in 1977, tortured, and driven manacled and naked over 700 miles to a police station, where he died on arrival. Mandela's strength, as it turned out, was in discerning more judiciously how to balance peaceful persuasion with violence.

Unbeknown to Mandela in his enforced isolation, the wind was turning in his favour. Ten thousand people attended Biko's funeral, this time including ambassadors from western countries. In neighbouring Rhodesia, the white regime gave way to a black government, and in Angola and Mozambique the Portuguese handed over to left-wing liberation leaders. At home, the regime was caught in a spiral of protests and violence, including the murder of police officers and officials, which it could contain only by ever-tougher repression.

In the west, the public were no longer ready to countenance their governments turning a blind eye to the excesses of a racist South African regime. Anti-racist movements organised boycotts against companies dealing with South Africa, and the U.N. voted for sanctions. By the 1980s, the white South African government was ostracised by much of the world, with only the United States and Britain holding out in half-hearted support.

The regime therefore began to look for ways out of the impasse which they had not considered before. This could only mean coming to some sort of arrangement with its enemies, but with whom? Not with the young firebrands who fought for black supremacy, nor with ANC leaders abroad, susceptible to foreign influence. It should be someone at home, of suitable stature. So, they came to the unlikely choice of a man then nearly 70 years old, whose spirit they had done their best to break during the prime of his life. In 1982, in recognition of this new status, Mandela was transferred with his political associates to a prison on the mainland, near Cape Town.

Then came a trap. In 1985, Prime Minister P.W. Botha announced that he would free Mandela if he renounced violence unconditionally. Mandela rejected the offer – the white regime was responsible for the violence, not him – and he delegated his daughter Zindzi to read a speech to a rally in Soweto. It was the first time in 20 years that his words had been heard in public:

> *"I cherish my freedom dearly, but I care even more for your freedom… I cannot sell my birth-right, nor am I prepared to sell the birth-right of the people to be free… Only free men can negotiate. Prisoners cannot enter into contracts. I cannot and will not give any undertaking at a time when you, the people, are not free. Your freedom and mine cannot be separated. I will return."*

The offer and the rebuff were part of a process that would be long drawn out, but persistent. On the mainland, the transferred prisoners were given better quarters and treated more humanely. One day, Mandela was surprised to be taken in a car for a tour, and when his escort left him alone for a few minutes, he was tempted to run away.

He resisted the urge however, since this would have made him a fugitive again. Moreover, he sensed the initiative was passing to him.

This was borne out when Mandela received an unannounced visit from the Justice Minister, Kobie Coetsee, while recuperating in hospital from an operation. The minister chatted as if they were old friends and wished him a speedy recovery. On his return to prison, Mandela was unexpectedly put into solitary confinement, but rather than fret, he exploited it to respond to the conciliatory gestures.

Isolation gave Mandela the liberty to pursue contacts with the regime without having to consult his imprisoned comrades. He suspected they would veto talks unless the ban on the ANC was lifted, and Mandela believed that holding out for this prior concession would risk thousands of lives. His ANC comrades-in-exile soon sniffed that something was up, and sent him worried messages. He reassured them he was working for the ban on the ANC to be lifted, but he was going it alone. It was risky.

When he was brought to a bungalow for meetings with Coetsee and other officials, he enunciated a list of demands for liberties and democratic rights for black people – including the lifting of the ANC ban.

"What's in it for us," one of the whites asked. "Nothing," Mandela replied, coolly. When they asked him to guarantee special rights for the white minority in a future South Africa, he refused – it would be equal votes for all. Prisoner though he still was, he knew he had the upper hand. But he assured them that "whites are Africans too," and added: "We don't want to drive you into the sea."

Next, he was invited to meet President P.W. Botha at an official residence. They only exchanged pleasantries, but

Mandela was struck that Botha smiled, shook his hand and offered him tea. It would have been unremarkable elsewhere, but in apartheid South Africa it was an extraordinary turnaround. In a state where most whites treated blacks as sub-humans, Mandela was being granted the dignities of an eminent citizen.

Overseas, he was meanwhile fêted like a rock star. In 1988, 100,000 people packed London's Wembley Stadium to celebrate his 70th birthday with a pop concert, broadcast to an audience of 600 million in 67 countries. He himself had to savour the occasion in his remote South African prison – a global celebrity, but still not free.

The collapse of the Soviet Union and the liberation of eastern Europe in 1989 hastened Mandela's journey to freedom. Moscow ceased trying to export revolution and western powers no longer feared that change would open the doors to Communism. As a new spirit of liberty spread abroad, South African President P.W. Botha had a stroke and ceded power in 1989 to F.W. de Klerk, who as a fresh face could make a new departure. No sooner was he appointed than de Klerk announced drastic change: South Africa would become a multi-racial society, and apartheid would be dismantled. He released seven of Mandela's co-prisoners with no pre-conditions, which meant they could speak and act as they wished; the ban on the ANC had effectively ended, and de Klerk had conceded the movement's two main demands.

Release and a Free Election

Then, in February 1990, de Klerk informed Nelson Mandela that he would be flown the next day to Johannesburg and released. Mandela sensed another trap: de Klerk would preside over his liberation as if it were an act of magnanimity rather than a restoration of his right. Mandela demanded time to inform the ANC, and he insisted that he walk free from his Cape Town prison. They bargained to and fro until compromising over a glass of whisky.

Mandela realised it was ridiculous to refuse to be freed, so the next day, 11th February 1990, he embraced his white warders and walked with a smile, hand-in-hand with his wife Winnie, up the driveway and through the prison gates. After a few moments of confusion, as he was engulfed by journalists and photographers, he raised his right fist, and there was a roar. "I had not been able to do that for twenty-seven years and it gave me a surge of strength and joy," he wrote later in his autobiography.[115]

Immediately, the question arose: what would Mandela do with his freedom? He had endured his captivity with dignity and courage, but the world would soon forget him if he devoted himself to personal pursuits. Worse, it would condemn him if he abused his freedom by succumbing to the temptations of greed and bullying, as many other African independence leaders had before him.

He chose to engage intensively with de Klerk in leading South Africa towards free elections, majority rule, liberation of political prisoners, lifting of the state of emergency, freedom of expression and an end to racial discrimination. With some misgivings, the ANC suspended its armed struggle. But it was a path full of pitfalls: many blacks wanted full-scale revolution, seizure of white assets and retribution for past oppression.

Ethnic differences burst to the surface, and fighting broke out between ANC supporters and Inkatha Zulus. Mandela suspected the whites were deliberately stirring up the trouble, and when de Klerk berated the ANC for carrying on with violence, Mandela publicly scorned him as the head of an illegitimate, discredited minority regime. As the death toll from police and Zulu attacks mounted, the ANC suspended negotiations and protesters called for armed struggle to resume.

Throughout, Mandela pressed home the message to his own people that freedom must be accompanied by peace, civility, rule of law and study, rather than violence and boycotts. "The time has come to accept in our hearts and minds that with freedom comes responsibility," he said.[116] To the whites, he refused special constitutional protections, but assured them that all who abandoned apartheid would have an honourable place in the new South Africa. De Klerk, for his part, never lost sight of the fact that he must work with Mandela to prevent South Africa from descending into the abyss. He too had to deal with doubting hardliners.

Although Mandela and de Klerk never hit it off, they were forced to cooperate, and in 1993 they were jointly awarded the Nobel Peace Prize. It was touch and go, but whenever there was a breakdown, negotiators met behind the scenes to get the process back on track. Finally, the two sides agreed to form a government of national unity, with elections set for 1994. On the eve of the vote, Mandela told his followers on television they could not build a new country through fighting. "But you can build a new country through voting. So go and vote!"

Vote they did, in peaceful masses, queuing from dawn to nightfall to exercise that basic democratic freedom: casting a ballot paper. For blacks such as Mandela himself, it was the first time ever. But the whites were proud too, that they were voting under truly free conditions, as never before, sharing the privilege with their black compatriots. The ANC won 62.6 per cent of the vote, and Nelson Mandela became president.

Reconciliation

Now the question became ever more insistent: what would Mandela make of his power? Many in the ANC wanted to seize advantages for themselves and push the whites out of positions of influence. Mandela, however, stuck to his line that the liberation struggle was not against a people, but a system of repression. He urged all South Africans to "unite and join hands and say we are one country, one nation, one people, marching together into the future."[117]

But how could blacks forget the killings, the tortures, the beatings, the oppression and the humiliations they had suffered at the hands of the whites? Should the culprits not be brought to justice? At this point, Mandela turned to another of South Africa's heroes in the liberation struggle: Archbishop Desmond Tutu, the black head of the South African Anglican Church. While Mandela was in prison, Tutu spoke out forcefully against apartheid, but as a churchman the regime could not touch him, and in 1984 he too won the Nobel Peace Prize.

Consequently, one of Nelson Mandela's first acts as president in 1994 was to designate Tutu as head of a Truth and Reconciliation Commission, set up to acknowledge the past honestly in a spirit of reconciliation. The Commission invited perpetrators of political crimes to recount before a tribunal what they had done. If the tribunal decided that he, or she, had made a full and frank admission, it granted an amnesty from prosecution. The Commission did not force anybody to appear, but gave a hearing to anybody who applied for amnesty. The most important sessions were shown live on television, exposing the nation to some harrowing confessions.

One policeman described how he and three others murdered a black lawyer. When the widow of Griffiths Mxenge saw her husband's body in a mortuary the next day, she observed: "Forty-five lacerations and stab wounds pierce his body, lungs, liver and heart. His throat is slashed. His ears are practically cut off. And his stomach is ripped open."[118]

Tutu tried to persuade P.W. Botha to testify to the Commission, but Botha dismissed it as "a circus" and refused to attend. He was put on trial before a black judge, and given a suspended prison sentence and a fine (later quashed on a technicality). Tutu commented: "He looked such a pathetic figure in court that I felt deeply sorry for him. His stubbornness provided some people with what they had been wanting to see – the leaders of the old dispensation getting a dose of retributive justice – but it happened against the Commission's wishes."[119]

The Commission's final report found the Botha government guilty of criminal misconduct, killing its political opponents, torture, abduction, arson and sabotage. On the other hand, it also concluded that the ANC's bomb attacks were "gross violations of human rights". The ANC was not happy and tried to block publication, backing down only when Tutu went on television to warn of "new tyrannies".

The process had its drawbacks. The main white and black leaders did not apply to testify, and most of those appearing were the "trigger-pullers". Opinion polls showed that South African whites were sceptical of its merits, However, blacks

were more positive, and its reconciliatory nature reinforced
Nelson Mandela's drive to deploy liberty for the purposes of
harmony and national unity.

The stature of Tutu and Mandela no doubt lent
authority to the undertaking, but they had a common touch
too, which appealed to the people. One was an outspoken
churchman with a mischievous grin, and the other appeared
in colourful African open-necked shirts so that he could mix
informally and use his charm.

What Tutu described later as an "electrifying moment"
came in 1995, when Mandela appeared in a Springboks jersey
for the final of the Rugby World Cup between South Africa
and New Zealand. Rugby was the white sport par excellence
in South Africa, and nearly all the crowd packing the
Johannesburg stadium were white. When Mandela walked
on to the pitch wearing a jersey with the same number on
the back as captain François Pienaar, the spectators rose to
their feet and chanted Mandela's name.

Then, after South Africa won, Mandela went back out,
still wearing his Springbok jersey, put his hand on Pienaar's
shoulder and said: "Thank you very much for what you
have done for our country." To which the captain replied:
"Mr President, it is nothing compared to what *you* have
done for our country." Mandela had found an unlikely soul
mate in the blonde, white rugby captain. When asked by
an interviewer about the 63,000 people cheering his team
on, Pienaar replied: "We didn't have the support of 63,000
South Africans today. We had the support of 42 million."
It was a powerful endorsement of Mandela's message that
freedom must lead to harmony.

The watching Archbishop Tutu remarked: "Quite
unbelievable, quite incredible, what happened. It had

the effect of just... turning around the country. It was an incredible transformation. An extraordinary thing. It said, yes, it is actually possible for us to become one nation."[120]

During his presidency, Mandela espoused another freedom too – the principle of a free-market economy. He had earlier been influenced by Marxist ideas, but once in power he chose not to narrow the gap in wealth between blacks and whites by rigid socialist planning. As a result, whites continued to control large parts of the economy, but it was relatively free to develop.

Mandela committed one last act that was out of the ordinary. Unlike the "Big Men" of the decades after Africa's decolonisation, he stood down as president in 1999, after just one term in office. Having brought freedom and a large measure of reconciliation to his people, he conformed with a due process of democracy – the timely passage of powers to a new leader.

From the beginning, Mandela correctly perceived that the position of the white apartheid regime was unsustainable before world opinion. All human beings make choices between freedom and security, but the whites opted overwhelmingly for security. That meant they could survive in power only by constantly oppressing the majority blacks and excluding them from fundamental liberties. Mandela realised this would lead them into a dead end, and he excelled in sensing the emerging cracks in the regime and boldly exploiting them. The price he paid was captivity for much of his adult life, but he was right to be confident that his fight for freedom would eventually prevail.

It was for his courage in waging this battle to a successful end that people around the world poured out their admiration for Nelson Mandela when he passed away in 2013, at the age of 95. He was celebrated for seeking harmony but not shirking the use of force against massive repression; and for deploying his inspirational authority to create tolerance, inclusiveness and forgiveness at a time when South Africa could have veered to disaster. In the light of the actions of his successors, it is legitimate to ask whether his legacy will last. However, he cannot be held responsible for that. During his lifetime, he succeeded better than all other African liberation leaders – and even Gandhi himself.

For these reasons, Nelson Mandela stands at the very forefront as a morally principled fighter for freedom. He waged the battle in his own way, and if anybody doubts that freedom is worth fighting for, Mandela showed that it is.

CHAPTER 15

THE ARAB SPRING

Salmiya, salmiya – Peaceful, peaceful.
– Tahrir Square protesters

Long Decline

I n 2011, people of the Arab world took to the streets and overthrew autocratic regimes in the name of freedom. Yet three years later, all but one of the uprisings had failed; civil war enveloped Syria and parts of Iraq, and Europe came under attack by terrorists from the Middle East. Does this mean that freedom is alien to the Arab world, or that Islamic fundamentalism will inevitably crush any moves towards democracy?

Nothing is less certain. The upheavals are representative of the battle in Arabs' hearts and minds between notions of freedom and human rights originating in the west and stricter traditions rooted in Islam. For most of the Middle Ages, Islam was the greatest power on earth – a multiracial civilisation governed according to the word of God, as revealed to the Prophet Muhammad. Its believers held Islam to be the final and perfect religion, and could not conceive that their system of administering human affairs could be bettered.

At this time, the Christian world in the west was ruled according to the word of God too, but it could not compete with the dynamism of Islam, and towards the end of the Middle Ages the authority of the Church began to be contested. Kings who tried to rule by divine right were removed, and wars between Protestants and Catholics were defused by shifting political power to secular authorities.

Released from the constraints of religion, Europeans could give free rein to their human creativity in governing, making money and exploiting scientific discoveries. In driving Islam out of Spain in 1492 and breaking a Turkish siege of Vienna in 1683, the western powers pushed Islam on to the back foot, and the advantage never stopped growing.

Unable to conceive of a need to change, Islamic rulers resisted new ideas and inventions coming from western "infidels" and rejected the principle of freedom as a challenge to holy law. Only when it was clear that the Muslim world was falling seriously behind did modernisers eventually gain the upper hand. At the end of the 19th century and the beginning of the 20th century, civilian governments modelled on western institutions were installed in several Arab countries, and western customs pervaded Muslims' lives. In Egypt, for example, the most populous Arab state, freedom of expression was allowed to flourish from as early as 1882.[121]

Democracy, however, never took firm root. From the 1950s, many Arab countries enforced socialism and ruling autocrats tolerated no dissent. When socialism proved unsustainable, reforms demanded by the International Monetary Fund in return for bailouts caused further distress: elimination of subsidies led to food riots, and privatisation merely moved ownership of state assets into the hands of the rulers' cronies and relatives. Autocrats stayed in power, but were increasingly corrupt and inept.

One response to these disasters has been an attempted return to the past, to the glorious days of Islamic supremacy when unchallenged holy law brought humanity a perfect religion. Islamic fundamentalists reject western influences as unholy and subversive, and apply their particularly severe interpretation of holy law with absolute rigour. The Shi'a religious dictatorship has imposed this radical conservatism in Iran since 1978, and today the self-styled Islamic State does likewise in the parts of Iraq and Syria it has seized by force of arms.

Grasping for Freedom

The other reaction has been the so-called Arab Spring – a series of popular uprisings for freedom which sought to overthrow the autocracies. From 2011, revolution threatened regimes ruling for decades in Tunisia, Egypt, Bahrain, Yemen, Sudan, Libya and Syria. Five leaders were overthrown, and the shock waves were felt throughout the Middle East.

The Arab Spring was ignited on 17th December 2010 by a young Tunisian named Mohamed Bouazizi, who sold fruit at a roadside stand. On that day, a municipal inspector declared Bouazizi's permit to be out of order and confiscated his wares. This petty act of official persecution, in a moribund economy, turned sullen discontent into violent outrage. Bouazizi doused himself with petrol and set himself alight; by the time he died of his burns on 4th January 2011, riots had spread all over Tunisia. The army made clear it would not fire on the people and, on 14th January Tunisia's president, Zine El Abidine Ben Ali, was forced to flee to Saudi Arabia.

Ben Ali had ruled for 24 years, during which time Tunisia consistently ranked near the bottom of international rankings for human rights and press freedom. To the west, however, he was a safe pair of hands and a bulwark against Islamic extremism. Now all of a sudden he was gone, swept away by a people liberating themselves from his despotism. Western media called it a "Jasmine Revolution" and, as in other revolutionary events, it moved very fast. Within months, all Ben Ali's supporters had been cleared out of office and in October 2011 the country held a free election, in which the previously banned Islamic party Ennahda won a majority.

The Egyptians moved just as fast; less than two weeks after Ben Ali's overthrow, crowds were out in Cairo's Tahrir Square demanding the removal of Hosni Mubarak, who had been in power for nearly 30 years. He was another old soldier favoured by the west, ruthlessly suppressing dissent, but at the age of 82 he was unable to manage the strains of a rapidly expanding population and unemployment.

Air force planes roared intimidatingly overhead, but crowds growing to several hundred thousand occupied the central square day and night, watched by television viewers around the world. Business owners gave workers time off to take part, and the employees worked through the night to make up time. Bakers offered cheap bread to the occupiers, and pharmacists discounted medicines. Social media and smartphones enabled the demonstrators to keep in touch with each other, outwitting police trying to stop them gathering. Then, when the police moved in with batons, the protesters chanted "*salmiya, salmiya* – peaceful, peaceful", just as the crowds had done in Prague and Berlin in 1989. They called for an end to "the regime" – that is, not only Mubarak and his government, but also all his corrupt hangers-on who were bleeding the state of its resources.

The police took scant notice of the appeals for peace, and some 800 people were killed in Cairo and other cities.

However, the army refrained from joining in the repression, since it had other plans. On 11th February, Mubarak resigned – or rather the army deposed him, having become disenchanted with his failing capacities and greedy ways. It was a coup, but the army only moved when the people rose up en masse to demand an end to the tyranny. After 18 days, the people had won, in the sense they had gained an opportunity for a radical new beginning. The demonstrators went home, and Cairo women came down on to the streets to clean away rubbish and put prised-up cobble stones back into place.

The Arab Spring then spread like wildfire, bringing regime change in Yemen and Sudan, and unrest in more than half a dozen other Arab countries. Within six days of the overthrow of Mubarak, disorders broke out in the city of Benghazi, in adjacent Libya, where Colonel Gaddafi had terrorised his people for four decades. Gaddafi launched ferocious attacks on the rioters, but within a short time he was no longer able to assert his authority. As civil war broke out, the United States, Britain and France launched aerial bombardments against Gaddafi's forces, under the aegis of a U.N. resolution.

After Gaddafi fled to his hometown of Sirte, a western air patrol attacked his convoy of cars, and rebels lynched him when he emerged from a rain gully where he took refuge. The last images filmed on rebels' smartphones showed a dishevelled and frightened man, aware that after 42 years of benighted misrule his end was nigh.

Then came the turn of Syria, where Bashar al-Assad had kept his people on a tight rein since succeeding his father as president in 2000. The Arab Spring's bacillus of freedom entered the country in the town of Daraa, on the border with Jordan, where 15 schoolchildren, aged between nine and 15, had seen TV broadcasts of protesters in Tahrir Square shouting: "Down with the regime." They scrawled the same slogan on their school wall and, on 6th March 2011 they were arrested and beaten. Local inhabitants tried to negotiate their release but the authorities refused, and troops killed four of a protesting crowd gathered outside a mosque.

With that, the fire of revolution was lit. A people longing for more freedom, a youthful attempt at liberty of expression, and an unnecessarily violent reaction by the authorities – it was a familiar cocktail. The Syrian army besieged Daraa with tanks and helicopters, causing thousands of casualties. Rebellions quickly spread to other towns, prompting ever more massive interventions by the military, and Assad's regime soon lost control of large parts of the country.

Freedom Crushed Again – except in Tunisia

At that point, the Arab Spring was at a crossroads. The people had freed themselves of tyrants who had misgoverned and allowed cronies to enrich themselves at public cost. Now the question was: what could the people do with their new-found freedom? The answer, alas, was not much.

In Egypt, the organisation of free presidential elections in 2012 at first boded well. However, the candidate representing the free-spirited occupiers of Tahrir Square, many of whom were educated professionals and students, narrowly failed to make the second round of voting. Elected with just 51 per cent of the vote in the second round was Mohammed Morsi of the Muslim Brotherhood movement.

Refusing to open up government beyond his own supporters, Morsi railroaded through a new constitution favouring Muslims, extended his powers by decree and sidelined the judiciary. Freely elected though he was, he proved no more capable of dealing with Egypt's economic woes than his predecessor. Blunders led to power cuts, shortages of food and petrol, and he could do nothing to relieve persistent joblessness, lack of housing and poor water supplies.

After scarcely a year of bungling Muslim Brotherhood rule, the people rose up once more and, at the end of June 2013, huge crowds of protesters gathered again in Tahrir Square. Five days later, the army deposed Morsi and imprisoned him along with thousands of other Brotherhood leaders. Millions turned out across the country to cheer and celebrate with fireworks, but the people's relief was short-lived. In the following years, courts condemned Morsi and over 1,000 other people to death at summary trials (though the death sentences had not been carried out by early 2016), and the army cracked down on opposition from any quarter, more harshly than Mubarak had ever done.

In a new presidential election, the army commander, General Abdel Fattah Al-Sisi, won 97 per cent of the vote, which none of the opposition parties contested. Egypt had again come under the rule of a general in dark glasses, preoccupied by security. He began buying expensive weapons abroad and steered resources to huge state-funded economic projects, leaving little scope for free enterprise to develop. Hardly what the Tahrir Square idealists had in mind, but they had no say any more and Egyptians had little choice but to fall into line.

Over the border in Libya, Gaddafi had left scarcely any state institutions, just instruments of repression and an education system designed to hinder people from thinking.

After his demise, Libyans elected a secular, moderate government, but it proved feeble and the country lapsed into an unruly contest between rival clans – all plentifully armed and one of them an extremist *jihadist* movement. If the Libyan people had hoped for more freedom, they now found themselves at the mercy of many tyrants instead of one.

In neighbouring Tunisia, with a relatively high level of education, the people bravely continued to put the ideals of the Arab Spring into practice. The secular Nidaa Tounes party won elections in 2014 and governed in coalition with the moderate Islamic Ennahda party, having worked together to draft a new democratic constitution. In contrast to Morsi, Ennahda's Rachid Ghannouchi reached out to secular parties rather than try to enforce Islamic supremacy.

But this successful exercise in cooperation and tolerance attracted revenge in 2015, when Islamic *jihadists* slaughtered over 70 people, many of them westerners, at two tourist locations. The attacks were clearly aimed at destabilising the new-found democracy and jeopardising an important source of national revenue. The Tunisian people were being punished for choosing a liberal way of life.

The Nobel Committee responded by awarding its 2015 Peace Prize to representatives of Tunisian trade unions, employers, human rights organisations and lawyers, who had worked together to ensure the new democracy was founded on consensus. It recognised Tunisia's success in establishing a civil society, enabling the free and constructive interplay of different interests.

Syria, Iraq and the Islamic State

Syria, meanwhile, went from bad to worse. When the 15 youngsters sprayed graffiti in a dusty frontier town in

2011, few people imagined that four years later civil war would have torn the country apart. Ancient cities were laid to waste, more than 200,000 people killed, and 10 million forced to flee their homes. The Syrian government slaughtered its population with huge barrel bombs dropped on cities from helicopters.

At the same time, the self-styled Islamic State of fanatical fundamentalists beheaded, raped, enslaved and terrorised in the name of their extreme version of Islamic law. The Islamic State equipped themselves with modern weapons and the swords of ancient Muslim warriors, paraded threateningly in black apparel, and amassed ransoms from kidnappings. They massacred the populations of captured towns, and forced young women to become brides of warriors. By simply calling itself Islamic State, it harked back to the Middle Ages when Islam recognised no national boundaries. As in those distant times, its shadowy leader, Abu Bakr al-Baghdadi, called himself caliph (the civil and religious head of a Muslim state). They embarked on an all-or-nothing holy war to restore the supremacy of Islam, denying any free choice to the people over whom they held sway.

Foreign intervention only added to the chaos. The west demanded the departure of Assad, but he hung on with the help of air strikes by Russia, to which he had granted a naval base on the Mediterranean. The Syrian regime's power base was a Shi'a minority, so Shi'a-dominated Iran also intervened with arms and logistical support for Assad. The Sunni-orientated authorities in Saudi Arabia, Qatar and Turkey meanwhile supported some of the rebels – but not the Islamic State. The United States, for its part, bombed the Islamic State, while at the same time rallying international support for Assad to go.

To complicate matters further, the Islamic State overran a number of towns in Iraq, including the oil-producing centre of Mosul. American-trained soldiers of the Iraqi government ran away under attack, further discrediting the United States' attempt to establish a free and democratic state in Iraq.

Chaos and international crisis in Syria and parts of Iraq, yet another military dictatorship in Egypt, tribal lawlessness in Libya, sectarian conflict in Yemen, a particularly aggressive form of Islam propagated from Saudi Arabia, and chronic instability in Lebanon – the picture was so dismal that the liberating spirit of the Arab Spring may seem to have been well and truly extinguished.

Instead of liberty, fundamentalist Islamic movements offer religious certainty and the promise of a return to Islam's long-lost supremacy. However, rigid application of holy law did not curtail the decline of Islam in the past, and such regimes offer no promising vision for the future. Moreover, recent polls have indicated that the fundamentalists lack popular appeal: in December 2015, a survey of 18,300 people in 12 Middle Eastern countries showed 89 per cent rejected the Islamic State.[122] In Lebanon, Jordan and Iraq, which are directly concerned, the percentages were between 99 and 97 per cent. Another poll, conducted throughout the Muslim world in 2013, showed only 13 per cent approving the other main radical movement, Al-Qaeda, with 57 per cent against.[123]

Secular dictatorships likewise have poor records and offer little prospect of improving the lives of their subjects. There is, therefore, reason to believe that Arabs will one day resume their pursuit of freedom, democracy and human rights. Since the collapse of Communism in 1989, these principles have empowered people all over the world, in ways scarcely dreamed of before. That also goes for the Muslim world; over 200 million Muslims live within a democracy in Indonesia, while countless others experience their religion as spiritual sustenance and a guide to good behaviour, shunning the intolerant practices of the fundamentalists. Only the liberal path offers promise for the future.

Five years after the Tahrir uprising, one of its prominent personalities, the blogger Alaa Abd El Fattah, wrote from prison: "I have nothing to say: no hopes, no dreams, no fears, no warnings, no insights; nothing, absolutely nothing… Now tomorrow will be exactly like today and yesterday and all the days preceding and all the days following, I have no influence over anything."

But he added: "One thing I do remember, one thing I know: the sense of possibility was real. It may have been naïve to believe our dream could come true, but it was not foolish to believe that another world was possible. It really was."[124]

More than 2,000 years ago, the Roman statesman Cicero was more sanguine: "Whoever tries to govern a country through fear is quite mad. For no matter how much a tyrant might try to overturn the law and crush the spirit of freedom, sooner or later it will rise up again either through public outrage or the ballot box. Freedom suppressed and risen again bites with sharper teeth than if it had never been lost."[125]

The Challenge to Europe

Whether this will prove true in the Middle East will be determined by the people who live there, but the Arab Spring has already had an impact much further afield. In 2011, movements in London, Madrid and New York emulated the occupations of Tahrir Square in protests against malfunctioning of the global economy. On Wall Street, campaigners asked passers-by: "Are you ready for a Tahrir moment?"

Four years later, the aftermath had even more drastic ramifications in Europe. Europeans may have felt settled in their traditions of democracy and freedom, but in 2015 an influx of hundreds of thousands of refugees fleeing the war in Syria and Iraq, and a massive terrorist attack on Paris, shook this assurance to the core.

In the summer of that year, a trickle of migrants turned into a flood; soon long lines of Syrian and Iraqi refugees carrying nothing but what they could take on their backs were trudging along roads, footpaths, railways tracks and open countryside, fleeing the tyranny and killings in their homeland. They did so in the hope of finding sanctuary in a peaceful and prosperous part of the world with a humanitarian tradition.

Quite how humanitarian Europeans really were would be duly tested. Within the European Union, people could circulate freely, take up jobs in member countries, trade freely across frontiers and enjoy legal protection of their democratic rights. The continent had a compassionate tradition going back to the foundation of the Red Cross in 1863, and the succour given to refugees from war and dictatorship in the 20th century.

Yet freedom of movement within the European Union was complemented by a fortress policy towards the outside world, repelling migrants who sought to enter to find work – in theory, that is, since many slipped in regardless along Mediterranean coasts. When hundreds of migrants drowned as their rickety boats sank, public opinion became indignant that governments were callously ignoring their fate. So in 2015 European naval patrols started rescuing them and bringing them ashore in European ports.

Many Europeans thus felt moved to offer a warm reception when hundreds of thousands of Syrians and Iraqis – men, women and children – began trudging their way to safety through south-east Europe. Chancellor Angela Merkel made clear they were welcome to settle in Germany, where the economy was flourishing but the population was declining. Special trains and buses were laid on, and thousands of Germans came to stations to applaud the refugees and offer them hot soup, blankets, teddy bears, shelter and kind words.

As winter drew in, the refugees stumbling ashore after sea crossings on over-crowded rubber-boats were visibly exhausted, frozen and traumatised. After fraught crossings from Turkey to the Greek island of Lesbos, grandmothers and infants were helped to safety by local rescuers, who wrapped them in thermal sheets against hypothermia. Hundreds did not survive these sea journeys: most poignantly, the lifeless corpses of small children were found washed up on rocks or drifting in surf lapping sandy beaches.

After more than 20 years of peace and stability, Europeans were shocked to see their roads and fields clogged by haggard figures queuing in mud and squalor, waiting to be processed by officials struggling to cope with the teeming masses. The sheer numbers were staggering. The European Commission estimated that three million refugees would come by 2017, and Germany itself took in over a million by the end of 2015. Many made their way also to refugee-friendly Sweden, but by the end of that year, Swedish officials said there were no more parish halls, schools or gyms available for shelter, and the country had run out of mattresses.[126]

This sharp influx caused considerable unease among Europeans that the migrants would swamp public services, cost a fortune to support and increase insecurity. Politicians accused Angela Merkel of propagating a "welcome culture", and there were widespread calls for the flow to be "managed", "controlled" or even stopped. Czech President Milos Zeman condemned the migration as "an organised invasion".

Barely had he spoken these hard words than gunmen of the Islamic State launched lethal attacks in Paris on the evening of Friday 13th November 2015, killing 130 people in outdoor restaurants and a rock concert hall over a period of several hours. It was the worst carnage in the French capital since World War II.

Inside the concert hall, the gunmen told their hapless victims they were avenging French air attacks on the Islamic State in Syria, but on a broader level it was an attack on France as a symbol of liberty. Paris on that Friday evening represented everything the Islamic State abhorred – men and women happily indulging in free conversation, tolerance, diversity, laughter, music and free love.

Europeans' first reaction was to refuse to bow to religious bigots, to go on with their lives regardless and to close ranks in solidarity with the common cause of freedom. When English organisers offered to call off a friendly football match between England and France a few days later in London, the French Football Association declined. When the French team management told French players they could pull out of the match, none did so. On the night, players of both nations lined up shoulder to shoulder, and London's Wembley Stadium was lit with France's red, white and blue tricolour. Screens displayed the slogan of the French Revolution, *Liberté, Egalité, Fraternité*, and the English crowd sang France's *Marseillaise* national anthem – in French.

Merkel fought back against her doubters by arguing that the refugees were so cruelly persecuted in Syria that they had little choice but to flee. To her critics in Germany she retorted: "If we start having to apologise for showing a friendly face in emergencies, then this is not my country… I have my vision and I will fight for it."[127] The German leader admitted the challenge was tough, but declared: "We can do it."

Many Europeans agreed with her, and continued to devote enormous resources to providing shelter and care for the never-ending flow of refugees. German theatres temporarily housed new arrivals, arranged professional advice and put on performances about their plight. European aid organisations rushed heated tents to protect thousands of migrants stranded amid ice and snow on the long trek across the Balkans.

Then, early in 2016, opinion polls started turning against the migrants after hundreds of women complained that they had been molested by asylum-seeking men of Middle Eastern and north African origin at a New Year celebration in Cologne. Did this signal that the refugees were undermining Europe's liberal values by importing repressive attitudes towards women? Political leaders reacted by abandoning their tolerance of cultural diversity in favour of new rules obliging immigrants to conform more strictly to local customs and laws. In Britain, it was pointed out that 22 per cent of Muslim women speak little or no English, often because their menfolk dissuade them. Although it could not be determined for sure who carried out the Cologne harassment, opinion-makers also spoke out against Muslim tribunals in Europe which treated women less liberally than state courts.

More urgently, public opinion demanded action to stem the flow of migrants. From the end of 2015, Hungary, Serbia, Croatia, Slovenia, Bulgaria, Greece, Britain and Spain were all protecting parts of their borders with rolls of razor-wire or wire fences. Long traffic queues began to build up at frontiers as states temporarily re-imposed identity checks for the first time in nearly 20 years, undermining the Schengen agreement, which otherwise allows over 400 million Europeans in 26 states to cross borders without being stopped.

The cause of greater security thus began restricting one of Europe's most significant freedoms – to travel around without being controlled. Ill-tempered, competing national interests began to threaten the whole principle of cooperation within a European Union based on common liberal ideas.

To prevent Europe disintegrating into national states sealed off from each other, leaders demanded that Europe secure its thousands of miles of external frontiers. "If Europe is not capable of protecting its own frontiers, it is the very idea of Europe that will be questioned," said French Prime Minister Manuel Valls. "The European project can die, not in decades or years, but very fast." Italian Prime Minister Matteo Renzi, complaining of lack of leadership, added bleakly: "Europe has gone missing in action."[128] Several years later little had changed.

Yet not everybody was so pessimistic. Some pointed out that the three million expected refugees represented less than one per cent of the European Union's population of 508 million, and include professionals capable of plugging labour shortages. Statistics also showed that immigrants eventually pay more taxes than locals, and London was cited as a multicultural city that is particularly thriving. Others believed Europe would never be able to stop the flow of migrants, and should focus instead on integrating them to good effect.

There was also an awareness of the drawbacks of abandoning freedom of movement across borders, to which citizens had grown accustomed. Conscious that their controls hindered commuting and transport of goods, border police in some places began filtering traffic at rush hours through selective spot checks.

By 2018, the tide in Europe was swinging further against those who wanted to stand up for liberty and welcome refugees from oppression. Voters were electing politicians set on curbing immigration in Britain, Italy, Austria, Hungary, Poland, the Czech Republic and Slovenia (but less so in Germany, France and Spain). The solidarity between member states of the European Union, which underpinned freedom of movement on the continent, began to crumble as states refused to cooperate in sharing the newcomers around, leaving Mediterranean states such as Italy and Greece to cope with enormous numbers. It is a division of opinions which has occurred many times in the fight for freedom.

This turmoil, taking place on a continent that prides itself as the heart of liberal civilisation, can be traced back to the Arab Spring. The Islamic State was spawned by the war in Syria, which itself began with children emulating revolutionary slogans they heard from demonstrators in Tahrir Square. That the aftershocks of the uprisings should also test Europe's values to the very core was an astonishing outcome that nobody foresaw.

CHAPTER 16

FIGHTING FOR FREEDOM TODAY – TRIUMPH AND DEFEAT

It is not power that corrupts but fear.
- Aung San Suu Kyi, 1991

Times have changed, the people have changed.
– Aung San Suu Kyi, 2015

A Lonely, Dusty Road

J ust a few days before the Islamic State delivered a devastating blow against one of Europe's great liberal civilisations in 2015, a 70-year-old woman won a glorious victory for freedom on the other side of the world. After 25 years of house arrest, discrimination and harassment, Aung San Suu Kyi triumphed in free elections in Myanmar (formerly Burma) and put an end to over half a century of military dictatorship. However her tale is a cautionary one about a hero's rise and fall.

Aung San Suu Kyi first took up the fight for freedom in the hallowed precincts of the University of Oxford, where men and women students were then segregated. They were obliged to be back in their respective colleges by 10pm and thereafter the gates were locked. By time-honoured tradition, most students felt compelled to break this rule and clamber back over the college walls after curfew. Not wishing to be excluded, Aung San Suu Kyi duly did her illicit late-night climbing but, unlike many of her fellow women students, she did not treat it as an amusing escapade. Aung San Suu Kyi did it for the principle.

Never again would she find it so easy to fight for freedom. She encountered one setback after another as she struggled to bring liberty and democracy to a country where such principles had scarcely ever been observed.

From a very early age, destiny beckoned. Her father Aung San led Burma to independence from Britain in 1948, but his path too was anything but straightforward. After the Japanese chased the British out of the country in 1942, Aung San fought briefly alongside the invaders as an anti-imperialist, but when the British started winning again, he changed sides.

To some this was opportunistic, but to his daughter it was merely a change in tactics in pursuit of the overriding goal of independence. With the war finished, the British hoped they could persuade the Burmese general to accept some form of autonomy while remaining in the British Empire, but Aung San insisted on full independence and the British conceded.

As with other former colonies, freedom from empire did not necessarily mean liberty from oppression. Just before independence in 1948, Aung San was shot dead by a jealous rival, and the new state came under strain from Communist insurgencies and its ethnic complexity. Besides the Burmese, the country is also populated by Kachin, Karens, Chinese, Bengalis and Rohinghyas, who have an uneasy relationship with the central government – such that today some 800,000 of its 55 million people are stateless.

As quarrels intensified among civilian politicians,

the military seized power, did away with parliamentary democracy and ruled the country on their own from 1962 to 2011. At first, they sought to push through a socialist revolution, but abandoned this when it led to economic crisis. The army leaders put down uprisings by students and Buddhist monks with increasing severity, and by the end of the 1980s they were in an impasse – unpopular at home and with no friends left abroad.

Aung San Suu Kyi's moment had come. Born in 1945, she had lived outside the country since the age of 15. In 1988 she returned home from Oxford to take over leadership of the National League for Democracy (NLD), and two years later stood in elections in opposition to the military government. It was anything but a fair campaign. On one occasion, an army captain ordered his soldiers to shoot unless Aung San Suu Kyi and her followers stopped walking down a road. She made her followers stand back and walked on alone towards the soldiers until, at the very last moment, a senior officer countermanded the order.

The NLD won a landslide victory with more than four-fifths of the seats in Parliament, but the military refused to accept the result, prevented Parliament from convening and placed Aung San Suu Kyi under house arrest. Apart from a few brief relaxations, she was confined to her home for the next 20 years. When her British husband Michael Aris was dying from cancer in England, the regime declined to give him a visa to visit her. When a cyclone blew off the roof of her home and cut its electricity, the military refused her a generator. For much of the time, she was not even allowed to receive visitors.

In response to continuing repression, the United States and the European Union applied sanctions against Myanmar, while the United Nations passed resolutions condemning human rights violations. Realising it was again blocked at home and abroad, the military regime released Aung San Suu Kyi in 2010 and, two years later, she was among 43 NLD candidates who won a by-election for 45 seats in Parliament.

While restrictions on the NLD were progressively relaxed, the military retained control of the organs of government and imposed a constitution banning anybody with foreign offspring from standing for the presidency. They thought that would prevent Aung San Suu Kyi from coming to power, since her two sons are British citizens. The military also reserved a quarter of seats in Parliament for unelected soldiers, who could be counted on to vote as a block. Moreover, with the generals still ruling in the run-up to new elections in 2015, she depended on their grudging willingness to let her campaign freely.

Aung San Suu Kyi also depended on the readiness of her people to seize their chance. During her long years of captivity, she came to believe that fear was the greatest obstacle hindering the people from fighting for freedom. In Myanmar, they had plenty to dread in the form of repression by the military dictatorship, but in a country with a volatile ethnic mix, they also feared for their own cultural identities should liberalisation unleash dangerous forces. The danger Aung San Suu Kyi saw was that her people would sink into apathy because of these fears. "Democracy, like liberty and justice, is not 'given', it is earned through courage, resolution and sacrifice," she declared, adding that, "it is not power that corrupts but fear."

In this, she was echoing two eminent predecessors: Franklin D. Roosevelt and Gandhi. In 1933, when millions of Americans were suffering in the Depression, Roosevelt

declared: "The only thing we have to fear is fear itself –
nameless, unreasoning, unjustified terror."[130] From Gandhi
came the sentiment: "The greatest gift for an individual or a
nation… is abhaya, fearlessness, not merely bodily courage
but absence of fear from the mind."[131] For Myanmar's
military, apathy born of fear was not unwelcome. For a
freedom fighter such as Aung San Suu Kyi, it was a curse.

Thus, nine months before the elections, her prospects of
gaining power were far from certain. However, as she trudged
along Myanmar's dusty roads and wended her way along its
twisting rivers, campaigning for freedom, democracy and a
"revolution of the spirit", it became clear that she retained
the allegiance of her people as much as when she first led her
party to election victory in 1990.

In November 2015, her NLD party won more than
two-thirds of the seats in Parliament, thus rendering the
block of non-elected officers impotent to restrain her
activities. The candidates who stood for election in the
party supporting the military won only 41 out of 664 seats,
and the landslide meant that Aung San Suu Kyi's party
could select a new president of its choice, though not by
obtaining a waiver of the constitutional bar to herself. The
election result was a defeat for the concept of "disciplined
democracy" promoted by the generals, and a decisive
victory for the free democracy for which Aung San Suu Kyi
sacrificed her own liberty for 20 years.

Her path to freedom was similar to that of Nelson
Mandela. Both were obliged to spend more than two decades
in the prime of their lives under arrest. Both bent repressive
regimes to their wills while languishing in captivity, and in
1991 Aung San Suu Kyi too won the Nobel Peace Prize. The
main difference between Mandela and Aung San Suu Kyi was

the latter kept to the path of nonviolence, acknowledging Gandhi as her inspiration.

After she assumed her country's leadership, it remained to be seen whether Aung San Suu Kyi would emulate Nelson Mandela also in using her newly won freedom to govern wisely, inclusively and tolerantly. In that however, she sorely disappointed. From 2015, the Burmese military launched a savage campaign of ethnic cleansing forcing hundreds of thousands of the Muslim Rohingya minority in the north to flee to neighbouring Bangladesh. Thousands were killed, raped and tortured and their villages were burned. While the military were clearly calling the shots, Aung San Suu Kyi apparently did nothing to hinder them, nor did she speak out on behalf of the victims. Indeed, she reacted angrily to protests from international leaders and humanitarian organisations, leading to speculation that she was siding with anti-Rohingya ethnic Burman nationalists.

Within a few years therefore, Aung San Suu Kyi lost her international reputation as a champion of liberty. In Oxford, she was stripped of her Freedom of the City award, and her old college at the University took down her portrait. The moral of this cautionary tale is that heroes of the fight for freedom may not be admirable people in themselves. Churchill was the man of the moment in World War II, but his political career was otherwise mediocre and he opposed freedom for the peoples of the British Empire. Aung San Suu Kyi undeniably fought for her people's freedom, but since succeeding she has omitted to use her authority to resist tyranny.

Russia and Ukraine

Unabashedly at the authoritarian end of the spectrum is a Russian leader who represses rather than tolerates, excludes rather than reaches out, generates conflict rather than harmony, and engages in armed intervention rather than democratic consensus. Russia's Vladimir Putin is motivated by the exercise of power, not freedom.

After the collapse of the Soviet Union in 1991, the world assumed that Russia had accepted a post-Cold War international settlement based on democracy, fundamental liberties and cooperation. The former east European satellites of the Soviet Union joined the European Union based on these principles, and the demise of Communism ended ideological disagreement.

However, the east European states doubted whether they could really trust Russia, and all joined NATO (North Atlantic Treaty Organisation) – the western defence alliance. Putin's past as a lieutenant-colonel of the Soviet KGB secret police lent weight to their suspicions, all the more since he soon made clear he rejected the post-Cold War consensus.

Presiding over Russia's fortunes since 1999, he projected a tough authority which struck a chord with his compatriots. Gorbachev allowed his authority to be freely challenged in public, and when he appeared on television debating with his opponents, Russians saw him as vacillating. Putin, by contrast, satisfied their desire for a strong leader who protected them from a hostile world and cherished their sense of great nationhood. To promote his hard, masculine image, Putin had himself photographed, stripped to the waist, striding over rugged terrain with a powerful hunting rifle and practising manly sports.

In building his power, Putin progressively eliminated political opponents. Banned from most of the Russian media, they were eased out of public life and in some cases killed. In 2006, journalist Anna Politkovskaya, an outspoken critic of the regime, was murdered in her apartment, where she was writing articles about Russia's controversial war in Chechnya. Alexander Litvinenko, a former secret service officer investigating organised Russian crime, suffered an agonising death from polonium radiation in the same year, after fleeing to London. A British public inquiry subsequently determined that he was murdered by a Russian secret service operation "probably" approved by Putin. Another former Russian agent living in Britain, Sergei Skripal, narrowly escaped with his life in 2018 after poisoning by a nerve agent. Again the British authorities pointed the finger at Russia.

Then in 2015, the most prominent political opponent, Boris Nemtsov, was gunned down on a bridge in the centre of Moscow. A former Deputy Prime Minister, Nemtsov was a charismatic figure who relentlessly criticised Putin's autocratic rule, laxity over corruption and troublemaking in Ukraine. He was killed a few days before he was due to address a protest rally. His close associate, Alexei Navalny, was repeatedly imprisoned and barred from standing for presidential election in 2018. Under such circumstances, democratic opposition was all but impossible. None of the murders were satisfactorily resolved, causing surviving opponents to fear for their lives.

In the winters of 2011 and 2012, crowds of up to 100,000 protested in Moscow against elections they claimed were fraudulent. But they were ineffective: police beat and detained ringleaders and in 2013 the protests fizzled out. They showed that the educated middle classes in the capital disliked Putin's autocracy, but only in St. Petersburg were there other large demonstrations. In the rest of Russia, which has almost never been ruled democratically, the campaign for a more liberal society raised few, if any, passions.

From 2008, Putin began flexing his muscles abroad, sending Russian troops into Georgia – a former Soviet state on the Black Sea – in order to dissuade it from rapprochement with the United States. Putin declared contemptuously that he wanted to hang the American-educated Georgian President, Mikheil Saakashvili, by his testicles.[133] Georgia backed down and ceded disputed territory to Russia; power politics triumphed, and the Georgian people were left with no say.

Next Putin turned his attention to a neighbouring country that Russian leaders have never quite accepted as independent. Lying along the south-west borders of Russia, Ukraine is a large country with a tormented history. The name means "borderland" and it was fortified by the Russian Tsars in the 18th century to protect themselves against foreign invaders. In the 1930s, Stalin persuaded himself that its peasants were disloyal to the Soviet Union, and subjected them to mass starvation by seizing their grain and selling it on foreign markets. Over three million perished as a result, in a country of rich arable soil.

When German armed forces invaded Ukraine in World War II, part of the Ukrainian population welcomed them as liberators, but after the Nazis were thrust back, returning Soviet security police meted out savage retribution. Between Russia and Ukraine there has been much bad blood.

Khrushchev, himself an ethnic Russian from Ukraine, sought to defuse the animosity in 1954 by allotting the Black Sea peninsula of Crimea to Ukraine, in the hope that this would bind Ukraine more closely into the Soviet Union.[134]

In 1994, after the Soviet Union broke up, Crimea remained within newly independent Ukraine, which in return decommissioned its nuclear weapons and allowed Russian warships to stay in Crimean ports. It seemed a tidy solution.

Until 2004, Ukraine was ruled by men of the post-Soviet mould: close to Moscow, amassing riches through corruption and allowing the population little chance to evolve freely. In presidential elections that year, however, the people took matters into their own hands. At first a pro-Moscow candidate was declared to have triumphed over the liberal front-runner, Viktor Yushchenko, but it was evident there had been widespread vote rigging, and huge crowds waving orange flags turned out in driving sleet in the capital of Kiev to protest. A re-run was ordered and, when Yuschenko was taken ill with dioxin poisoning, the "Orange Revolution" burst out with renewed force. Yushchenko won the new election and began opening up to the west to unleash his people's potential.

That brief taste of freedom soon turned sour, as the government foundered in futile quarrels. In 2010, Yushchenko's opponent of six years earlier, Viktor Yanukovych, was elected in his place, and Ukraine once again fell into step with Russia. Corruption continued, jerry-built buildings from the Soviet era crumbled away, roads became pitted with potholes, oligarchs manipulated the media, and one of the leading lights of the "Orange Revolution", Yulia Tymoshenko, was put in prison. Young people had little opportunity to learn foreign languages, no money to travel and no visas for western countries. They were imprisoned in a repressive, decaying society.

Pent-up demand for an opening to the west intensified, however, and in 2013 Yanukovych declared readiness to sign a Cooperation Agreement with the European Union. For Putin, that was too much. That the Ukrainian people may have wanted such a rapprochement was of no concern to him: he interpreted the move only as a geopolitical challenge to Russia's influence.

Putin forced Yanukovych to renege, prompting a new uprising on the streets of Kiev and a return of the protesting crowds of 2004, this time waving banners of the European Union. All over the world, television viewers watched a mass of shadowy figures, milling around barricades lit by flickering flames, on the dark February nights of 2014. Riot police with truncheons and metal shields tried to push the main square clear, but had to retreat. Factions negotiated, agreements were announced and then promptly broken, and all at once it turned nasty. Yanukovych decreed emergency laws and snipers on rooftops killed several dozen people. A pizza restaurant opened its doors as a clinic, and a hotel and a shoe shop served as makeshift morgues.

Then, all of a sudden, it was over. The police disappeared abruptly on 23rd February, and the next thing anybody knew was that Yanukovych had fled. One moment he was president, with luxurious trappings and a legion of security forces; the next he had vanished on a plane, his protectors merging innocuously back into the civilian population. He later turned up in Rostov-on-Don in Russia and disappeared from view. In Kiev, Parliament convened and began preparing a new election.

The uprisings of 2004 and 2014 were classical revolutions for freedom. Over a few giddy days and nights, Ukrainians rose up en masse to rid themselves of despotism, and in 2014 they took a decisive step towards a society based on the liberal principles of the European Union. This was unacceptable to a Russian leader for whom Ukraine was always a strategic "borderland", and Putin had his next move ready.

As soon as the 2014 Sochi Winter Olympics on the Russian Black Sea were over, armed men in balaclavas began to appear at key points of Crimea. They occupied cities, airports, army bases and the port of Sevastopol, where the Russian Black Sea fleet was based. They wore no badges on their military fatigues, but their weapons were modern, they were well organised and they spoke Russian. They were obviously special services sent from Russia and operating clandestinely.

Putin blandly asserted to alarmed western leaders that the interlopers were locals who bought their uniforms in stores. He did not expect to be believed and made it clear that he did not care. He alleged that Russians in Ukraine were under threat, which was not apparent to anybody else, but bore a nasty resemblance to Hitler's similar claims of threats to Germans in Czechoslovakia before he invaded that country in 1939.

Within a week or so, Crimea was under the control of the gunmen. Shortly afterwards, to popular acclamation in Moscow and Crimea, Putin formally incorporated the territory back into Russia. Western leaders protested and refused to recognise the transfer, but Putin correctly calculated they would do nothing to stop him, and his bravado won him kudos with the Russian public. To strike fear into local objectors, a Russian court sentenced Oleg Sentsov, a prominent Ukrainian film director who organised protests there, to 20 years imprisonment in Siberia. When the soccer World Cup started in Russia in June 2018, Sentsov had been on hunger strike for 32 days.

Next, similar gunmen began appearing in eastern

Ukraine, where much of the population was ethnically Russian, and the central government lost control of the south-east corner, including the regional capital of Donetsk. When the new government in Kiev held presidential elections on 25th May 2014, rebels prevented the poll from taking place in the east. By contrast, in the western half of the country, bands played the national anthem, priests recited the Lord's Prayer and women wept as they cast their votes.[135] After years of corrupt, authoritarian rule, people in that part of the country once again saw a vision of freedom.

The west imposed economic sanctions on Russia, which certainly hurt, but Putin gambled that he had achieved his goal; he had made it clear that if Ukraine wanted to be independent and close to the west, he could render part of it ungovernable. Thereby, he took Russia back to its old role of asserting power through military force, now reinforced by a modernised nuclear arsenal and international cyber-warfare.

Western leaders realised that a chasm had opened up. German Chancellor Angela Merkel, brought up under the Communists, declared that the Ukraine crisis was over values – in this case, the right of a people to freedom and self-determination. She insisted on the inviolability of individual human dignity, and added: "From that grows acknowledgement of one's freedom and self-realisation, of freedom of opinion and art. Russia is setting other accents, as we see not only in the Ukraine crisis."[136]

Vladimir Putin did indeed intend to upset the apple cart. By seizing the Crimean peninsula and a pocket of eastern Ukraine, he tore up the post-1989 settlement in Europe and indicated his ambition to rival the United States as a superpower. First in Georgia, then in Crimea and Ukraine, and later in intervening in the Syrian war, he was trying to reassert Russia's influence and push back the west.

Instead of a system based on cooperation and respect for people's democratic choices, Putin, smarting with offended Russian pride, resurrected the old concept of nations engaged in a Darwinian struggle for superiority. Contrasting his authoritarian principles with "effete" western democracy, Putin returned to the practices of Russia (and other great powers) before World War I, under which the fates of nations were determined by governing elites regardless of the people's choice.

Underlying this vision of inevitable great power conflict is a deep scepticism about the ability of individuals to exercise freedom. It also ignores that the outcome of a dispute can be a win for both sides. Putin's is the zero-sum philosophy, under which one side can win only at the expense of the other.

Among Russian masses cynical about the merits of freedom, such a strong-arm approach found favour, but most Ukrainians uncoupled themselves from Russian ways of thinking. In the west of the country, they were aware that neighbouring Poland, Slovakia and Hungary, as members of the European Union, had established democracies and grown their economies much faster than Ukraine's. An opinion poll in 2015 showed that only 30 per cent of Ukrainians still felt positive towards Russia, compared with 88 per cent in 2013.[137] Throughout Ukraine, people desired more access to the open world, freer travel, freedom from abuse of authority and more opportunities to learn English. They had none of these and, while Russia could not fulfil these wishes, the European Union could.

Whether the European Union *wanted* to do much for Ukraine, however, was another matter, since none of its member governments envisaged Ukraine as a full member in the foreseeable future. Its legal system, economy and living standards remained out of kilter, and EU states showed little willingness to relieve its grinding poverty. Nor was Ukraine likely to be admitted as a full member to NATO, since this would imply a readiness by other NATO states to make war on Russia in order to protect it. However, for people who have twice gone to the barricades in this century, only the west could offer the sort of freedoms the Ukrainian people have struggled for.

In June 2014, newly elected president, Petro Poroshenko, duly signed the Cooperation Agreement with the European Union, and in September his party won the largest number of seats in Parliament. Russia refused to recognise the new Ukrainian government, and its undeclared clandestine war in the east ground on, ruining towns and villages and killing over 6,000 people.[138] By the end of 2015, Putin had destroyed the rule of Ukrainian law in the eastern part of the country, but failed to offer its suffering people there a viable substitute.

Putin denied any involvement by Russian troops but, according to an investigation by Boris Nemtsov, several hundred regular Russian soldiers were among the casualties. By the time his report was published in May 2015, Nemtsov too was dead.

CHAPTER 17

FIGHTING ON

Man is free at the moment he wishes to be.
– Voltaire

The fight for freedom has swung to and fro for 2,500 years: freedom is there, and then it is not. Will there ever be a winner in the endless struggle between those who desire it and those who do not? In recent years, popular uprisings in the Arab world have overthrown tyrants but led to chaos and massacres, and a Russian strongman has emerged to assert the principle that might is right. If the fight for freedom is a roller coaster, it may be argued we are on a downward plunge.

Up to 30 million people today are slaves, according to various estimates, and it costs as little as $90 to buy a human being.[139] Many bonded labourers from south Asia building skyscrapers in the Gulf owe their first year's wages to a recruitment agent, and during this time their money and passports are withheld. In India alone, 452,679 cases of child trafficking for domestic labour were reported between 2008 and 2012, and the Thai fishing industry is said to rely on "systematic and pervasive" use of forced labour from Myanmar and Cambodia.[140]

Fundamental Islamists reject freedom of opinion and tyrannise blameless people with holy wars, while their regressive societies discriminate against women. Nuclear-armed North Korea cruelly regiments its people and threatens its neighbours. China denies its 1.4 billion citizens political liberties, and Africa, despite having put the worst behind it, still exposes millions of inhabitants to exploitation and persecution. Even Americans and Europeans, who championed freedom in the past, have elected populist leaders who care more for aggressively asserted national interests than shared liberal values.

Every day the media serves up fresh reports of oppression, but we should beware of the media's natural focus on the negative. If a woman is stoned to death in a remote village, it is normal that a journalist should report that rather than the uneventful lives of millions of liberated women elsewhere. The media earn their living by reporting the exceptional and the shocking, but that does not mean they convey an accurate overall view of reality.

In fact, the balance between liberty and oppression is not entirely weighted against liberty. On the contrary, over the centuries the achievements of those who have fought for freedom have been immense. Starting with the Athenians' victory over the Persians in 480 BC, there has been one advance after another: Magna Carta protected against abuse of sovereign power, Parliament involved ordinary people in government, Americans devised a regime based on fundamental liberties and rights, Enlightenment thinkers defeated religious dogmatism through reason, and the French Revolution overthrew a monarchy misruling by divine right.

In more recent times, Allied armies liberated Europe from Nazi totalitarianism, Gandhi put an end to British rule in India through civil disobedience, Mandela defeated apartheid in South Africa, peaceful protesters brought down

Communist dictatorships in eastern Europe, and women made big advances in winning equal rights, as did the black community in America. Hardly any nation now seeks to impose its law and culture over foreign peoples, as in the days of imperial rule.

Even the appalling fact that some 30 million people today are slaves reflects some improvement on times when slaves made up a substantial part of mankind. In a world of 7.2 billion people, 30 million is a tragically large number, but it represents a much smaller proportion of the population than it once did. Slavery was the norm for much of human history, but in the 19th and 20th centuries Wilberforce, Lincoln, Martin Luther King and others banished it to the fringes of world society. In this respect, the world has made giant steps forwards. Millions of people who would quite normally have spent their lives in servitude now evolve as free individuals.

This persistent expansion of the boundaries of freedom, in the face of countless obstacles, indicates a fundamental urge to be free in the human psyche. If that were not so, liberty would not have prevailed, since plenty of people have wanted to restrain it – to protect vested interests, conquer empires, enforce religious beliefs or to impose political ideologies. Some people also resist freedom out of fear – of their neighbours, another ethnic group or another state – or because they do not feel up to the challenge of acting freely. Erich Fromm, a Jewish psychoanalyst who fled Nazi tyranny, asserted in 1941 that Germans supported Hitler because they preferred to submit to a strongman, rather than choose freedom fraught with dangers and unwelcome responsibilities.[141]

Post-war Germans embraced liberty, nonetheless, but Fromm was right in noticing that some people just did not want freedom. If life has moved against you and there seems little chance of doing better, liberty may seem a bitterly hollow promise. Believing that freedom is an illusion comforts the pessimist in his hopelessness. As Voltaire put it, "man is free at the moment he wishes to be" – but not otherwise. By contrast, an optimist confident in mankind's capacity for good is likely to welcome the opportunities that freedom offers.

We may wish to be free, but we know that we can never achieve it totally. Willingly we forego some liberties for the sake of protection – against murder or theft, for example – or because we give precedence to social justice. The constraints of law and order provide stability, justice, a safe framework for one's life and protection against mankind's baser instincts. We must forever live somewhere between freedom and restriction.

For hundreds of years, societies have been trying to establish an appropriate balance. John Locke asserted that governments should exercise power over citizens on the basis of a freely consented social contract, and John Stuart Mill argued that liberty should never be curtailed unless it is shown to do harm. Other societies are less trustful, putting more emphasis on security and order, but this has serious drawbacks. An authoritarian ruler, claiming to keep chaos at bay, typically imprisons large numbers of people, stifles debate and rejects new thinking that might benefit his people. The law and order camp is safe but fearful, well-regulated but confining, stable but stultifying.

Freedom, by contrast, is bold and innovative. Enterprising spirits have never been content to sit in safety. Since earliest times, people have been ready to take risks, think the unthinkable, push the boundaries of the permissible, and make use of a capacity unique to us humans.

As in the times of the Gutenberg printing press, new and ever-more sophisticated communication technology is helping the freedom fighters. Social media such as Twitter and Facebook enable anybody with an internet connection, or a mobile device, to spread news and views around the world. In parts of rural Asia and Africa, where 30 years ago people knew very little beyond their immediate environment, today hundreds of millions of people can exchange information with unparalleled freedom. People no longer depend on mainstream media for their information or forming opinions. Through social media, everybody can act as a journalist – news often breaks first on Twitter.

As always, authorities try to suppress or censor what people say in the media, and new social media platforms are not immune. China has partly succeeded in doing this (so far), but elsewhere authorities struggle to put the genie of free expression back into the bottle. In Thailand, a military government that seized power in a coup blocked Facebook for a few hours, but stopped after an outcry among the country's 24 million users. Even when governments manage to control the flood of free information, new means of dissemination are constantly invented. People are awed by their new powers and do not want to give them up.

Able now to converse freely on a massive scale, people no longer always need to fight to achieve liberty. Increasingly, they assume their freedom and invent new ways of living without reference to laws, policy or theory. The masses have taken to social media without the experts understanding what is at stake, and have adopted the new practices as individuals, regardless of whether the societies they live in are liberal or authoritarian.

For better or for worse, people increasingly shape their

own lives and citizens do not wish to be ruled from the top down. Terms of address amongst people have become more familiar, and schools increasingly teach pupils how to think, not just to learn. While experts debate the pros and cons, doctors and families discreetly practise euthanasia if they judge a person is suffering intolerably. Freedom pervades our lives, whether we like it or not. "Just do it" is a slogan known the world over.

There will always however be an inherent conflict between freedom and authority. Freedom in itself is neither good nor bad, and it is vain to believe that a liberal order is pre-ordained. There will always be those who believe mankind's evil tendencies need to be curbed by authoritarian rule, whether or not the people agree.

As in 1940, when nearly all Europe was suppressed by Nazi tyranny, liberty at times may seem banished forever. However if history has any continuity, it teaches us that freedom fighters will always return. The story of this book is of freedom advancing as if on a ratchet, with gains outweighing setbacks in the long run. Nothing is ever granted: freedom will always have to be fought for. But we can be sure that a large number of people will keep striving for it, aware that this is one of their basic functions as a human being. By definition it will be out of control, and it offers no utopia, but it presents the chance to realise one's life to the full.

North America, the British Isles and continental Europe generally enjoy the greatest liberty and democracy, but although the fight for freedom started earlier in the west, it has not been confined to that part of the world. Moreover, western nations are no paragons: nearly all at one time or another restrained the liberties of other peoples. Gandhi, Martin Luther King and Mandela achieved their great victories precisely in liberating their peoples from white domination. India has established the world's largest democracy and even in China, the people have shown they will rise up against oppression when given the chance. The desire for liberty knows no geographical boundaries.

The struggle for freedom has brought the greatest benefits to mankind when accompanied by tolerance, respect for others and goodwill. Many of the great freedom fighters have come from backgrounds where education, religious upbringing or leadership positions have conditioned them to feel concern for others. The great Athenians were philosophers, an Archbishop of Canterbury drafted Magna Carta, Enlightenment intellectuals drew up America's Declaration of Independence, Gandhi was trained in law and Hindu wisdom, Martin Luther King had a university doctorate, Nelson Mandela was the educated son of a traditional chief, and Aung Sang Suu Kyi graduated from Oxford.

When a vacuum of power is instead filled by leaders unconcerned for the well-being of their people, the outcome of a fight for freedom can be disastrous; as was the case for a few years during the French Revolution, for 30 to 40 years in newly independent Africa, and today in parts of the Middle East. In communities that have remained primitive, people are more likely to be cynical, suspicious and barely aware of interests beyond their own society. So when authority is taken away, they may choose to revert to clan rivalry or religious conflict rather than liberty, as happened several hundred years ago also in today's more liberal societies. We can thus be thankful for the people who fought for freedom for noble reasons, and made good use of it. Among them are some of the finest spirits in history.

Let us therefore acclaim those who let freedom ring

from the mountainsides, who sang hymns as they were burnt at the stake for their beliefs, who shackled themselves to railings to win votes for women, who spoke out against Nazism when nobody else dared, who inspired people to give "blood, sweat and tears" for liberty, who took to the streets against the might of the Soviet Red Army, who held up tanks in Beijing armed only with shopping bags, who braved threatening rifles to campaign for democracy, and all the other unknown men and women who, at one time or another, risked everything in the cause of freedom.

Such heroes make humans special. In seeking freedom as they did, they have lent hope and vigour to the human race.

If you have enjoyed this book, the author would welcome a review on Amazon.

ENDNOTES

1. Berlin, Isaiah, *Two Concepts of Liberty,* Oxford University Press, 1969

2. Strauss, Barry, *The Battle of Salamis,* Simon & Schuster, New York, 2004, pp 59, 61, 65

3. As related by the Greek playwright Aeschylus, who took part in the battle.

4. Strauss, op.cit. p 247

5. Demosthenes, *Third Philippic, 31*

6. Cicero, *Pro Cluentio,* 53, 146; Marcus Aurelius, *The Meditations,* Book 1

7. Battles of Bibracte and Vesontio

8. Plutarch's Lives, Everyman's Edition, 1910, reprinted 1953, (Dryden translation), vol. ii, p 551

9. This draws on the account of Boadicea's uprising by the Roman historian Tacitus, the son-in-law of Gnaeus Julius Agricola, a military tribune who served in Britain at the time.

10. Decimate is derived from the Latin decem, which means ten.

11. Strauss, Barry, *The Spartacus War,* Phoenix, 2009, p 165

12. Luke 6:20, 24, Matthew 19:24

13. Cf Crossan, John Dominic, *Jesus,* ebook

14. 1 Corinthians 14:14-15

15. Muller, Herbert J., *Freedom in the Ancient World,* Secker & Warburg, 1961, pp 263, 310

16. www.huffingtonpost.com/cullen-murphy/10-questions-about-the-inquisition_b_1224406.html

17. Raphael's Madonna hangs in the Zwinger gallery in Dresden, and Fra Filippo Lippi's in the Uffizi museum in Florence.

18. Begun in 1559, the Index was finally abolished in 1966.

19. Reed, T.J., *Light in Germany*, University of Chicago Press, 2015, p 6

20. Hampson, Norman, *The Enlightenment*, 1990, ebook

21. A Royal Charter granted to the first settlement in Jamestown, Virginia.

22. Rousseau, Jean-Jacques, *On the Origin of the Inequality of Mankind*, Second Part

23. Thomas Jefferson, drafter of the American Declaration of Independence, was U.S. ambassador to France at the time.

24. Mill, John Stuart, *On Liberty*, John D. Parker and Son, London, 1859

25. www.victorianweb.org/history/riots/luddites.html

26. Reed, John, *Ten Days That Shook The World*, Penguin, 1926, p 108

27. Black, Jeremy, *Slavery: a New Global History*, Robinson, London, 2011, p 14

28. Black, op.cit. pp 7-17

29. http://www.bbc.co.uk/history/british/empire_seapower/white_slaves_01.shtml

30. Library of Congress, The Thomas Jefferson Papers, http://memory.loc.gov/ammem/collections/jefferson_papers/mtjprece.html

31. International Museum of Slavery, Liverpool

32. Black, op.cit. pp 22-9

33. Kolchin Peter, *American Slavery 1619-1877*, Penguin, 1993, p 126

34. Kolchin, op.cit. pp 33, 38, 52

35. Welles, Jonathan, *The Complete History of Slaves*, ebook

36. Abbott, Elizabeth, *Haiti: An insider's history of the rise and fall of the Duvaliers*, Simon & Schuster, 1988, p viii

37. Study by University College of London, published by The Independent, 24 February 2013, and Welles, op.cit.

38. Kristof, Nicholas D. & Wudunn, Sheryl, *Half The Sky*, Hachette Digital, 2010

39. Invented in 1793, the cotton gin was a machine which separated cotton fibres from seeds.

40. Former slave Frederick Douglass, quoted in International Museum of Slavery, Liverpool.

41. Bury, J.B. *A History of Freedom of Thought*, 1912, ch. 7

42. Applebaum, Anne, *Gulag: a History*, Penguin, 2003, p 521. Gulag was the name of the Soviet institution administering forced labour camps.

43. Including Leon Trotsky, Gregory Zinoviev, Lev Kamenev, Nikolai Bukharin and Sergei Kirov.

44. Snyder, Timothy, *Bloodlands*, ebook, p 3

45. Applebaum, op.cit. p 4

46. New York Times, 4 August 2008

47. Applebaum, op.cit. p 468

48. Matthew 26:33

49. *The Speeches of Winston Churchill*, Penguin, p 165

50. Quoted by the Yugoslav Partisan leader Milovan Djilas after a meeting with Stalin

51. Ungváry, Kristián, *Battle for Budapest*, I.B. Tauris, 2003, pp 279-303. Also Mazower, Mark, *Hitler's Empire*, Penguin, 2008, p 541

52. Interview by the author

53. www.britannica.com/EBchecked/topic/285821/Indian-Mutiny

54. Apart from some territories which remained under allied Indian rulers after 1857.

55. Some 74,000 Indian soldiers died in World War I, according to Indian government figures.

56. A significant minority of Indians living in slums and remote villages are in practice excluded from democratic participation because they have no legal rights.

57. Meredith, Martin, *The State of Africa*, The Free Press, London, 2005, p 21

58. Meredith, op.cit. p 92

59. Meredith, op.cit. p 92

60. Meredith, op.cit pp 96-7

61. Meredith, op. cit. p 99

62. https://www.marxists.org/reference/archive/mao/works/red-book/ch22.htm

63. The Economist, 12 October 2013, p 110

64. McCrittick, David, The Independent, 20 April 2014
www.independent.co.uk/news/world/europe/irelands-war-of-independence-the-chilling-story-of-the-black-and-tans-475005.html

65. Told to a visitor in 2013 by Che's former personal secretary

66. www.npr.org/2014/12/18/371597743/cubans-react-to-u-s-moves-to-normalize-relations-with-cuba

67. As part of the 2014 agreement, Cuban authorities released 53 political prisoners, but a further 60 remained in jail.

68. Meredith, op.cit. p 163

69. Meredith, op.cit. pp 162-5, 169

70. Meredith, op. cit. p 340

71. Former Zaire is now known as the Democratic Republic of the Congo.

72. Meredith, op.cit. p 526

73. BBC4 documentary, 16 January 2014

74. Meredith, op.cit. p 228

75. Meredith, op.cit. p 515

76. African Development Bank Group, Millennium Development Goals (MDG), 2013, Summary

77. The Economist, 2 May 2013

78. https://freedomhouse.org/report/freedom-world-2014/map-freedom-2014#.VSwiENQueRa

79. Schweizer Monatshefte, *Ungarn 1956/2006,* Zürich, February 2006, p 31

80. Nemzeti dal (National song), translation by A. Makkai

81. Mićunović, Veljko, *Moscow Diary,* Doubleday, 1980, pp 131, 141, 144.

82. Robinson, Jane, *Bluestockings,* Viking, 2009, pp 84-7, 202-16

83. Mill, op.cit. pp 5-6

84. www.abolishforeignness.org/blog/emancipation-of-women

85. Steinbach, Susi, *Women in England 1760-1914*, Phoenix, 2004, p 316

86. Robinson, Jane, *In the Family Way*, Viking, 2015, The Oxford Writer, May 2015

87. The World Today, April & May 2015

88. Magnus, George, *The Economist*, 17 May 2014, p 18

89. Kristof/Wudunn, op.cit. p 10

90. Kristof/Wudunn, op.cit. p 79

91. Associated Press, 28 May 2014

92. Tribune de Genève, 19 May 2015

93. Kristof/Wudunn, op.cit. pp 92-3, 97,

94. Kristof/Wudunn, op.cit. p 177

95. Lennox, Annie, The Guardian, 6 March 2015

96. Kristof/Wudunn, op.cit. p 220

97. Kristof/Wudunn, op.cit. p 167

98. El-Feki, Shereen, *Sex and the Citadel*, Chatto & Windus, 2013, pp 13, 151

99. Qur'an 4:19, 4:34, 2:228, 2:282, 4:11

100. Deuteronomy, 22:13-21

101. In 2015, two men were sentenced in Pakistan to 25 years in prison for the attack on Malala, including the one who shot her, but eight other men charged were freed.

102. Kristof/Wudunn, op.cit. p 181

103. Kristof/Wudunn, op.cit. p 233-4

104. Kristof/Wudunn, op.cit. p 221

105. Kristof/Wudunn, op.cit. p 271

106. New York Times, 22 May 2015

107. King, Martin Luther, *The Words of Martin Luther King Jr*, selected by King, Coretta Scott, William Collins & Sons & Co Ltd, 1986, pp 71, 73

108. *The Autobiography of Martin Luther King Jr.,* edited by Clayborne Carson, IPM + Grand Central Publishing, 1998, ebook

109. *The Autobiography…* op.cit.

110. *The Autobiography* … op.cit.

111. King, Martin Luther; King, Coretta Scott. The Words of Martin Luther King, Jr.: Second Edition. Newmarket Press, 2008, p. 95. http://www.archives.gov/press/exhibits/dream-speech.pdf marked "Copyright 1963 Martin Luther King, Jr."

112. http://millercenter.org/president/speeches/speech-4034 Speech on 6 August 1965

113. Montefiore, Simon Sebag, *Speeches that Changed the World: The Stories and Transcripts of the Moments that Made History,* Quercus, 2006, p 155

114. The small South African Communist Party did support the ANC, but its influence was limited.

115. Mandela, Nelson, *Long Walk To Freedom,* ebook, 1995

116. Closing address in the debate on the State of the Nation address, Parliament, Cape Town, 24 February 1995

117. Mandela, op.cit.

118. Tutu, Desmond, *No Future Without Forgiveness,* Rider, 1999, pp 94-7

119. Tutu, ibid, pp 201-2

120. www.theguardian.com/sport/2007/jan/07/rugbyunion.features1

121. Lewis, Bernard, *What Went Wrong? Western Impact and Middle Eastern Response,* OUP, 2002, p 46

122. Arab Center for Research and Policy Studies, 22 December 2015

123. Pew Research Global Attitudes Project, quoted in Gelvin, James A., *The Arab Uprisings: What Everybody Needs To Know,* OUP, 2012, p 172

124. The Guardian, 23 February 2016

125. Cicero, Marcus Tullius, *How To Run A Country*

126. Interview BBC Radio 4, 12 November 2015

127. Reuters, 14 November 2015

128. BBC 22 January 2016 & The Guardian 21 January 2016

129. Le Temps, Switzerland, 5 November 2015

130. Roosevelt, Franklin D., Inaugural Address, March 4, 1933, published in Samuel Rosenman, ed., *The Public Papers of Franklin D. Roosevelt, Volume Two: The Year of Crisis, 1933,* New York, Random House, 1938, pp 11–16.

131. Aung San Suu Kyi, *Freedom From Fear,* Penguin, 1991, pp 176, 297, 184

132. www.news.bbc.co.uk, 13 November 2015

133. www.bbc.co.uk/news/world-europe-23010526

134. Decree of the USSR Supreme Soviet, 17 February 1954

135. Interview by the author with Joanna Hanson, OSCE election observer, 4 June 2014

136. Interview Frankfurter Allgemeine Zeitung, 16 May 2014

137. The Economist, 20 June 2015, quoting the Kiev International Institute of Sociology

138. According to a U.N. report.

139. Chatham House, 17 October 2013; Monique Villa, Thomson-Reuters Foundation, 3 December 2013

140. Human Rights Watch, quoted by The Observer, 2 March 2014

141. Fromm, Erich, *Escape From Freedom,* Owl Books, New York, 1941, p xiii

SELECTED BIBLIOGRAPHY

Abbott, Elizabeth, *Haiti: An insider's history of the rise and fall of the Duvaliers,* Simon & Schuster, 1988

Acton, Lord, *The History of Freedom,* Public Domain Book, 1907

Applebaum, Anne, *Gulag: a History,* Penguin, 2003

Applebaum, Anne, *Iron Curtain,* Allen Lane, 2012

Armstrong, Karen, *Islam,* Weidenfeld & Nicolson, 2000

Aung San Suu Kyi, *Freedom From Fear,* Penguin, 1991

Barr, Stringfellow, *The Pilgrimage of Western Man,* Gollancz, 1950

Beevor, Antony, *Berlin: the Downfall 1945,* Viking, 2002

Berlin, Isaiah, *Two Concepts of Liberty,* Oxford University Press, 1969

Bishop, Morris, *The Middle Ages,* Horizon-New Word City, 1968

Black, Jeremy, *Slavery: a New Global History,* Robinson, London, 2011

Blandenier, Jacques, *Martin Luther & Jean Calvin,* Editions Je Sème, 2008

Bryant, Arthur, *Triumph in the West 1943-1946,* W.M. Collins & Sons Ltd, 1959

Chang, Jung & Halliday, Jon, Mao: the Unknown Story, Vintage, 2006

Chomsky, Noam, *Problems of Knowledge and Freedom,* Pantheon, 1971

Chua, Amy, *World On Fire,* Arrow Books, Random House ebooks, 2002

Clark, Christopher, *The Sleepwalkers: How Europe Went to War in 1914,* Allen Lane, 2012

Coogan, Tim Pat, *1916: The Easter Rising,* Phoenix, 2001

Crossan, John Dominic, *Jesus: a Revolutionary Biography,* HarperCollins e-books, 1994

Davies, Norman, *Europe,* Oxford University Press, 1996

Davies, Norman, *Europe at War 1939-1945,* Macmillan, 2006

El-Feki, Shereen, *Sex and the Citadel,* Chatto & Windus, London, 2013

Ferguson, Niall, *Empire,* Allen Lane 2003

Fest, Joachim, *Hitler,* Ullstein, 1973

Fest, Joachim, *Ich Nicht (Not I),* Rowohlt, 2006

Fromm, Erich, *Escape From Freedom,* Owl Books, New York, 1941

Gelvin, James L., *The Arab Uprisings,* Oxford University Press, 2012, 2015

Gladwell, Michael, *The Tipping Point,* Little, Brown & Co, 2000

Hampson, Norman, *The Enlightenment,* ebook, 1990

Hannan, Daniel, *Inventing Freedom,* ebook, 2014

Jones, Dan, *Magna Carta,* Head of Zeus, 2014

Judt, Tony, *Post War: a History of Europe Since 1945,* Pimlico, 2007

King, Martin Luther (editor Carson, Clayborne), *The Autobiography of Martin Luther King,* IPM, 1998

Kolchin Peter, *American Slavery 1619-1877,* Penguin, 1993

Kristof, Nicholas D. & Wudunn, Sheryl, *Half The Sky,* Hachette Digital, 2010

Leas, Allan, *The Abolition of the Slave Trade,* Curriculum books, 2013

Lewis, Bernard, *What Went Wrong? Western Impact and Middle Eastern Response,* OUP, 2002

Lings, Martin, *Muhammad,* George Allen & Unwin, 1983

Macmillan, Margaret, *The War That Ended Peace,* Profile Books, 2013

Mandela, Nelson, *Long Walk To Freedom,* ebook, 1995

Mazower, Mark, *Dark Continent,* Penguin, 1998

Mazower, Mark, *Hitler's Empire,* Penguin, 2008

McCullough, David, *1776,* Simon & Schuster, 2006

Meredith, Martin, *The State of Africa,* The Free Press, London, 2005

Mićunović, Veljko, *Moscow Diary,* Doubleday, 1980

Mill, John Stuart, *On Liberty,* John D. Parker and Son,

London, 1859

Montefiore, Simon Sebag, *Speeches that Changed the World,* Quercus, 2006

Muller, Herbert J., *Freedom in the Ancient World,* Secker & Warburg, 1961

Reed, John, *Ten Days That Shook The World,* Penguin, 1926

Reed, T.J., *Light in Germany,* University of Chicago Press, 2015

Roberts, J.M., *The French Revolution,* Oxford University Press, 1978

Robinson, Jane, *Bluestockings,* Viking, 2009

Robinson, Jane, *In the Family Way,* Viking, 2015

Sharp, Gene, *Sharp's Dictionary of Power and Struggle,* Oxford University Press, 2012

Snyder, Timothy, *Bloodlands*, ebook

Steinbach, Susi, *Women in England 1760-1914,* Phoenix, 2004

Strauss, Barry, *The Battle of Salamis,* Simon & Schuster, 2004

Strauss, Barry, *The Spartacus War,* Phoenix, 2009

Taubman, William, *Khrushchev,* W.W. Norton & Company, 2003

Tutu, Desmond, *No Future Without Forgiveness,* Rider, 1999

Ungváry, Kristián, *Battle for Budapest,* I.B. Tauris, 2003

Welles, Jonathan, *The Complete History of Slaves,* ebook

Williams Anne & Head Viviane, *Freedom Fighters,* Canary Press eBooks Limited, 2013

Wright, Robert, *Nonzero,* Vintage, 2001

Yousafzai, Malala (with Lamb, Christina), *I Am Malala,* Weidenfeld & Nicolson, 2013

INDEX

Also by
Crux Publishing

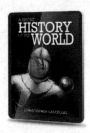

A Short History of the World

by Christopher Lascelles

"A clearly written, remarkably comprehensive guide to the greatest story on Earth - man's journey from the earliest times to the modern day. Highly recommended."
**Dan Jones, author of The Plantagenets:
The Kings Who Made England**

There is an increasing realisation that our knowledge of world history – and how it all fits together – is far from perfect. *A Short History of the World* aims to fill the big gaps in our historical knowledge with a book that is easy to read and assumes little prior knowledge of past events. The book does not aim to come up with groundbreaking new theories on why things occurred, but rather gives a broad overview of the generally accepted version of events so that non-historians will feel less ignorant when discussing the past.

While the book covers world history from the Big Bang to the present day, it principally covers key people, events and empires since the dawn of the first civilisations in around 3500 BC. To help readers put events, places and empires into context, the book includes 36 specially commissioned maps to accompany the text. The result is a book that is reassuringly epic in scope but refreshingly short in length. An excellent place to start to bring your historical knowledge up to scratch!

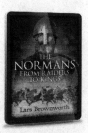

The Normans: From Raiders to Kings

by Lars Brownworth

"An evocative journey through the colourful and dangerous world of early medieval Europe"
Jonathan Harris, author of Byzantium and the Crusades

There is much more to the Norman story than the Battle of Hastings. These descendants of the Vikings who settled in France, England, and Italy - but were not strictly French, English, or Italian - played a large role in creating the modern world. They were the success story of the Middle Ages; a footloose band of individual adventurers who transformed the face of medieval Europe. During the course of two centuries they launched a series of extraordinary conquests, carving out kingdoms from the North Sea to the North African coast.

In *The Normans*, author Lars Brownworth follows their story, from the first shock of a Viking raid on an Irish monastery to the exile of the last Norman Prince of Antioch. In the process he brings to vivid life the Norman tapestry's rich cast of characters: figures like Rollo the Walker, William Iron-Arm, Tancred the Monkey King, and Robert Guiscard. It presents a fascinating glimpse of a time when a group of restless adventurers had the world at their fingertips.

The Sea Wolves: A History of the Vikings

by Lars Brownworth

"An axe age, a wind age, a wolf age". Thus the Vikings described Ragnarok – the end of the world – a time of destruction and death that would follow three bitter years of ice and snow without the warmth of a summer. To Western Europeans during the two and a half terrifying centuries of Viking attacks, Ragnarok seemed at hand. The long winter began in the eighth century, when Norse warriors struck the English isle of Lindisfarne, and in the traumatized words of the scholar Alcuin "laid waste the house of our hope, and trampled on the bodies of saints in the temple of God."

Wave after wave of Norse 'sea-wolves' followed in search of plunder, land, or a glorious death in battle. Much of the British Isles fell before their swords, and the continental capitals of Paris and Aachen were sacked. Turning east, they swept down the uncharted rivers of central Europe, captured Kiev and clashed with mighty Constantinople, the capital of the Byzantine Empire.

But there is more to the Viking story than brute force. They were makers of law - the term itself comes from an Old Norse word – and they introduced a novel form of trial by jury to England. They were also sophisticated merchants and explorers who settled Iceland, founded Dublin, and established a trading network that stretched from Baghdad to the coast of North America.